Institutional Vulnerability in Law

Ius, Lex et Res Publica
Studies in Law, Philosophy and Political Cultures

Edited by Barbara Janusz-Pohl

Vol. 44

Monika Jagielska / Barbara Mikołajczyk / Piotr Pinior (eds.)

Institutional Vulnerability in Law

PETER LANG
Berlin · Bruxelles · Chennai · Lausanne · New York · Oxford

Bibliographic Information published by the Deutsche Nationalbibliothek
The Deutsche Nationalbibliothek lists this publication in the Deutsche Nationalbibliografie; detailed bibliographic data is available online at http://dnb.d-nb.de.

Library of Congress Cataloging-in-Publication Data
Names: Jagielska, Monika editor | Mikołajczyk, Barbara editor | Pinior, Piotr editor
Title: Institutional vulnerability in law / Monika Jagielska, Barbara Mikołajczyk, Piotr Pinior [eds.].
Description: First edition. | Berlin ; New York : Peter Lang, 2025. | Series: Ius, lex et res publica. studies in law, philosophy and political cultures, 2191-3250 ; vol. 44 | Includes bibliographical references.
Identifiers: LCCN 2025031638 (print) | LCCN 2025031639 (ebook) | ISBN 9783631931752 hardcover | ISBN 9783631931769 pdf | ISBN 9783631943427 epub
Subjects: LCSH: Discrimination--Law and legislation | Discrimination--Law and legislation--European Union countries | Minorities--Legal status, laws, etc. | Victims of crimes--Protection--Law and legislation | International law and human rights | Vulnerability (Personality trait) | Resilience (Personality trait)
Classification: LCC K3242 .I57 2025 (print) | LCC K3242 (ebook) | DDC 342.08/7--dc23/eng/20250721
LC record available at https://lccn.loc.gov/2025031638
LC ebook record available at https://lccn.loc.gov/2025031639

This publication was financially supported by the University of Silesia in Katowice, Poland.

UNIWERSYTET ŚLĄSKI
W KATOWICACH

ISSN 2191-3250
ISBN 978-3-631-93175-2 (Print)
ISBN 978-3-631-93176-9 (E-PDF)
ISBN 978-3-631-94342-7 (E-PUB)
DOI 10.3726/b23213

Published by Peter Lang GmbH, Berlin (Germany)

info@peterlang.com

This publication has been peer reviewed.

www.peterlang.com

Table of Contents

Preface

Vulnerability intensifies during wars, disasters, and conflicts, though it can also occur in ordinary circumstances due to an abuse of power by a majority or by institutions. It frequently occurs in connection with characteristics such as race, nationality, gender, age, or sexual orientation, though it can occur in many different circumstances, such as economic hardship, service subordination, and participation in judicial or administrative proceedings. In addition, vulnerability and being in a disadvantageous position affect not only individuals, but also groups of individuals and other entities, including legal entities. The various facets of vulnerability may also be related to technological progress, environmental degradation, or climate change, or may result from a disadvantaged position in some structure (e.g. in a company) and do not need to involve a breach of the law or the principles of social co-existence. In this particular sense, the issue of vulnerability in a legal context seems inexhaustible.

With this in mind, this book aims to analyse the various aspects of vulnerability that are or should be identified in different legal systems, international law, European law, and national law. The central assumption of this book is that vulnerabilities, which are often not visible at first glance, are multi-layered and intersectional, and therefore require a cross-cutting approach and a step-by-step case study. The various forms of vulnerability can prove challenging for those who create laws, as well as those who implement and enforce them. The responsibility of all actors in the legal sphere is therefore crucial to the quality of the law and its educational role. Civil society and the private sector must be sensitive to various weaknesses in order to evaluate the actions of policymakers and law enforcement.

On the other hand, not every disadvantage creates vulnerability or means discrimination, so it is not always necessary to introduce special protection or compensatory measures for the entity in question. The authors of this book are trying to answer whether and to what extent weaker entities should be protected. They conduct their research from the perspective of diverse fields of law, all approaching vulnerability and disadvantage differently. This spectrum of research and concepts is undoubtedly a significant asset of this book.

The book is divided into three parts, each presenting a different perspective on vulnerability. First, theoretical considerations aim to describe the various, often hidden and even deceptive, faces of vulnerability. Second, vulnerability is presented as powerlessness in the face of legal solutions for which the needs of specific individuals or groups of individuals are simply invisible. The third part of the book aims to make the reader aware that the vulnerable may be individuals and entire groups of people, enterprises, and even local government units. Everything depends on the context and individual legal solutions in various fields of law as well as in practice.

The three parts mentioned above consist of 12 chapters. The initial chapter is devoted to theoretical issues of discrimination and vulnerability. The book's key features include considering critical legal concepts such as the vulnerability theory from the perspective of constitutional law, criminal law, civil law, and public law. In particular, the authors present their views on the intersection of vulnerability in the legal decision-making process, the situation of weaker entities in the private and public sectors and before criminal courts, as well as vulnerability in the digital world in the context of the development of artificial intelligence. Despite the diversity of the addressed issues and nuances of vulnerability, each proposed chapter has a similar structure. First, the nature and specifics of the vulnerability of particular groups or entities is pointed out, as well as the phenomena that cause their vulnerability. Second, the authors search for a legal response to vulnerability and its various aspects. Finally, they track legal solutions in the analysed area, identify legal gaps, and propose *de lege ferenda* solutions.

In this way, the readers learn about various aspects of vulnerability and other specific actors, such as criminal victims, AI users, public sector users, municipal units, and minority shareholders, as well as about the vulnerability of various actors from the perspective of environmental and climate change regulations. Therefore, the proposed book offers a broad perspective, not only due to research conducted on international, European, and national law, but also because the authors are scientists representing research institutes from Poland, Portugal, and Spain. Moreover, they are specialists in various fields of law, including international public law, constitutional law, commercial law, criminal law and criminology, administrative law, and financial law. The authors share with the reader various viewpoints, approaches, and specifics of the legal issues discussed. In this context, the book is fully comparative and expresses scientific diversity.

Editors: Monika Jagielska, Barbara Mikołajczyk,
Piotr Pinior

PART I

Faces of Vulnerability

Discrimination and Vulnerability – Old Problems and New Questions

*Olga Sitarz**

Abstract: In recent years the equality principle and the prohibition of discrimination generated a lot of heated political and social discussions, and the anti-discrimination measures still raise numerous doubts. It is a challenging issue, which may be evidenced by Article 15 of Council Directive 2000/78/EC establishing a general framework for equal treatment in employment and occupation. This provision is entirely devoted to Northern Ireland; it limits anti-discrimination actions with respect to recruitment to the police and employment in education due to religious and historical reasons. The publication itself is not about analysing anti-discrimination regulations (international or national); these are referred to only for illustrative purposes. The author answers the fundamental questions underlying all anti-discrimination regulations: 1. What is the essence of discrimination from a human rights perspective? 2. What factors should be taken into account when qualifying a given phenomenon as discrimination (at the level of lawmaking and application)? 3. What problems with regard to discrimination are caused by social, cultural, and civilisational changes? 4. Which criterion should be used to assess whether members of a particular social group belong to the conceptual category of 'vulnerable persons', 5. What is the role of the law in eliminating discrimination, bearing in mind that both discrimination and its prohibition constitute a restriction of human rights?

Keywords: the essence of discrimination, the criteria of vulnerable persons, the role and importance of anti-discrimination regulations

1. Introduction

In human rights theory and practice, the principle of equality and non-discrimination, regardless of whether it is treated jointly or as two separate principles, is considered one of the general principles of international human rights law. The European Court of Human Rights (ECtHR) defines it as a fundamental principle that, together with the rule of law and values such as tolerance, forms the basis for the European Convention on Human Rights. It has a complex normative nature because it may be considered as one of the protected independent subjective rights, but is primarily a general clause

* Professor at the Faculty of Law and Administration, University of Silesia in Katowice. ORCID: 0000-0002-2075-5307

that is an interpretative directive of particular relevance to the application of substantive guarantees.[1]

In a sense, the history of law is a history of discrimination; law has introduced and preserved social inequalities. At the same time, the evolution of law shows its efforts to rise above prejudices to respect equality and diversity, and to recognise human rights. Consequently, international declarations, conventions, and constitutions are cited as the first anti-discrimination instruments.[2] It should therefore be strongly emphasised that previous instruments removing unjustified inequality before the law are also anti-discrimination regulations.[3] Although this analysis does not aim to interpret specific anti-discrimination provisions, it is helpful to return to fundamental issues in discussions on the significance and prevention of discrimination. An example of this can be found in Article 15 of Directive 2000/78/EU, entirely devoted to Northern Ireland and allowing for religious differences in recruitment in the police service and teachers in schools ('furthering the reconciliation of historical divisions between the major religious communities there').

The adoption of such a regulation clearly shows that the issue of discrimination and anti-discrimination measures remains a dynamic problem and drawing the boundaries between the freedoms of individuals and social groups, while respecting the equality principle, is an extremely difficult task. The provision devoted entirely to Northern Ireland confirms the argument that many issues must be assessed and resolved individually, separately, almost

1 Agnieszka Bień-Kacała, Julia Kapelańska-Pręgowska, "Niższy wiek emerytalny kobiet: przywilej czy dyskryminacja? Perspektywa prawnomiędzynarodowa i konstytucyjna", Praca i Zabezpieczenie Społeczne 01/2022, p. 13. See: Colm O'Cinneide, The Principle of Equality and Non-discrimination within the Framework of the EU Charter and Its Potential Application to Social and Solidarity Rights in: Making the Charter of Fundamental Rights a Living Instrument, Giuseppe Palmisano (eds), Brill Nijhoff 2014, (pp. 199–221), Elise Muir, The Essence of the Fundamental Right to Equal Treatment: Back to the Origins, German Law Journal (2019), 20, pp. 817–839. doi:10.1017/glj.2019.64

2 Stuart Casey-Maslen, Christof Heyns, "In The Right to Life under International Law: An Interpretative Manual" (pp. 1–6) "An Historical Introduction to the Right to Life)". Cambridge: Cambridge University Press 2021

3 For example, The General Charter of Jewish Rights, known as the Statute of Kalisz, of 1264, prescribed in §17 that "Any Jew may freely and safely walk or ride a horse without permission or hindrance in our kingdom. They will pay the usual tolls, just like other Christians." <https://dziedzictwo.ekai.pl/@@statut_kaliski_tekst>.

on an *ad hoc* basis. Finally, a social problem of an entirely different nature than discrimination itself may be one reason for commonly accepted (sic) discriminatory behaviour.

This article seeks to answer four fundamental questions that underlie any anti-discrimination regulation and decisions on whether discrimination has occurred:

1. What is the essence of discrimination from the point of view of human rights?
2. What protected grounds should be taken into account when classifying a phenomenon as discrimination and what is the relationship between discrimination and vulnerability?
3. What is the relevance of social, cultural, and civilisational changes to the essence of discrimination?
4. What is the role of law in eliminating discrimination, given that both discrimination and its prohibition are a restriction of human rights?

2. The essence of discrimination from the point of view of human rights

It is crucial to define the phenomenon of discrimination with regards to its identification and prevention. Walter E. Williams writes: 'discrimination might be operationally defined as the act of choice or selection. All selection necessarily and simultaneously requires non-selection. In other words, choice requires discrimination (…)'. And the author rightly notes that the essence of discrimination is the selection criterion.[4] Not every infringement of human rights and freedoms is discrimination; not every restriction of access to certain goods or services can be described as such. It is generally assumed that discrimination is an unfair, harmful, selective, inappropriate treatment of a person based on their membership of a socially identifiable group, identified based on one or more characteristics.[5] It is a situation where

[4] Walter E. Williams, "Discrimination: The Law vs. Morality", *Cornell Journal of Law and Public Policy*, Vol. 13, Issue 1, Fall 2003, p. 113, <https://scholarship.law.cornell.edu/cgi/viewcontent.cgi?article=1061&context=cjlpp>.

[5] Zofia Jabłońska [in:] Karolina Kędziora, Krzysztof Śmiszek (eds.), "Ustawa o wdrożeniu niektórych przepisów Unii Europejskiej w zakresie równego traktowania. Komentarz", Warszawa 2017, p. 17.

a person, because of various characteristics, is treated less favourably than another person would be treated in a comparable situation.[6] Discrimination also means any preference based on specific characteristics that has the purpose or effect of nullifying or impairing the recognition, enjoyment, or exercise, on an equal footing, of human rights and fundamental freedoms in the political, economic, social, cultural, or any other field of public life.[7] Discrimination also includes a denial of reasonable accommodation.[8]

In his classic work on the nature of prejudice, Gordon W. Allport pointed out that discrimination aims to remove specific individuals from certain places or spheres of social life. It is a purposeful, recurrent, and long-lasting action.[9] In his socio-cognitive concept of prejudice in discourse, Teun A. van Dijk distinguishes 'the seven Ds of discrimination'. They are: 'dominance, differentiation, distance, diffusion, diversion, depersonalisation or destruction, and daily discrimination'.[10]

In analytical terms, the following features of discrimination can be identified:

- a restriction of the rights and freedoms of a human being;
- due to or because of their specific characteristic(s) common to a specific group of people;
- without reasonable and legitimate justification;
- long-lasting;
- in a specific field of social (public) life.

In essence, discrimination is an arbitrary, egoistic, unjust and unfair from the perspective of (universal and recognised) social and cultural norms – resolution of a conflict of goods based on an irrelevant (in given circumstances)

---

6 See: comments by the Commissioner for Human Rights. <https://bip.brpo.gov.pl/pl/content/czym-jest-dyskryminacja>.

7 See: Article 1 of the International Convention on the Elimination of All Forms of Racial Discrimination of 1966 (Journal of Laws of 1969, No. 25)

8 See: Article 2 of the Convention on the Rights of Persons with Disabilities, adopted in New York on 13 December 2006, Journal of Laws of 2012, item 1169.

9 Gordon W. Allport, "The Nature of Prejudice", Addison-Wesley, London 1979 as quoted by: Aleksandra Winiarska, Witold Klaus, Dyskryminacja i nierówne traktowanie jako zjawisko społeczno-kulturowe, Studia BAS Nr 2(26) 2011, p. 11

10 As quoted by: Martin Reisigl, "Dyskryminacja w dyskursach", Tekst i dyskurs 3/2010, p. 32.

characteristic of a person (or group of people). The conflict arises from, on the one hand, the rights and freedoms of a discriminated actor in the form of access to specific goods, services, possibilities, and, on the other hand, a discriminating actor in the form of the freedom to pursue its own beliefs (based on prejudices and stereotypes) and to maximise its own material and non-material benefits. The narrowing of human autonomy in the social dimension may therefore be called discrimination.

A characteristic being a criterion for discrimination may be innate (being innate to personal identity) or may result from a choice made by a given person (or a group of people). States are given a wider margin of assessment in the latter case.[11] The characteristic discriminated against is non-culpable, regardless of whether it is immutable or has been chosen.[12] The question arises whether the individuals in respect of whom restrictive behaviour is undertaken could avoid putting themselves at a severe disadvantage compared with others by taking a specific action (for example, acquiring specific skills required by their employer, sacrificing a particular aspect of their ethnicity, or giving up an aspect of their freedom to express religious beliefs) may complain about a measure giving rise to that disadvantage. In the opinion of O. de Schutter, it is obvious that, in a situation where a change in behaviour would mean the abandonment of one of the characteristics by which an ethnic or religious minority is defined, it would be inadmissible to reject an allegation of discrimination on the grounds that, by failing to 'comply' with a contested requirement, the victim would be waiving the right to complain.[13] In social terms, it is important that a restriction of rights is no fault of the person subjected to the restriction.

---

11 So Yeon Kim, "Les vulnérables: evaluating the vulnerability criterion in Article 14 cases by the European Court of Human Rights", Legal Studies (2021), 41, p. 620, doi:10.1017/lst.2021.21

12 Differently: Iyiola Solanke, "The anti-stigma principle and legal protection from fattism", Fat Studies 10/2021, pp. 128 and 136–137, who argues as follows: "Victims of discrimination have no control and are therefore 'innocent', deserving of state protection through the use of law" and "Weight discrimination occurs with impunity because of the widespread assumption that fat is mutable – behavioural public policies that promote weight loss encourage such views that fat individuals are to blame for their size."

13 See: Olivier de Schutter, "Three Models of Equality and European Anti-Discrimination Law", Northern Ireland Legal Quarterly Vol. 57, No 1, p. 18.

The key to the term discrimination is certainly a lack of reasonable and legitimate justification for the differentiation of the legal and social situation of individuals. From this perspective, discrimination is an arbitrary decision[14] based on prejudices and stereotypes. For example, the different treatment of women and men may be considered to be in conformity with the Convention, in principle, only when it is supported by 'very weighty reasons'.[15] US legislation provides for the possibility of being free from a charge of discrimination on the basis of *bona fides* occupational qualification.[16] In this context, reference can be made to an assessment given by the Polish Constitutional Tribunal stating that the requirement of a clean criminal record is not a form of discrimination, but an upgrading of employee requirements in the public interest.[17] It should be pointed out that a reasonable justification is based on universal values consistent with the concept of human rights, fairly balancing the conflict of rights, taking into account the proportionality principle and the *ultima ratio*.

The issue of proportionality (on many levels) is part of a reasonable justification. The importance and relevance of a restriction must be taken into account in contextual terms when anti-discrimination regulations are designed. For example, the Court of Justice held that a prohibition on wearing the Islamic headscarf does not constitute direct discrimination on the grounds of religion or belief within the meaning of Article 2, para. 2, letter a, of Directive 2000/78/EC, because the prohibition set out in the work regulations covers all manifestations of such beliefs and applies equally to

---

14 Referring to the words of Walter E. Williams quoted earlier ("Discrimination: The Law vs. Morality") – discrimination is a choice based on prejudices and stereotypes; an illegitimate choice.

15 See: among others, judgements in the cases of: J.D. and A. v. UK — applications Nos 32949/17 and 34614/17, judgement of 24 October 2019, point 89; Konstantin Markin v. Russia — application No 30078/06, judgement of 22 March 2012, point 127.

16 Irmina Miernicka, "Dyskryminacja w zatrudnieniu ze względu na wygląd" [in:] Joseph Roger Carby-Hall, Zbigniew Góral, Aneta Tyc (eds.), "Różne oblicza dyskryminacji w zatrudnieniu", Warszawa 2021, p. 409.

17 After: Stefan Płażek, Karalność pracownika a dyskryminacja w zatrudnieniu [in:] Joseph Roger Carby-Hall, Zbigniew Góral, Aneta Tyc (eds.), "Różne oblicza dyskryminacji w zatrudnieniu", Warszawa 2021, p. 412.

all employees.[18] It can be concluded that such a solution fails to take into account the proportionality principle. The situation is quite different where the requirements of a given religion in the area of religious symbols are so firm and rigorous that non-compliance excludes one from a religious community compared to a situation where a lack of religious symbols does not violate the canons of one's religion.

Moreover, proportionality means taking into account the interests of all the parties who bear the costs of discrimination and anti-discrimination measures (proportionality between the burden of discrimination and the interest of the discriminating party).[19] This approach may be illustrated by the following measure: 'In order to guarantee compliance with the principle of equal treatment of persons with disabilities, reasonable accommodation is provided for. This means that the employer shall take appropriate measures, taking into account the needs of the particular situation, to enable a person with a disability to have access to, perform, or advance in employment or have training, provided that these measures do not impose a disproportionate burden on the employer. That burden is not disproportionate if it is sufficiently compensated by existing measures within the framework of a policy pursued by a given Member State in favour of persons with disabilities'.[20]

Discrimination, which is a value in the name of which anti-discrimination measures are taken, stands in opposition to equality and respect for diversity.

In today's dynamic world, the principle of respect for diversity takes on particular significance. It is not and cannot be treated as synonymous to the equality principle. It gives the equality principle a specific characteristic – it is the rational core of anti-discrimination action and sets its limit. The UNESCO Convention on the Protection and Promotion of the Diversity of Cultural Expressions emphasises in the preamble the significance of diversity

---

[18] Helena Szewczyk, "Dyskryminacja ze względu na przekonania religijne: glosa do wyroku Trybunału Sprawiedliwości z 14.03.2017 r., C-157/15, Samira Achbita i Centrum voor gelijkheid van kansen en voor racismebestrijding przeciwko G4S Secure Solutions NV", Europejski Przegląd Sądowy 2017, No 10, pp. 42–49.

[19] Anna Olmińska, "Dyskryminacja jako przykład nierównego traktowania pracownika", Roczniki Administracji i Prawa nr XVII, p. 341.

[20] After: Wojciech Burek, Witold Klaus, "Definiowanie dyskryminacji w prawie polskim w świetle prawa Unii Europejskiej oraz prawa międzynarodowego", Problemy Współczesnego Prawa Międzynarodowego, Europejskiego i Porównawczego, vol. XI, A.D. MMXIII, p. 78.

from the perspective of the individual person, but also of entire societies benefiting from cultural diversity.[21] A similar significance of diversity can be read with reference to culture (culturalism). Respect for all diversity is a condition for individual and collective existence. Considerable doubts are raised in this connection by a (previously cited) judgement delivered by the Court of Justice of the European Union (EU) that considered the significance of a total prohibition on wearing of visible political, worldview, or religious symbols in the workplace placed in the work regulations of a private sector company. The Court of Justice held that the prohibition on wearing the Islamic headscarf is not direct discrimination on grounds of religion or belief within the meaning of Article 2, para. 2, letter a, of Directive 2000/78/EC, because the prohibition set out in the work regulations covers all manifestations of such beliefs and applies equally to all employees.[22] One may wonder whether referring to the equality principle did not breach the principle of respect for diversity. Human beings differ, among other things, in terms of their attitude to religion and there are no rational reasons to conceal it. The question is whether compliance with the prohibition on discrimination is to be based on levelling or concealing differences. The idea of the negation of discrimination is to respect diversity. Instead, all religious symbols should perhaps be allowed in the public space without making any of them dominant. I. Solanke correctly observed 'that it is the social meaning that we need to be blind to not the characteristic itself'.[23]

On the essence of discrimination, account must be taken of its social and individual consequences. An extensive body of research spanning multiple disciplines shows that perceived discrimination is associated with increased rates of stroke, high blood pressure, cardiovascular disease, morbidity, anxiety, depression, and a range of other negative physical and mental

---

[21] It was adopted in Paris on 20 October 2005.

[22] Helena Szewczyk, Dyskryminacja ze względu na przekonania religijne: glosa do wyroku Trybunału Sprawiedliwości z 14.03.2017 r., C-157/15, Samira Achbita i Centrum voor gelijkheid van kansen en voor racismebestrijding przeciwko G4S Secure Solutions NV "Europejski Przegląd Sądowy" 2017, No 10, pp. 42–49.

[23] Iyiola Solanke, "Discrimination as Stigma. A theory of Anti-discrimination Law", Oxford and Portland, Oregon 2017, pp. 208–209

health outcomes.[24] Discrimination results in marginalisation, exclusion, and the inability of people from a discriminated group to exercise their own rights. A restriction in one sphere of human life frequently leads to a deprivation of needs in other spheres of human life. As a social phenomenon, discrimination leads to social unrest and disrupts the security and harmonious coexistence of individuals who differ in certain characteristics. It limits the development of individual people, social groups, society, and ultimately humanity.

The social context means that there can be no discrimination within the family or private contacts. Parents do not have a duty to provide the same level for all their children. Similarly, 'If we wish to befriend only people of a certain religion, we are free to do so, and if we wish to give handouts only to homeless people of certain races, we are likewise free to do that'.[25] It may be a problem to draw the boundary between the private sphere understood in this way and the social/public sphere.

The element of social context has another meaning. For example, Article 27 of the Convention on the Rights of Persons with Disabilities provides that State Parties will take appropriate steps to employ people with disabilities in the public sector and to promote the employment of people with disabilities in the private sector through appropriate policies and measures, which may include affirmative action programmes, incentives, and other measures.

3. Protected grounds and the conceptual category of 'vulnerable persons'

In general, discrimination means different treatment based on a difference that results from a protected ground. 'A protected ground' is a human characteristic that should not be regarded as essential for different treatment or for gaining specific benefits. A protected ground is an identifiable, objective, or personal characteristic or a 'status' according to which individuals or groups

---

[24] Matthew A. Andersson, Catherine E., Harnois, "Higher exposure, lower vulnerability? The curious case of education, gender discrimination, and Women's health", Social Science & Medicine, Volume 246, February 2020.

[25] See: Sophia Moreau, "What is discrimination?", Philosophy and Public Affairs 38 (2)/2010 pp. 160–161.

of individuals can be distinguished from one another.[26] The doctrine and the judicature make use of the following terms: differentiating grounds, criteria for differentiation, legally protected grounds, reasons for discrimination.

These grounds define very strongly who an individual is in the social sense based on primary identities (skin colour) and on secondary identities (marital status).[27] Being aware of its controversial nature, it is necessary to analyse another human characteristic that is occasionally cited as a criterion for discrimination. This is behaviour associated with a particular group, behaviour that is, in essence, group-specific and specific to a characteristic that distinguishes that group (for example, the prayer of the faithful, breast-feeding, and the cultivation of traditions). We believe that the inability to pursue it does not constitute discrimination, even when it is positively or neutrally interpreted. It is not a question of not having access to specific goods, services, or employment, but rather the impossibility of exercising one's rights in a specific place at a specific time (singing psalms during work, wearing traditional regional costumes exposing female breasts, breast-feeding in class in college), just like a member of a non-discriminated group cannot always exercise all of their rights (e.g. drink alcohol at work, sleep at work, etc.). This approach may be supported, among other things, by an argument put forward by J. Maliszewska-Nienartowicz, who rightly pointed out that it is clearly evident from the provision of Article 4, para. 1, of Directive 2000/78/EC that it is not the reason for the different treatment, but a characteristic connected with that reason that constitutes a relevant and determinant professional requirement permitting different treatment.[28]

In the opinion of W. Burek and W. Klaus, an analysis of documents and international agreements shows that the following protected grounds are expressly listed in them: sex, race, skin colour, mother tongue, religion/belief, political or other opinion, nationality, social origin, national and ethnic origin, disability, civil status, financial situation, birth, or membership of

[26] Handbook on European non-discrimination law, Publications Office of the European Union, 2018, <https://rm.coe.int/fra-2018-handbook-non-discrimination-law-2018-en/1680a2b52b>.

[27] Zofia Jabłońska, p. 17.

[28] Justyna Maliszewska-Nienartowicz, "Dyskryminacja ze względu na religię, niepełnosprawność, wiek lub orientację seksualną. Dyrektywa 2000/78 i orzecznictwo TS UE. Komentarz", Warszawa 2013, p. 27

national minorities.[29] This list seems to be incomplete from today's perspective, but it must be considered whether every criterion for discrimination needs to be explicitly included. For example, as regards fattism, I. Solanke observes: 'Despite the prevalence of weight discrimination in society, there are few jurisdictions that provide legal protection. There has never been legal protection against weight discrimination in the UK and in Europe. In the USA, only one state – Michigan – explicitly bans weight discrimination'.[30] It should be recalled that many international and national instruments use an open list of protected grounds or use the term 'for any reason'.[31]

Notably, respect for or a violation of human dignity is not a decisive criterion[32] in the process of identifying discrimination. This is argued, for example, by M. Zima-Pierjaszewska: 'The obligation to respect the dignity of another person and their rights should be seen as the source of the prohibition on discriminatory behaviour based on prejudice and stereotypes relating to various social groups, especially those considered 'minorities''.[33] In turn, M. Kułak argues that linking unequal treatment to identity makes it possible to recognise the special connection between the prohibition on discrimination and human dignity.[34] Some jurisdictions even offer special damage awards to the claimant for 'injury to dignity, feelings, and self-respect'.[35] It should be pointed out that the 'dignity' argument may be relied on by both

---

29 Wojciech Burek, Witold Klaus, pp. 80–81.

30 Iyiola Solanke, "Discrimination…", p. 127.

31 At the same time, one cannot lose sight of the issue of centrality and the multipronged nature of status vulnerability, positionality, and relational power within institutional and organizational environments – see e.g. Vincent J. Roscigno, "Discrimination, Sexual Harassment, and the Impact of Workplace Power", Socius, 5/2019, <https://journals.sagepub.com/doi/10.1177/2378023119853894>

32 See also: Conor O'Mahony, "There is no such thing as a right to dignity", *International Journal of Constitutional Law*, Volume 10, Issue 2, 30 March 2012, pp. 551–574, <https://doi.org/10.1093/icon/mos010>.

33 Monika Zima-Pierjaszewska, "Zakaz dyskryminacji a uchybienie godności studenta," Studia Iuridica 84, p. 47.

34 Maciej Kułak, "Zakaz dyskryminacji w dostępie do dóbr i usług a prawa podstawowe usługobiorców i usługodawców w prawie Unii Europejskiej. Rozprawa doktorska", Warszawa 2020, p. 164. <https://wpia.uw.edu.pl/uploads/media/5ee31b739a3a4/zakaz-dyskryminacji-w-dostepie-do-dobr-i-uslug-a-prawa-podstawowe-uslugobiorcow-i-uslugodawcow-w-prawie-unii-europejskiej.pdf/>.

35 Sophia Moreau, p. 146.

parties to the conflict and that anti-discrimination prohibitions apply to goods that are frequently associated with human dignity. Consequently, whose dignity is to be protected – that of the individuals intending to register a same-sex partnership or that of the registrar opposing such behaviour? In terms of the essence of discrimination seen as a conflict of goods, the protection of dignity becomes an argument of little practicality.

A justification of restrictions, i.e. justification of discrimination, should not invoke the conscience clause. This is part of the characteristic of social distinctiveness, referring to behaviour that does not presuppose discrimination. The opposite is the case in the area of socially relevant behaviour, invoking the conscience clause is in fact discrimination, as the service or good in question becomes inaccessible to those who 'do not fit' with the beliefs and views of the service provider or employer. An example of this is a physician who, according to the precepts of his religion, cannot touch female patients, a pharmacist whose religion forbids them to sell contraceptives, or a teacher who does not 'believe' in the theory of evolution. The prohibition on acting according to one's convictions is not discrimination because the public aspect of professional activity demands respect for the deliberative freedom of others.

Referring to the essence of discrimination, the conflict of goods is generally resolved by or in favour of the stronger party at the expense of the weaker party. The weaker parties are frequently members of vulnerable groups. The ECtHR has identified negative social attitudes, dependency on the state, historical prejudice, and social exclusion as markers of vulnerable groups. In contrast to the suspect categories approach, the vulnerability criterion subdivides the most disadvantaged groups within the suspect categories. For example, Roma individuals are identified as part of a vulnerable group, although discrimination against them can be broadly categorised as racial discrimination.[36] The ECtHR has often invoked the vulnerability criterion to overcome the drawbacks of cases concerning Article 14 of the European Convention on Human Rights, the prohibition on discrimination. This new criterion, allowing the court to favour applicants, highlights the applicants' group affiliation. However, in the opinion of So Yeon Kim, the

---

36 So Yeon Kim, p. 621.

vulnerability criterion was initially used to fix the drawbacks of Article 14, but eventually backfired.[37]

At the same time, in the context of helping vulnerable people, there is increasing mention of targeting them. The criteria for assessing vulnerability are indicated. In essence, the longer the list of vulnerability criteria used, the higher the likelihood of an inclusion error.[38] There is no clear definition of vulnerability. A generally agreed upon definition of vulnerability is the diminished capacity of an individual or group to anticipate, cope with, resist, and recover from the effect of natural, human-induced, or human-made disaster or conflict. People are, or become, more vulnerable to hazards due to a combination of physical, social, environmental, and political factors. However, vulnerability is not a fixed state or category. Among the affected population, individuals with the same characteristics will not experience the same level of vulnerability.[39] B. Hoffmaster builds the definition of vulnerability from Whitehead's definition of a human being. According to B. Hoffmaster, vulnerability is a loss to three urges of being a human: urges '(1) to live, (2) to live well, and (3) to live better'.[40] The court has not provided any definition of vulnerability or vulnerable group. Instead, it has identified the markers of vulnerability, namely social disadvantages, dependence on the state, and historical prejudice and stigmatisation.[41] However, even in this case, one must be cautious of over-easy automatisation. A violation of the rights of a vulnerable person does not always have to be discrimination and not being a member of a vulnerable group does not *a priori* rule out discrimination.

One must bear in mind that grouping applicants as 'vulnerable' and requiring special protection for them can lead to paternalism and stigmatisation (labelling). The court's paternalism is inevitable as long as the court invokes the vulnerability criterion. This is because the court demands that the respondent state provide 'special protection' to the group the vulnerable applicant

---

37 So Yeon Kim, p. 624.

38 <https://sheltercluster.s3.eu-central-1.amazonaws.com/public/docs/vulnerability_criteria_guideline.vf4_.pdf>.

39 <https://sheltercluster.s3.eu-central-1.amazonaws.com/public/docs/Vulnerability%20Criteria.pdf>.

40 Barry Hoffmaster 'What does vulnerability mean?' (2006) 36 Hastings Center Report 38 at 42 after: So Yeon Kim, p. 625.

41 So Yeon Kim, pp. 625–626.

belongs to. This is a common trap to fall into when facing a vulnerable individual – when someone is vulnerable to serious harm, it is unobjectionable to think in terms of trying to protect them. Despite good intentions, when this protection is elevated to the level of social intervention, it may cause a pathogenic source of vulnerability, with 'the relationships of domination and inequality among members of a community or between the state and citizens' being perpetuated.[42] S.Y. Kim argues that the court has also failed to provide a non-paternalistic form of protection to vulnerable individuals. S.Y. Kim cites three criteria for a non-paternalistic form of protection: (1) the protection should receive universal support from all individuals; (2) the protection should be conceived as applying to all individuals, rather than specific individuals or groups, and; (3) the protection should not give government officials any power to control the protected individuals.[43] It should be added that a non-paternalistic protection requires respect for the autonomy of the persons to be protected. That approach takes on special significance, not for the identification of discrimination but for the proposed anti-discrimination measures.

4. Impact of social, cultural, and civilisational changes on the understanding of the essence of discrimination

The main macro-social cause for the emergence of marginalisation is a social change occurring too rapidly. A diversified access to a certain type of goods, both tangible and intangible, is the root cause of inequality. The following is also indicated: a great disparity in income, power, prestige, and participation in culture.[44]

There is a belief in sociology that human societies are constantly changing at all levels of their intrinsic complexity. The change takes place at the macro, the intermediate, and the micro level.[45] From the perspective of the subject-matter

[42] So Yeon Kim, pp. 626–627.

[43] So Yeon Kim, pp. 628–629.

[44] Anna Nowak, "Pojęcie, istota, przyczyny, mechanizmy marginalizacji i wykluczenia społecznego", Chowanna 1/2012, pp. 26–27.

[45] Piotr Sztompka, "Socjologia zmian społecznych", Kraków 2005, p. 67.

of this article, a further observation is called for – society is not a whole, but a set of multilevel, interrelated processes and a 'trans-temporal phenomenon'.[46] It is thought that the primary factors for the occurrence of social change are: changes in the natural environment, demographic, technological changes, cultural diffusion, emergence of new ideas, and a social conflict.[47]

As a result of social changes in a modern society, it is necessary to indicate its key features, the existence of which is important for a subsequent identification of discrimination. P. Sztompka lists the following features: individualism (which he calls a megatrend), differentiation both in the sphere of work and consumption, rationality in the operation of organisations and institutions, economism, and the expansiveness of modernity.[48] These key features should be complemented by social changes in the field of politics – the increasing role of the state in assuming new functions, the rule of law, the broadening of the category of citizenship, and the importance of human rights. To provide a cognitive perspective, the following social changes relevant for the assessment of discriminatory behaviour should also be indicated: secularisation and the declining importance of religious beliefs and values stemming from them, the growing importance of science, the democratisation of education, the emergence of mass culture, and the separation of work time and free time with the increasing scope of the latter.[49]

The significance and the list of protected grounds are not a constant value. The new view of the human being, their rights and status, mean that the concept of discrimination and its scope constantly require a very thorough examination.

Without entering into details, it is worth mentioning certain protected grounds that have recently become particularly important in scholarly reflection. These include intelligence level, skills and competences (including language skills), name, surname, age,[50] having/not having children, obesity ('fattism' has been described as the 'last great acceptable prejudice'[51]), and even a beard.[52] It is difficult to assess situations where an employer refuses to

---

46 Ibidem.
47 So Yeon Kim, pp. 617–632.
48 Piotr Sztompka, pp. 82–83.
49 Ibidem, p. 84.
50 Anna Zawidzka-Łojek, "Zakaz dyskryminacji ze względu na wiek w prawie Unii Europejskiej", Warszawa 2013, p. 69.
51 For more, see: Iyiola Solanke, "Discrimination as Stigma", pp. 125–143.
52 See: the case of Sadruddin v. City of Newark after: Irmina Miernicka, p. 409.

recruit an applicant because of a criminal record, the incapacitation process and, in the future, the consent (or lack thereof) for microchip implants. Climate protection involves dynamically imposed restrictions that are most frequently connected with economic discrimination (means of transport, heating, and tourist places will be available at an appropriately high price).

Hence, a continuous extension of the list of criteria for unacceptable discrimination can be observed, which is a proof of increasing respect for fundamental rights.[53] It is no surprise that the list of protected grounds is open because (…) basically any attribute that the dominant group considers undesirable in a given situation may lead to discrimination against any minority group characterised by that attribute,[54] but restrictions that were considered normal in the past have lost that value and require a reasonable justification for their legitimacy (e.g. jobs prohibited for women).

5. Role of law in eliminating discrimination

M. Domańska rightly pointed out that anti-discrimination law has a dynamic nature. The balance of power in society is constantly changing, the identified needs are evolving and do not lend themselves to long-term categorisation.[55] The issue is further compounded by the fact that the rights of a minority, discrimination, and combating it frequently become an object of political calculation[56] and even populism.

S. Moreau argued that the three commonly recognised types of anti-discrimination laws are (i) prohibitions on what in the United States is known as 'disparate treatment' and in the United Kingdom, as 'direct discrimination'; (ii) prohibitions on what in the United States is known as 'disparate impact' and in the United Kingdom, as 'indirect discrimination'; and (iii) special

---

53 Łukasz Wacław, "Wyjątki od zakazu dyskryminacji ze względu na religię lub przekonania w zatrudnieniu pracowniczym na gruncie Article 4 dyrektywy 2000/78/we," Studia z Prawa Wyznaniowego, Tom 24/2021, p. 475.

54 Aleksandra Winiarska, Witold Klaus, pp. 10–11

55 Monika Domańska, "Zakaz dyskryminacji ze względu na więcej niż jedno zabronione kryterium", Warszawa 2019, p. 363.

56 Norbert Wons, "Mniejszości narodowe w Polsce – pomiędzy dyskryminacją, tolerancją a uprzywilejowaniem" [in:] Józef Kupny, Aniela Dylus, Tomasz Biedrzycki, "Dyskryminacja jako nowa kwestia społeczna", Katowice 2007, p. 132.

accommodation requirements for individuals with certain traits, such as disabilities. That author observed:

Anti-discrimination laws are a familiar feature of our legal landscape. In the private sector, they operate in certain contexts – for instance, the provision of goods and services, rental housing, and employment – to prohibit us from singling out individuals for less favourable treatment because of certain traits, such as their race, age, gender, or religion. They also sometimes prohibit us from adopting rules or practices that do not explicitly exclude anyone on the basis of a prohibited ground but nevertheless have the effect of disproportionately disadvantaging some groups on this basis, such as aerobic capacity tests that exclude women at a higher rate than men. And some anti-discrimination laws, such as the Americans with Disabilities Act, require us not just to avoid disadvantaging people on the basis of a prohibited ground of discrimination but also to provide the facilities and services they need.[57]

It is clear that anti-discrimination law attempts to give deliberative freedoms to all, because each of us has an independent entitlement to them. It attempts to give them to us by preventing our employers, service providers, landlords, and others from acting in ways that deny us opportunities because of these traits, so that when we deliberate about such things as where to work and where to live, we do not have to think about these traits as costs.[58] One should not overlook the fact that anti-discrimination provisions restrict the freedom of actors making a decision on the access to goods, services, or employment. Both discrimination and its prohibition restrict human rights.

When making anti-discrimination law, it is necessary to be aware of what rights are restricted in the name of respecting the equality principle and respect for diversity. They certainly include:

- economic and para-economic activity;[59]
- the freedom to manifest one's worldview and engage in behaviour consistent with it in the public space – freedom of the press, freedom of socio-cultural events;
- the freedom of artistic creation.

---

[57] Sophia Moreau, pp. 143–154.

[58] Sophia Moreau, p. 147.

[59] Aniela Dylus, "Dyskryminacja. Między faktycznością a normatywnością" [in:] Józef Kupny, Aniela Dylus, Tomasz Biedrzycki, "Dyskryminacja jako nowa kwestia społeczna", Katowice 2007, pp. 48–52.

These restrictions result from abandoning the absolute principle of fighting for one's own good in favour of giving support to weaker actors. That approach is a measure of civilisation and humanism.

At the same time, equality and diversity are not absolute values. Restrictions of the equality principle and respect for diversity can result from the need to respect such things as:

- the right to life and health, security, the provision of which requires specific competences;
- freedom of speech;
- religious freedom;
- ownership right, under which the costs of ensuring respect for diversity and equality must not unduly burden others.

The following regulation is obvious: 'This Directive does not require the recruitment, promotion, maintenance in employment or training of an individual who is not competent, capable and available to perform the essential functions of the post concerned or to undergo the relevant training, without prejudice to the obligation to provide reasonable accommodation for people with disabilities'.[60] The literature typically defines these provisions as 'exceptions to the prohibition on discrimination'. However, it follows from the literal wording of the cited provision that, as Ł. Wacław rightly pointed out, a different treatment of employees due to certain characteristics foreseen by the directive is not an exception to the prohibition on discrimination, but simply 'does not constitute discrimination'.[61]

A. Dylus argues that there are instances where well-intentioned anti-discrimination measures are inadequate in scope, content, or form and, consequently, become distorted, occasionally giving rise to discrimination and exploitation *a rebours*.[62] The problem of omitting or ignoring

---

60 Council Directive 2000/78/EC of 27 November 2000 establishing a general framework for equal treatment in employment and occupation, *Official Journal L 303* (preamble, point 17). See also Article 4 para. 1 of the directive.

61 Ibidem.

62 Aniela Dylus, pp. 29–30.

anti-discrimination regulations by obligated entities (e.g. employers) should be left aside.[63]

With reference to the elements of discrimination indicated earlier, it is possible to create a set of legal problems that the legislature dealing with discrimination has to resolve:

- What is the nature of protected grounds – are they man-dependent or independent, culpable or non-culpable?
- Should there be a list of protected grounds, can such a list be revised, or should it be universal and timeless?
- How far should the causality between the protected ground and the decision we potentially consider discriminatory go?
- What are the criteria for justifying unequal treatment and how should proportionality be constructed within their framework?
- What is a list of goods that have to be restricted to counteract discrimination?
- Is the duration of a particular phenomenon relevant to the identification of discrimination and is it a social or individual perspective?
- How does one establish the boundary between social (public) and private life?

The answers to these questions must be included not in the definitions and glossaries found in particular legal instruments, but in the specific provisions.

In situations of depriving or significantly impairing opportunities for the exercise of human rights by a person or group of people, international law obliges states to undertake affirmative action aimed at ensuring equal enjoyment of rights and freedoms, i.e. seeking to achieve substantive equality (equality *de facto*).[64] Such action is frequently referred to as temporary special measures, but also 'positive measures', 'positive discrimination', 'reverse discrimination', 'preferential treatment', or 'positive action'.[65] I believe these regulations can be called justifications – secondarily removing the discriminatory

---

[63] Dana Corina Deselnicu, Andreea Barbu, Marius-Ionel Anton, Discrimination Against Vulnerable Personnel in the Workplace, Proceedings of the International Conference on Business Excellence July 202418(1):1007–1017, DOI: <http://dx.doi.org/10.2478/picbe-2024-0088>.

[64] Agnieszka Bień-Kacała, Julia Kapelańska-Pręgowska, p. 13.

[65] Ibidem, p. 17.

nature of certain undertakings. Their aim is social and cultural change, not the creation of new rights. It is also necessary to take into account the context, meaning that they should be abandoned once the assumed real equality has been achieved.[66] Although former Commissioner for Human Rights Ewa Łętowska observed that affirmative action is entangled in politics, ideology, manipulation, and ignorance, she asks herself the question. "How does one protect oneself from having a legitimate preference aimed at egalitarianism turn into a tool for discriminating against members of another/different social group'.[67] It is underlined that such measures aim to shape the position of people in different areas of social life (public life, employment, and education) in such a way as to reduce or eliminate existing inequalities and enable the full enjoyment of human rights. Their temporary, individual, and specific nature is stressed.[68] However, a reversal of trends, though right and fair, leads – in the name of historical justice – to individual injustice in relation to specific members of dominant, more powerful groups who have previously exploited their advantage. This harms individuals with no access to goods or services and it produces effects similar to the effects of 'ordinary discrimination'; among other things, it may also be a source of new conflicts and unrest. The literature review shows counterarguments to anti-discrimination measures – the risk of 'secondary discrimination', violation of individual freedoms, humiliation of representatives of supported groups, reinforcement and perpetuation of social prejudices and stereotypes and economic losses; as well as the ineffectiveness or illusory nature of the compensatory nature of positive discrimination and the manifestation of paternalism (not always justified).[69]

It appears that temporary special measures are a sort of shortcut. The declared cultural and systemic changes can be introduced differently, but these are long and costly undertakings.

---

[66] Ibidem, p. 17.

[67] Ewa Łętowska, "Szczodrość deklaracji – skąpstwo realizacyjne, czyli o prawach kobiet w konstytucji" http://konsulty.pl/szczodrosc-deklaracji-skapstwo-realizacyjne-czyli-o-prawach-kobiet-w-konstytucji/, December 18, 2023.

[68] Katarzyna Sękowska-Kozłowska, "Między obowiązkiem a przyzwoleniem. Środki wyrównawcze na rzecz kobiet jako instrument realizacji praw człowieka", Warszawa 2021, pp. 220–221.

[69] Aniela Dylus, p. 53.

6. Conclusions

E. Łętowska is right to argue that 'equality' cannot simply mean 'applying' a male role model to women. In turn, the differentiation of law by the legislature falls into the trap of false protectionism: it either discriminates against men in relation to women, and/or makes women, for example, unattractive as competitors to men in the labour market.[70] This conclusion applies to all areas of discrimination.

The above considerations allow a final conclusion. Regulations that are too detailed, casuistic, depriving discriminated individuals of their autonomy, and interfering too much in the autonomy of discriminating actors, not taking into account the situational context and dynamic social changes, are a trap for the fight against discrimination. At the level of making and applying anti-discrimination law, immense significance lies in the principle of equity, which allows the full individualisation of assessment and maximum respect for the autonomy of free people. W. Dziedziak correctly argues that equity is a corrective value in the application of law – rectifying, perfecting, and complementing the law while fulfilling justice. At the same time, the author points out that equity opposes law-making relativism, which in essence also applies to instruments of interpretation and application of law.[71]

One must recall the words of J. Elliott: 'We learn to be racists, which means we can also learn how not to be them. There is no gene for racism'.[72] The phenomena of marginalisation and exclusion can also be mitigated and regulated. Social pedagogics developed at least two roads to demarginalisation. The first may be supportive care based on the principles of social solidarity. The second is the belief that the best mechanism for demarginalisation is education.[73]

---

70 Ewa Łętowska, 18 December 2023.

71 Wojciech Dziedziak, "Słuszność jako wartość prawa", Studia Iuridica Lublinensia 2011/15, pp. 71–81.

72 Nora Lester, "Niebieskoocy. Podręcznik do prowadzenia zajęć w organizacjach", Stowarzyszenie Kobiet Konsola 2006, p. 5.

73 Anna Nowak, p. 31.

Bibliography

Andersson M. A., Harnois C. E., "Higher exposure, lower vulnerability? The curious case of education, gender discrimination, and women's health", Social Science & Medicine, Volume 246, February 2020.

Bień-Kacała A., Kapelańska-Pręgowska J., "Niższy wiek emerytalny kobiet: przywilej czy dyskryminacja? Perspektywa prawnomiędzynarodowa i konstytucyjna", Praca i Zabezpieczenie Społeczne 01/2022.

Burek W., Klaus W., "Definiowanie dyskryminacji w prawie polskim w świetle prawa Unii Europejskiej oraz prawa międzynarodowego", Problemy Współczesnego Prawa Międzynarodowego, Europejskiego i Porównawczego, vol. XI, A.D. MMXIII.

Casey-Maslen S., Heyns C., "In The Right to Life under International Law: An Interpretative Manual" Cambridge University Press 202.

O'Cinneide C., "The Principle of Equality and Non-discrimination within the Framework of the EU Charter and Its Potential Application to Social and Solidarity Rights" in: "Making the Charter of Fundamental Rights a Living Instrument", G. Palmisano (Eds.), Brill Nijhoff 2014.

"Handbook on European non-discrimination law", Publications Office of the EU, 2018, <https://rm.coe.int/fra-2018-handbook-non-discrimination-law-2018-en/1680a2b52b>.

Deselnicu D. C., Barbu A., Anton M.-I, Discrimination Against Vulnerable Personnel in the Workplace, Proceedings of the International Conference on Business Excellence July 202418(1):1007–1017, <http://dx.doi.org/10.2478/picbe-2024-0088>.

Domańska M., "Zakaz dyskryminacji ze względu na więcej niż jedno zabronione kryterium", Warszawa 2019.

Dziedziak W., "Słuszność jako wartość prawa", Studia Iuridica Lublinensia 2011/15.

Dylus A., "Dyskryminacja. Między faktycznością a normatywnością" in: J. Kupny, A. Dylus, T. Biedrzycki, "Dyskryminacja jako nowa kwestia społeczna", Katowice 2007.

Jabłońska Z. in: Kędziora K., Śmiszek K. (Eds.), "Ustawa o wdrożeniu niektórych przepisów Unii Europejskiej w zakresie równego traktowania. Komentarz", Warszawa 2017.

Kułak M., "Zakaz dyskryminacji w dostępie do dóbr i usług a prawa podstawowe usługobiorców i usługodawców w prawie Unii Europejskiej. Rozprawa doktorska", Warszawa 2020.

Kim S.Y., "Les vulnérables: evaluating the vulnerability criterion in Article 14 cases by the European Court of Human Rights", Legal Studies (2021), 41, p. 620. doi:10.1017/lst.2021.21.

Lester N., "Niebieskoocy. Podręcznik do prowadzenia zajęć w organizacjach", Stowarzyszenie Kobiet Konsola 2006.

Łętowska E., "Szczodrość deklaracji – skąpstwo realizacyjne, czyli o prawach kobiet w konstytucji", <http://konstytucyjny.pl/szczodrosc-deklaracji-skapstwo-realizacyjne-czyli-o-prawach-kobiet-w-konstytucji/>, 18 December 2023.

O'Mahony C., "There is no such thing as a right to dignity", *International Journal of Constitutional Law*, Volume 10, Issue 2, 30 March 2012.

Miernicka I., "Dyskryminacja w zatrudnieniu ze względu na wygląd" in: Carby-Hall J. R., Góral Z., Tyc A. (Eds.), "Różne oblicza dyskryminacji w zatrudnieniu", Warszawa 2021.

Maliszewska-Nienartowicz J., "Dyskryminacja ze względu na religię, niepełnosprawność, wiek lub orientację seksualną. Dyrektywa 2000/78 i orzecznictwo TS UE. Komentarz", Warszawa 2013.

Moreau S., "What is discrimination?", Philosophy and Public Affairs 38 (2)/2010.

Muir E., "The Essence of the Fundamental Right to Equal Treatment: Back to the Origins", German Law Journal (2019), 20, pp. 817–839. doi:10.1017/glj.2019.64.

Nowak A., "Pojęcie, istota, przyczyny, mechanizmy marginalizacji i wykluczenia społecznego", Chowanna 1/2012.

Olmińska A., "Dyskryminacja jako przykład nierównego traktowania pracownika", Roczniki Administracji i Prawa nr XVII.

Płażek S., "Karalność pracownika a dyskryminacja w zatrudnieniu" in: J. R. Carby-Hall, Z. Góral, A. Tyc (Eds.), "Różne oblicza dyskryminacji w zatrudnieniu", Warszawa 2021.

Reisigl M., "Dyskryminacja w dyskursach", Tekst i dyskurs 3/2010.

Roscigno Vincent J. , "Discrimination, Sexual Harassment, and the Impact of Workplace Power", Socius, 5/2019, <https://journals.sagepub.com/doi/10.1177/2378023119853894>.

de Schutter O., "Three Models of Equality and European Anti-Discrimination Law", Northern Ireland Legal Quarterly Vol. 57, No. 1.

Sękowska-Kozłowska K., "Między obowiązkiem a przyzwoleniem. Środki wyrównawcze na rzecz kobiet jako instrument realizacji praw człowieka", Warszawa 2021.

Solanke I., "The anti-stigma principle and legal protection from fattism", Fat Studies 10/2021.

Solanke I., "Discrimination as Stigma. A theory of Anti-discrimination Law", Oxford and Portland, Oregon 2017.

Szewczyk H., "Dyskryminacja ze względu na przekonania religijne: glosa do wyroku Trybunału Sprawiedliwości z 14.03.2017 r., C-157/15, Samira Achbita i Centrum voor gelijkheid van kansen en voor racismebestrijding przeciwko G4S Secure Solutions NV", Europejski Przegląd Sądowy 2017, no. 10.

Sztompka P., "Socjologia zmian społecznych", Kraków 2005.

Wacław Ł., "Wyjątki od zakazu dyskryminacji ze względu na religię lub przekonania w zatrudnieniu pracowniczym na gruncie Article 4 dyrektywy 2000/78/we", Studia z Prawa Wyznaniowego, Tom 24/2021.

Williams W. E., "Discrimination: The Law vs. Morality", *Cornell Journal of Law and Public Policy*, Vo. 13, Issue 1, Fall 2003.

Winiarska A., Klaus W., "Dyskryminacja i nierówne traktowanie jako zjawisko społeczno-kulturowe", Studia BAS Nr 2(26) 2011.

Wons N., "Mniejszości narodowe w Polsce – pomiędzy dyskryminacją, tolerancją a uprzywilejowaniem" in: Kupny J., Dylus A., Biedrzycki T., "Dyskryminacja jako nowa kwestia społeczna", Katowice 2007.

Zawidzka-Łojek A., "Zakaz dyskryminacji ze względu na wiek w prawie Unii Europejskiej", Warszawa 2013.

Zima-Pierjaszewska M., "Zakaz dyskryminacji a uchybienie godności studenta", Studia Iuridica 84, p. 47.

Vulnerable Groups and Supermajority Rules in Constitutional Adjudication: From a Theoretical Insight to a Comparative Perspective

Mauro Arturo Rivera León[*,1]

Abstract: Constitutional courts are deemed to be deliberative bodies adjudicating constitutional questions, usually through a simple majority vote. Nonetheless, in comparative scholarship, several instances of supermajorities exist. For example, the Supreme Courts of Nebraska and North Dakota in the United States employ supermajority rules, as do the constitutional courts of South Korea, the Czech Republic, Peru, the Dominican Republic, and Chile, among others. Despite having existed since the 1900s, the theoretical validity of supermajority rules has only recently been explored, mainly through the works of Shugerman, Caminker and, to some extent, Waldron. A contemporary debate has arisen regarding their validity, with several objections raised. It is often argued that supermajorities make it harder for courts to fulfil their task of protecting human rights, thereby impacting vulnerable groups, and that supermajorities obstruct the courts' functioning or may allow political branches to control courts through selective court packing. This chapter seeks to analyse the vulnerability objection through a theoretical discussion of its underlying assumptions. It suggests that the argument relies on the disputable assumption that supermajorities significantly prevent courts from striking down legislation, disproportionally affecting vulnerable groups. It also presupposes that constitutional court judges ideologically tend to align with vulnerable groups in a significantly higher proportion than elected legislatures and executives, which is a contingent claim context-dependent.

Keywords: supermajority rules, constitutional adjudication, vulnerability, constitutional review, human rights

* Ph.D., Assistant Professor at the Faculty of Law and Administration of the University of Silesia in Katowice, Poland. ORCID: 0000-0003-4964-7086.

1 The research leading to these results has received funding from the Norwegian Financial Mechanism 2014–2021, under Research Project No 2020/37/K/HS5/02758, titled "Qualified majorities in counter-majoritarian mechanisms: Towards a new theory of supermajorities in judicial review."

1. Introduction

Scholarship has often described judicial review as a deliberative forum for principled discussion.[2] Nonetheless, courts often disagree on the meaning of the constitution and the constitutionality of statutes. In cases of disagreement, most constitutional courts or judicial bodies performing judicial review resolve cases through majority voting. Majority voting is the prevailing method in the supreme courts of the United States and India, as well as in formal constitutional courts, such as those in South Africa, Germany, Spain, Italy, and Poland. As Waldron has pointed out,[3] there is scarce analysis on the validity of majority voting within courts, although recent scholarship has begun to take on the task.[4]

Conversely, some jurisdictions employ a supermajority rule in determining the constitutionality of statutes, or even, as in the case of the Dominican Republic and formerly in Peru in 1982, require a supermajority for the court to make any decision. Although the theoretical validity of supermajority rules in constitutional adjudication has just recently been re-examined,[5]

---

2 John Rawls, *Political Liberalism* (Columbia University Press 1993); Ferejohn, John and Pasquino, Pasquale, 'Constitutional Courts as Deliberative Institutions: Towards an Institutional Theory of Constitutional Justice' in Sadurski, Wojciech (Ed.), *Constitutional Justice, East and West. Democratic Legitimacy and Constitutional Courts in Post-Communist Europe in a Comparative Perspective* (Springer 2002); Conrado Hübner Mendes, *Constitutional Courts and Deliberative Democracy* (Oxford University Press 2013).

3 Jeremy Waldron, 'Five to Four: Why Do Bare Majorities Rule on Courts' (2014) 123 The Yale Law Journal 1692.

4 Favouring majority voting, see Guha Krishnamurthi, 'For Judicial Majoritarianism' (2019) 22 University of Pennsylvania Journal of Constitutional Law 1201. For a contrary view, see Cristóbal Caviedes, 'Is Majority Rule Justified in Constitutional Adjudication?' (2021) 41 Oxford Journal of Legal Studies 376.

5 Supermajority rules, particularly those pertaining to legislative procedures, have previously been discussed alongside absolute majority rules. See Adrian Vermeule, 'Absolute Majority Rules' (2007) 37 British Journal of Political Science 643; Keith L Dougherty and Julian Edward, 'The Properties of Simple Vs. Absolute Majority Rule: Cases Where Absences and Abstentions Are Important' (2010) 22 Journal of Theoretical Politics 85; King, Brett, 'The Use of Supermajority Provisions in the Constitution: The Framers, the Federalist Papers and the Reinforcement of a Fundamental Principle' (1998) 8 Seton Hall Constitutional Law Journal 363; Melissa Schwartzberg, 'The Arbitrariness of Supermajority Rules' (2010) 49 Social Science Information 61; Melissa Schwartzberg, *Counting the Many: The Origins and Limits of Supermajority Rule* (Cambridge University Press 2013).

supermajority rules for ruling on the constitutionality of statutes have existed since the early 1900s.

During the progressive era in the United States, Ohio,[6] North Dakota,[7] and Nebraska[8] all adopted supermajority rules, in 1912, 1919, and 1920, respectively, while the Czechoslovak Constitutional Court, which came into being in 1920, employed a supermajority to strike down statutes and ordinances.[9] Despite the empirical experience, scholarship offered limited analysis of supermajority rules.

In the early 2000s, contributions by Shugerman[10] and Caminker[11] unleashed a discussion, heated subsequently by Waldron's questioning of majority rule in courts.[12] Contemporarily, a broader discussion is emerging on the feasibility of supermajority rules and their advantages for constitutional adjudication.[13]

---

6 W Rolland Maddox, 'Minority Control of Court Decisions in Ohio' (1930) 24 American Political Science Review 638; Carl L Meier, 'Power of the Ohio Supreme Court to Declare Laws Unconstitutional' (1931) 5 U. Cin. L. Rev. 293. However, in the case of Ohio, the supermajority was repealed in 1968 by the Modern Courts amendment. William W Milligan and James E Pohlman, 'The 1968 Modern Courts Amendment to the Ohio Constitution' (1968) 29 Ohio St. LJ 811.

7 Fite, Katherine B. and Rubinstein, Louis Baruch, 'Curbing the Supreme Court – State Experiences and Federal Proposals' (1937) 35 Michigan Law Review 762, 779–80.

8 Paul W Madgett, 'The Five-Judge Rule in Nebraska' (1968) 2 Creighton Law Review 329.

9 Jana Osterkamp, *Verfassungsgerichtsbarkeit in der Tschechoslowakei (1920–1939): Verfassungsidee, Demokratieverständnis, Nationalitätenproblem* (V Klostermann 2009) 68. See also Tomáš Langášek, *Ústavní Soud Československé Republiky a Jeho Osudy v Letech 1920–1948* (Vydavatelství a nakladatelství Aleš Čeněk 2011) 32–33.

10 Jed Handelsman Shugerman, 'A Six-Three Rule: Reviving Consensus and Deference on the Supreme Court' (2003) 37 Georgia Law Review 893.

11 Evan H Caminker, 'Thayerian Deference to Congress and Supreme Court Supermajority Rules: Lessons from the Past' (2003) 78 Indiana Law Journal 73.

12 Waldron (n 3). Waldron did not explicitly advocate for supermajority rules. However, he questioned majority rule as a natural decision-making rule in courts, observing that legislatures were often being depicted as dominated by majoritarianism despite courts employing the same decisional mechanism.

13 Pablo Castillo-Ortiz, 'The Dilemmas of Constitutional Courts and the Case for a New Design of Kelsenian Institutions' (2020) 39 Law and Philosophy 617; Yaniv Roznai, 'Introduction: Constitutional Courts in a 100-Years Perspective and a Proposal for a Hybrid Model of Judicial Review' (2021) 14 ICL Journal 355; Cristóbal Caviedes, 'A Core Case for Supermajority Rules in Constitutional Adjudication' (2022) 20

Supporters of supermajority rules generally contend that such rules may supplement deference to legislation, diminishing the counter-majoritarian nature of judicial review. Supermajorities are said to produce more accurate decisions from a Condorcetean perspective and even foster dialogue, deliberation and consensus among the courts.[14]

On the other hand, detractors of supermajorities consider that such rules may be epistemically dubious by preventing majorities from deciding,[15] which may lead to court paralysis[16] or may allow political branches to unduly control the court.[17] Finally, there are those who have posited that supermajorities may place an insurmountable obstacle to courts in their duty to enforce constitutional rights, thus having a disproportional effect on vulnerable groups, which are likely to be more dependent on courts for guaranteeing the enforcement of their rights.

While some scholars have tackled theoretical objections to supermajority rules and others have begun to address some of the more practical concerns

---

International Journal of Constitutional Law 1162; Cristóbal Caviedes, *Supermajority Voting in Constitutional Courts: The Problem of Majority Rule for Democracy and Legislation* (Routledge 2024); Mauro Arturo Rivera León, 'Judicial Review of Supermajority Rules Governing Courts' Own Decision-Making: A Comparative Analysis' (2024) 13 Global Constitutionalism 79; Mauro Arturo Rivera León, 'Control and Paralysis? A Context-Sensitive Analysis of Objections to Supermajorities in Constitutional Adjudication' (2024) 22 International Journal of Constitutional Law 134; Mauro Arturo Rivera León, *Supermajorities in Constitutional Courts* (Routledge 2024).

14 For a theoretical outline of the advantages of supermajorities, see Caviedes' recent piece: Caviedes, 'A Core Case for Supermajority Rules in Constitutional Adjudication' (n 13).

15 Krishnamurthi (n 4) 1238.

16 Sandra Zellmer and Kathleen Miller, 'The Fallacy of Judicial Supermajority Clauses in State Constitutions' (2015) 47 University of Toledo Law Review 73, 87; Venice Commission, 'Opinion No. 833/2015 On Amendments to the Act of 25 June 2015 on the Constitutional Tribunal (CDL-AD(2016)001' (Venice Commission 2016) CDL-AD(2016)001; Venice Commission, 'Preliminary Opinion 849/2016 on the Amendments to the Organic Law on the Constitutional Court and to the Law on Constitutional Legal Proceedings' (Venice Commission 2016) CDL-PI(2016)005.

17 Rivera León, 'Control and Paralysis? A Context-Sensitive Analysis of Objections to Supermajorities in Constitutional Adjudication' (n 13) 13.

of their functioning,[18] scholarship has yet to address, theoretically or comparatively, the objection concerning the rights of vulnerable groups. This chapter attempts to fill that gap by undertaking a defence of supermajorities in view of the vulnerability objection.

The remainder of the chapter is structured as follows. Section 2 outlines a core formulation of the vulnerability argument and highlights the origin of its inception in the scholarship and policymaking arena. The section shows that the vulnerability argument is based on at least two disputable assumptions regarding the relationship between judicial review and vulnerable groups. Section 3 tackles the vulnerability argument by dissecting its assumptions. On the one hand, the section argues that, empirically, it is not proven that supermajorities will prevent courts from enforcing the rights of vulnerable groups to a significant extent. Furthermore, it disputes the assumption that instances in which supermajority rules prevent striking down legislation will disproportionately affect vulnerable groups. It also contests that the implicit claims that judges better guard the rights of vulnerable groups than legislatures rely on non-proven ideological assumptions. The section shows this to be a contingent claim, proven by the fact that the first supermajority requirements in constitutional adjudication in the United States were introduced to prevent courts from striking progressive regulations and thereby providing rights to vulnerable groups. Finally, Section 4 provides concluding remarks and offers a roadmap to a future research agenda.

2. The core formulation of the vulnerability argument

Several scholars have expressed concerns about introducing a supermajority rule on constitutional adjudication, due to its potentially harmful impact on the ability of courts to fulfil their role as protectors of human rights. Some have criticised supermajorities, claiming that supermajorities dubiously instate a presumption of unconstitutionality 'against the citizen [seeking

---

[18] Regarding objections of court control and court paralysis, see Rivera León, 'Control and Paralysis? A Context-Sensitive Analysis of Objections to Supermajorities in Constitutional Adjudication' (n 13). On the general functioning of supermajority rules and the formal and informal institutions surrounding their applications, see Rivera León, *Supermajorities in Constitutional Courts* (n 13).

to defend his rights]'[19] and that simple majorities are more favourable to fundamental rights.[20]

Zellmer and Miller considered that a supermajority requirement 'undermines the ability of the court to protect the constitutional rights of vulnerable individuals and groups'.[21] They considered that unpopular racial and religious minorities, along with other viewpoints disfavoured by majority groups, become vulnerable as their rights are susceptible to infringement by political majorities already represented by Congress and the Executive Branch.[22]

Recently, when considering a reformulation of Kelsenian constitutional courts, Castillo-Ortiz deemed that supermajorities were an adequate option to supplement restraint to courts, institutionalising a clear mistake rule. Nonetheless, he considered that supermajorities could potentially undermine an essential value of constitutional courts, namely their ability to protect democracy and human rights.[23]

The argument is not only of a scholarly nature. It has even featured in the first examples of supermajorities established in constitutional adjudication. In the Nebraska Constitutional Convention (1919–1920), Deputy Oleson, opposing the introduction of a supermajority, considered that raising the threshold to declare statutes unconstitutional directly endangers constitutionally guaranteed rights. Oleson considered it even more logical to require a supermajority to declare statutes constitutional.[24]

While scholarship has offered other arguments against supermajority rules worthy of attention, the scholars mentioned above have raised objections to them due to their disproportionate impact on vulnerable groups and the function of judicial review in defending fundamental rights. I will categorise this objection as the 'vulnerability argument'. To address the argument, I will first establish its core case.

---

19 Joaquín Brage, *La acción abstracta de inconstitucionalidad* (IIJ-UNAM 2005) 347.

20 Acosta, Hermógenes, 'El Proceso de Amparo En El Nuevo Modelo de Justicia Constitucional Dominicano' in Eto, Gerardo (ed), *Treinta años de jurisdicción constitucional en el Perú* (Centro de Estudios Constitucionales 2014) 185.

21 Zellmer and Miller (n 16) 85.

22 ibid.

23 Castillo-Ortiz (n 13) 640.

24 Clyde H. Barnard (ed), *Journal of the Nebraska Constitutional Convention (1921)* (The Kline Pub Co 1921) 1135.

The vulnerability argument may be summarised as follows: constitutional courts and other institutions primarily performing judicial review are usually tasked with the defence of rights. By heightening the decisional threshold, supermajorities create judicial inertia disproportionally favouring the elected branches – Executive and Legislative – which already represent majority views through their connection with the electorate. Judges are then less likely to invalidate legislation enforcing fundamental rights. Since fundamental rights are usually presumed to be minority triumphs against majoritarian will, the mechanism tilts the odds in favour of majoritarianism, adversely to vulnerable groups.

This core case leads to a number of assumptions pertaining to judicial review. In the first place, it considers normatively rights enforcement to be a primary function of judicial review. Second, it makes an empirically verifiable claim that a higher threshold will result in considerably fewer decisions favouring rights, which will substantially impact vulnerable groups. Finally, it also assumes that courts are more prone to enforcing rights than legislatures, and that, *ceteris paribus*, judges will be more prone to enforcing the rights of vulnerable groups than elected legislatures.

From the three outlined assumptions, at least the second and third are disputable. Although some scholars have formulated substantive relevant objections to the existence of judicial review by claiming that, in functional societies, democratic legislatures may better protect rights than a non-elected judiciary,[25] I am going to assume here that, where functional institutions of judicial review exist in a given jurisdiction, the enforcement of individual rights is a relevant contribution of those institutions. Section 3 will address the vulnerability objection by disputing the remaining two assumptions.

3. Addressing a theoretical objection

3.1 Supermajorities will prevent courts from enforcing the rights of vulnerable groups

One disputable assumption of the vulnerability argument is that courts will render substantially fewer decisions enforcing the rights of vulnerable groups

[25] Jeremy Waldron, 'The Core of the Case against Judicial Review' (2006) 115 The Yale Law Journal 1346.

if a supermajority threshold exists. This assertion requires unpacking. Courts discuss, deliberate and vote on making decisions. In courts functioning under a majority rule, decisions are taken in accordance with the opinion of half plus one of the judges, either of the court or, ordinarily, of those present and voting, provided that quorum requirements have been introduced.

This assumption posits that the higher threshold will necessarily impact rights protection, since it will be mathematically harder to attain a supermajority of judges than a majority of them in favour of a given proposition. Paradoxically, this argument also partially functions in cases of majority rule. It is theoretically possible to have problems reaching a majority of judges, even in systems in which supermajorities are not required. For example, ties may arise in courts with an even number of members,[26] and the same situation may occur in odd-member courts when judges are recused or absent. Furthermore, there are courts in which ties favour the constitutionality of legislation – presumably, adversely to the rights of vulnerable groups, as the objection would claim – such as in the German Constitutional Court. In other courts, several impasse rules allow taking non-majority decisions that will not necessarily favour rights, such as an affirmance by an equally divided court in the United States,[27] or decisions governed by the Chief Justice's casting vote, such as in the Italian or Spanish Constitutional Courts.[28]

Despite the above, no relevant objection has been formulated against majority voting as a decisional mechanism, for example, favouring a plurality vote, based on the fact that it produces a higher probability of rendering decisions adverse to the interests of vulnerable groups. One possible explanation is that situations in which the majority vote reaches such decisional impasses are rare, meaning it is not a significantly relevant objection based

---

[26] Ernst, Wolfgang, 'The Fine-Mechanisms of Judicial Majoritarianism' in Birke Häcker and Wolfgang Ernst (Eds.), *Collective Judging in Comparative Perspective: Counting Votes and Weighing Opinions* (Intersentia 2020) 15.

[27] Generally, see Hartnett, Edward, 'Ties in the Supreme Court of the United States' (2002) 44 William and Mary Law Review 643.

[28] For Italy, see Raffaele Bifulco and Davide Paris, 'The Italian Constitutional Court', *The Max Planck Handbooks in European Public Law: Volume III: Constitutional Adjudication. Institutions* (Oxford University Press 2020) 460. In Spain, the casting vote has been critically examined. Santaolalla, Fernando, 'El Voto de Calidad Del Presidente Del Tribunal Constitucional' [2009] Revista Española de Derecho Constitucional 201.

on its de facto statistical occurrence. Can a similar claim be formulated in the case of supermajority rules?

Considering that supermajority rules are bound to prevent striking down a certain number of statutes, the higher threshold would, unquestionably to some degree, prevent decisions favouring the rights of vulnerable groups – although supermajority critics should also concede that they are bound statistically to also protect such rights in some instances, for example, by safeguarding protective statutes from being struck down by restrictive courts. Thus, for the objection to be valid, there must be some significant degree of incidence of supermajority rules in procedures in which the rights of vulnerable groups are settled. That is an empirically verifiable claim.

Scholarship has not delved systematically into the empirical impact of supermajority rules until recently.[29] Analysing the jurisdictions of Ohio, North Dakota, Nebraska, the former Czechoslovakia, the Czech Republic, Peru, the Dominican Republic, and Mexico, recent studies have posited that supermajority rules tend to have a minor impact on courts.[30] In many jurisdictions, the rate at which such rules affect courts is less than or equal to 5% of the decisions in which supermajority rules are applicable.[31] This rate also covers decisions not pertaining to the rights of vulnerable groups and statutes that favoured the rights of such groups (thus being protected by the supermajority not allowing the respective statute to be invalidated). Statistically, the effect is unlikely to be perceivable in view of the arguable behaviour that courts in such jurisdictions would possess under majority rule.

Fractional decreases in the percentages of decisions that may favour vulnerable groups by invalidating statutes seem not to be a convincing argument for discarding the validity of a voting system, particularly when supermajorities offer other advantages that should be pondered when considering their possible shortcomings.

---

29 There are two exceptions that provide some information that allows making statistical inferences, although neither of them focuses significantly on the issue. Fite, Katherine B. and Rubinstein, Louis Baruch (n 7); Joon Seok Hong, 'Signaling the Turn: The Supermajority Requirement and Judicial Power on the Constitutional Court of Korea' (2019) 67 The American Journal of Comparative Law 177.

30 Rivera León, *Supermajorities in Constitutional Courts* (n 13).

31 ibid 198.

A second, more nuanced version of the assumption could posit that, even though statistically the rule's occurrence in cases pertaining to vulnerable groups is not significant, there is an added substantive impact that vulnerable groups would take. Since vulnerable groups are underrepresented in traditional political discourse, their rights ought to be perceived as controversial, so a supermajority is likely to affect them with a higher propensity than others. That is also a claim addressable from an empirical perspective.

Given the fact that several datasets exist highlighting instances in which supermajorities have prevented courts from declaring the unconstitutionality of legislation,[32] a starting point from an empirical discussion could be initiated by classifying the provisions protected by the supermajority rule in various jurisdictions, considering whether the rights pertaining to vulnerable groups would have been affirmed without the qualified threshold. Such research would also allow a more precise overview of the rate at which the voting protocol obstructs decisions favouring such groups.

A partially similar exercise was undertaken for Mexico, reporting that most provisions protected by the supermajority rule concerned the realm of electoral law or administrative governmental regulations, followed by criminal and tax law regulations.[33] Provisions pertaining to human rights, covering those held by vulnerable and non-vulnerable groups alike, had a minor incidence.[34] Replicating a more precise version of this research in other jurisdictions would be clarifying.

While such an exercise would not definitively confirm that supermajorities do not hinder vulnerable groups, it could prove that some of the critical

32 See, generally, ibid 205.

33 Mauro Arturo Rivera León, 'La Mayoría Calificada En La Invalidez de Normas En Materia Electoral: Un Análisis de Su Comportamiento Empírico' in Rubén Lara Patrón (Ed.), *La acción de inconstitucionalidad en materia electoral* (Tirant lo Blanch 2023) 458.

34 As stated previously, such work only partially illustrates the probable empirical results. Although a category for "rights" was drafted, it concerned statutes solely regulating constitutional rights. It is possible that rights, even those pertaining to vulnerable people, had been discussed in rulings classified as "criminal law" or "tax law". For example, several of the decisions on criminal law accounted for by the 2023 study referred to the rights of victims of crime, usually considered a vulnerable group. Other regulations affected prisoners, who are considered a vulnerable group on several accounts.

assumptions of the vulnerability argument are factually inaccurate – for example, their alleged propensity to impact vulnerable groups.[35]

3.2. Are Judges more prone to protect rights than Legislatures? A complex assumption

The final assumption of the vulnerability argument is that judges are generally more prone to protect rights than legislatures, and so having judges able to reverse decisions made by the political branches through a softer threshold will strengthen the protection of vulnerable groups. Conversely, raising the threshold will leave the rights of vulnerable groups more often in the hands of the elected branches, whose interests tend to be less aligned with the former.

Who are vulnerable groups, and why should judges be presumed to be ideologically prone to ensure their rights more than legislatures?

The concept of vulnerability itself is generally considered vague, as it is its application to defining vulnerable groups. Scholarship has pointed out that the notion of vulnerability may be linked to greater difficulty in exercising rights and being underrepresented in dominant discourses. Conditions of vulnerability 'affect the group as a whole and their individual members specifically'.[36]

There is no generally legally binding definition of vulnerable groups in international law, which would not be subject to variation across jurisdictions.[37] Nonetheless, as a soft law, Section 2.1(3) of the Brasilia Regulations Regarding Access to Justice for Vulnerable People defines them as 'those who, due to reasons of age, gender, physical or mental state, or due to social,

[35] However, nuanced versions of the vulnerability argument could still be theoretically defended. In a nuanced version of the arguments, detractors of supermajority rules could claim that, although statistically non-significant, the few decisions in which supermajorities tilted the odds against vulnerable groups produce a particularly strong intromission in defence of their rights, as they are already underrepresented in the traditional political channels.

[36] Ingrid Nifosi-Sutton, *The Protection of Vulnerable Groups under International Human Rights Law* (first issued in paperback, Routledge, Taylor & Francis Group 2019) 5.

[37] For an attempt to reconstruct the concept of vulnerable groups based on the European Courts of Human Rights case law, see Lourdes Peroni and Alexandra Timmer, 'Vulnerable Groups: The Promise of an Emerging Concept in European Human Rights Convention Law' (2013) 11 International Journal of Constitutional Law 1056.

economic, ethnic and/or cultural circumstances, find it especially difficult to fully exercise their rights before the justice system as recognised to them by law'.

Attempting to provide a typology on the root causes of vulnerability, Ippolito and Iglesias consider the shared characteristics of classic vulnerability groups that make them perceived as inherently vulnerable – for example, disabilities. A second group would encompass vulnerability stemming out of a position of being a minority in terms of the dominant cultural, social or sexual orientation positions in society. A third classification would rely on the position that states grant to non-nationals. A fourth position would consider vulnerable groups caused by human behaviour, such as trafficked migrants and victims of crime, among others. In contrast, a fifth and final group would be constituted by prisoners, irregular immigrants and socially vulnerable people who have a contingent situation of vulnerability.[38]

Regardless of the theoretical problems in providing a conclusive list of vulnerable groups, several scholars have considered that the following groups are generally identified as vulnerable: people with a disability, indigenous people, refugees, people affected by conflicts, ethnic and religious minorities, women, children, older people, and people with several life-endangering diseases, such as HIV/AIDS.[39]

The vulnerability argument would claim that judges better protect these groups than legislatures, and thus, every requirement that increases the decision-making costs of the courts to enforce those rights by striking down statutes that restrict them directly hinders the protection of such interests. The example of transgender rights in the Czech Republic could be paradigmatic of the situation the vulnerability argument claims supermajorities may foster.

---

38 Francesca Ippolito and Sara Iglesias Sánchez, 'Introduction' in Francesca Ippolito and Sara Iglesias Sánchez (Eds.), *Protecting vulnerable groups: the European human rights framework* (Hart Publishing 2015) 5–6.

39 I reconstructed the groups based on the examples provided in Agnė Limantė and Artūras Tereškinas, 'Definition of Vulnerable Groups' in Agnė Limantė and Dovilė Pūraitė-Andrikienė (eds), *Legal Protection of Vulnerable Groups in Lithuania, Latvia, Estonia and Poland*, vol 8 (Springer International Publishing 2022); Francesca Ippolito and Sara Iglesias Sánchez (Eds.), *Protecting Vulnerable Groups: The European Human Rights Framework* (Hart Publishing 2015).

In 2020, the Czech Constitutional Court, functioning under a supermajority, was unable to declare the unconstitutionality of a provision of the Act on the Population Record that required disabling the reproductive function and transforming the genitalia as a condition to perform gender reassignment surgery. A bare majority of the court considered the restriction unconstitutional. Given the supermajority requirement, the court fell one vote short of the required threshold. The dissenting opinion considered that the self-restraint of the court endangered the protection of the rights of transgender people,[40] a clearly identified minority and vulnerable group.

Although a seductive example, the argument remains contingent on the ideological position of courts, which may vary across time and jurisdictions. For a counterexample, take the US Supreme Court. A supermajority would have a very different effect on abortion rights under the Burger Court than under the Roberts Court. A supermajority would have constrained results traditionally associated with the protection of vulnerable groups in the Burger or the Warren Court, but would prevent outcomes that would be likely classified as disfavouring rights were it to be imposed on the Roberts Courts.

Abortion offers a perfect example of how supermajority rules may be on both sides of the coin: protecting vulnerable groups or preventing the enforcement of their rights, depending on the temporary ideological leaning of judges. In 2000, the Mexican Supreme Court divided 6:5 regarding the unconstitutionality of the 'Robles Law', a statute allowing abortion in cases of rape in Mexico City.[41] The supermajority requirement prevented the court from invalidating that piece of legislation. Vulnerable groups preserved their right because of the requirement to reach a qualified eight-vote majority. Conversely, in 2014, the 4:1 supermajority requirement in North Dakota prevented the state Supreme Court from striking down a regulation restricting abortion rights in *MKB Management Corp v. Burdick*.[42]

---

40 Doubek, Pavel, 'Sterilization of Transgender People: A Worrying Judgement of the Czech Constitutional Court' (*ECHR Blog*) <https://www.echrblog.com/2022/04/sterilization-of-transgender-people.html>.

41 Steven Gow Calabresi, *The History and Growth of Judicial Review, Volume 2: The G-20 Civil Law Countries*, vol 2 (Oxford University Press 2021) 239.

42 2014 N.D. 197 (N.D. 2014). For a brief commentary on the case, see North Dakota: North Dakota Law Review Associate Editors, 'North Dakota Supreme Court Review' (2014) 90 North Dakota Law Review 637, 639.

As an institution, per se, judicial review is not necessarily bound to side with vulnerable groups. If anything, it at least partially tends to ideologically lean toward the policy preferences of justices, as often claimed by political science scholarship. Such preferences are contingent and not fixed. Considering this objection, Zellmer and Miller exemplify multiple cases in which the Supreme Court has rendered decisions favouring rights due to the majority rule in decision-making, such as in *Miranda vs Arizona*,[43] or declared the unconstitutionality of restrictions to same-sex marriages in *Obergefell vs Hodges*.[44] They conclude that judges have mostly produced desired outcomes from the perspective of rights. Nonetheless, the US Supreme Court has also produced controversial decisions such as *Citizens United v. Federal Election Commission*,[45] *New York State Rifle & Pistol Association, Inc. v. Bruen*,[46] or *Dobbs v. Jackson Women's Health Organization*.[47] Even recently, many scholars claim that the current majority of the US Supreme Court has undermined key precedents pertaining the protection of rights.[48] Perhaps the argument of Zellmer and Miller applies to courts that generally render decisions protective of vulnerable groups, which is not a universal feature of all courts consistent through time.

It is often forgotten, but the first functional model of supermajorities in constitutional adjudication, introduced in Ohio in 1912, was defended on the basis that courts had grown overly conservative and were striking progressive regulations.[49] Delegates explicitly complained about the fact that courts struck down regulations on working hours, safety laws in child labour, and miner's

---

[43] 384 U.S. 436 (1966).

[44] 135 S. Ct. 2584 (2015).

[45] 558 U.S. 310 (2010) (striking down restrictions from the Bipartisan Campaign Reform Act that attempted to prevent corporate interests from unions and corporations in elections by limiting their finances).

[46] 597 U.S. 1 (striking down a New York state law that imposed limitations on pistol concealed carry licences).

[47] 597 U.S. 215 (overturning Roe v. Wade and thus limiting a long-standing line of precedents upholding the right to abortion).

[48] Stephen I Vladeck, *The Shadow Docket: How the Supreme Court Uses Stealth Rulings to Amass Power and Undermine the Republic* (Basic Books, Hachette Book Group 2023).

[49] Rivera León, *Supermajorities in Constitutional Courts* (n 13) 33.

payments protection.[50] The supermajority was meant to protect rights from the courts themselves.

Moreover, the fact that the political branches often choose or appoint constitutional court judges in many jurisdictions already guarantees a certain degree of possible ideological alignment[51] between them. The scholarship does not neglect this relationship. One of the long-known standard methodologies from political science employs the party of appointment as a proxy of judicial ideology to test the attitudinal model or other judicial ideology-related inquiries. Although scholarship has developed more sophisticated methods to measure judicial ideology,[52] the fact that the party of appointment remains a central element in such an analysis already hints that a strong ideological departure between constitutional court judges and the elected branches[53] is not a common feature observed in many jurisdictions.

Finally, the assumption also seems to be generally unaware that supermajority rules may be imposed neutrally. In some jurisdictions, such as the Dominican Republic, a supermajority is required for the constitutional court to make any decision. In the case of such models, the impact on vulnerable groups is nuanced. While a supermajority would be required to strike down a law that disfavours them, the same supermajority would be needed to

50 "Ohio's 1912 Constitutional Convention. Fifty-Second Day (Legislative Day of April 2)" 1089. See Delegate Anderson's intervention, claiming that Courts were striking a great deal of desirable progressive statutes based on alleged economic freedoms.

51 For example, Sunstein et al. performed an empirical analysis in the United States, concluding: "We have found striking evidence of a relationship between the political party of the appointing president and judicial voting patterns. " Cass R Sunstein and others, *Are Judges Political? An Empirical Analysis of the Federal Judiciary* (Brookings Institution Press 2006) 147.

52 Maoz Rosenthal and Shai Talmor, 'Estimating the "Legislators in Robes": Measuring Judges' Political Preferences' (2022) 43 Justice System Journal 373. Similarly, see Adam Bonica and Maya Sen, 'Estimating Judicial Ideology' (2021) 35 Journal of Economic Perspectives 97. Bonica and Sen posit that "It was not until the last few decades that researchers tackled the question of how best to measure judicial ideology beyond simply using the party of the appointing president as a proxy. " ibid 97.

53 See further Ronen Shamir, '"Landmark Cases" and the Reproduction of Legitimacy: The Case of Israel's High Court of Justice' (1990) 24 Law & Society Review 781, 782. Shamir summarises the literature that posits that Judges have a natural tendency to support the government.

uphold those statutes, helping to ensure that no extremist position within the bench prevails.

4. Conclusions

Supermajorities in constitutional adjudication are currently being theoretically re-examined. Emerging new theories of judicial review and the self-limitation of judges have led to several theoretical examinations of deferential mechanisms to ensure that judges do not substitute policy values of the elected branches with their own. As several scholars have noted, supermajorities embody a unique system that allows institutionalising deference (a clear-mistake rule) through the aggregative mechanism of voting rather than entrusting individual justices to supplement it via the classical presumption of constitutionality internally.[54] Nonetheless, the vast majority of constitutional courts and bodies performing constitutional adjudication employ majority rule.[55] Natural inertia favours simple majorities, with some even considering majority rule as an inherent principle in courts.[56] In this regard, critical voices have emerged in the debate questioning the theoretical validity of supermajorities in constitutional adjudication.

Common objections to supermajorities reside in their alleged induced court paralysis or that supermajorities may presumably facilitate court capture and control by virtue of their heightened standard. The scholarship is beginning to analyse such objections either from a theoretical or empirical perspective. Nonetheless, several objections and potential shortcomings of supermajorities remain unexplored. This chapter focused on the vulnerability objection, a common claim stating that, since constitutional courts are tasked with enforcing rights, increasing the threshold to strike down legislation significantly tilts the balance of power in favour of the elected branches, which means that, given that the elected branches are commonly chosen through some form of majority rule, naturally under-represented vulnerable groups

---

[54] Caminker (n 11).

[55] Caviedes provides several examples of prominent constitutional and apex courts employing majority rule. See Caviedes, "Is Majority Rule Justified in Constitutional Adjudication? " (n 4) 377.

[56] Amar, Akhil Reed, *America's Unwritten Constitution: The Precedents and Principles We Live By* (Basic Books 2012) 357–58.

are disfavoured by the mechanism, since the ordinary political process is unfavourable towards defending their rights.

I have argued that such an objection makes several disputable assumptions from a theoretical and empirical perspective. From the latter's perspective, I have claimed that the argument presupposes a substantial impact on courts and a distinguishable disproportional effect on vulnerable groups, while from the former's, it assumes that judges are more likely to enforce rights in cases that produce outcomes favourable to vulnerable groups. I have shown that both assumptions rely on problematic premises.

First, recent research has proven that supermajorities commonly affect only a handful of contested decisions.[57] While it is true that such conclusions were formulated on a partial sample of all models currently or formerly employing supermajority rules, it is arguably sufficiently representative to claim that other models may be expected to behave similarly. Although a more nuanced version of the argument could claim that vulnerable groups are expected to be overly affected by supermajority rules, even in those limited cases in which it occurs, the chapter outlined the possibilities for empirically verifying such a claim.

Second, the assumption that judges are expected to predominantly embrace positions that favour vulnerable groups has yet to be proven. Although studies accounting for judicial ideology are common, studies are yet to demonstrate whether or not, ideologically, judges at constitutional courts tend to rule in favour of the interests of vulnerable groups at a significantly higher rate than legislators enact legislation expanding or restricting their rights. Finally, the chapter pointed out that it is generally accepted in the scholarship that there is a probable ideological linkage between the elected branches and constitutional court judges through the appointment mechanism.

In conclusion, although a relevant objection at first sight, the vulnerability argument can be countered by theoretical and empirical considerations and does not appear to be an objection conclusively refuting the feasibility of supermajority rules in constitutional adjudication.

---

57 Rivera León, *Supermajorities in Constitutional Courts* (n 13) 198.

Bibliography

Acosta H, 'El Proceso de Amparo En El Nuevo Modelo de Justicia Constitucional Dominicano' in Eto, Gerardo (Ed.), *Treinta años de jurisdicción constitucional en el Perú* (Centro de Estudios Constitucionales 2014).

Amar AR, *America's Unwritten Constitution: The Precedents and Principles We Live By* (Basic Books 2012).

Bifulco R and Paris D, 'The Italian Constitutional Court', *The Max Planck Handbooks in European Public Law: Volume III: Constitutional Adjudication. Institutions* (Oxford University Press 2020).

Bonica A and Sen M, 'Estimating Judicial Ideology' (2021) 35 Journal of Economic Perspectives 97.

Brage J, *La acción abstracta de inconstitucionalidad* (IIJ-UNAM 2005).

Calabresi SG, *The History and Growth of Judicial Review, Volume 2: The G-20 Civil Law Countries*, vol 2 (Oxford University Press 2021).

Caminker EH, 'Thayerian Deference to Congress and Supreme Court Supermajority Rules: Lessons from the Past' (2003) 78 Indiana Law Journal 73.

Castillo-Ortiz P, 'The Dilemmas of Constitutional Courts and the Case for a New Design of Kelsenian Institutions' (2020) 39 Law and Philosophy 617.

Caviedes C, 'Is Majority Rule Justified in Constitutional Adjudication?' (2021) 41 Oxford Journal of Legal Studies 376.

——, 'A Core Case for Supermajority Rules in Constitutional Adjudication' (2022) 20 International Journal of Constitutional Law 1162.

——, *Supermajority Voting in Constitutional Courts: The Problem of Majority Rule for Democracy and Legislation* (Routledge 2024).

Clyde H (ed), *Journal of the Nebraska Constitutional Convention (1921)* (The Kline Pub Co 1921).

Doubek P, 'Sterilization of Transgender People: A Worrying Judgement of the Czech Constitutional Court' (*ECHR Blog*) <https://www.echrblog.com/2022/04/sterilization-of-transgender-people.html>.

Dougherty KL and Edward J, 'The Properties of Simple Vs. Absolute Majority Rule: Cases Where Absences and Abstentions Are Important' (2010) 22 Journal of Theoretical Politics 85.

Ernest W, 'The Fine-Mechanisms of Judicial Majoritarianism' in Birke Häcker and Wolfgang Ernst (Eds.), *Collective Judging in Comparative Perspective: Counting Votes and Weighing Opinions* (Intersentia 2020).

Ferejohn J and Pasquino P, 'Constitutional Courts as Deliberative Institutions: Towards an Institutional Theory of Constitutional Justice' in Sadurski W (Ed.), *Constitutional Justice, East and West. Democratic Legitimacy and Constitutional Courts in Post-Communist Europe in a Comparative Perspective* (Springer 2002).

Fite K and Rubinstein LB, 'Curbing the Supreme Court - State Experiences and Federal Proposals' (1937) 35 Michigan Law Review 762.

Hartnett E, 'Ties in the Supreme Court of the United States' (2002) 44 William and Mary Law Review 643.

Hong JS, 'Signaling the Turn: The Supermajority Requirement and Judicial Power on the Constitutional Court of Korea' (2019) 67 The American Journal of Comparative Law 177.

Hübner Mendes C, *Constitutional Courts and Deliberative Democracy* (Oxford University Press 2013).

Ippolito F and Iglesias Sánchez S, 'Introduction' in Francesca Ippolito and Sara Iglesias Sánchez (Eds.), *Protecting vulnerable groups: the European human rights framework* (Hart Publishing 2015).

—— (Eds.), *Protecting Vulnerable Groups: The European Human Rights Framework* (Hart Publishing 2015).

King B, 'The Use of Supermajority Provisions in the Constitution: The Framers, the Federalist Papers and the Reinforcement of a Fundamental Principle' (1998) 8 Seton Hall Constitutional Law Journal 363.

Krishnamurthi G, 'For Judicial Majoritarianism' (2019) 22 University of Pennsylvania Journal of Constitutional Law 1201.

Langášek T, *Ústavní Soud Československé Republiky a Jeho Osudy v Letech 1920–1948* (Vydavatelství a nakladatelství Aleš Čeněk 2011).

Limantė A and Tereškinas A, 'Definition of Vulnerable Groups' in Agnė Limantė and Dovilė Pūraitė-Andrikienė (eds), *Legal Protection of Vulnerable Groups in Lithuania, Latvia, Estonia and Poland*, vol 8 (Springer International Publishing 2022).

Maddox WR, 'Minority Control of Court Decisions in Ohio' (1930) 24 American Political Science Review 638.

Madgett PW, 'The Five-Judge Rule in Nebraska' (1968) 2 Creighton Law Review 329.

Meier CL, 'Power of the Ohio Supreme Court to Declare Laws Unconstitutional' (1931) 5 U. Cin. L. Rev. 293.

Milligan WW and Pohlman JE, 'The 1968 Modern Courts Amendment to the Ohio Constitution' (1968) 29 Ohio St. LJ 811.

Nifosi-Sutton I, *The Protection of Vulnerable Groups under International Human Rights Law* (Routledge 2019).

North Dakota Law Review Associate Editors, 'North Dakota Supreme Court Review' (2014) 90 North Dakota Law Review 637.

'Ohio's 1912 Constitutional Convention. Fifty-Second Day (Legislative Day of April 2)'.

Osterkamp J, *Verfassungsgerichtsbarkeit in der Tschechoslowakei (1920–1939): Verfassungsidee, Demokratieverständnis, Nationalitätenproblem* (V Klostermann 2009).

Peroni L and Timmer A, 'Vulnerable Groups: The Promise of an Emerging Concept in European Human Rights Convention Law' (2013) 11 International Journal of Constitutional Law 1056.

Rawls J, *Political Liberalism* (Columbia University Press 1993).

Rivera León MA, 'La Mayoría Calificada En La Invalidez de Normas En Materia Electoral: Un Análisis de Su Comportamiento Empírico' in Lara R (Ed.), *La acción de inconstitucionalidad en materia electoral* (Tirant lo Blanch 2023).

——, 'Control and Paralysis? A Context-Sensitive Analysis of Objections to Supermajorities in Constitutional Adjudication' (2024) 22 International Journal of Constitutional Law 134.

——, 'Judicial Review of Supermajority Rules Governing Courts' Own Decision-Making: A Comparative Analysis' (2024) 13 Global Constitutionalism 79.

——, *Supermajorities in Constitutional Courts* (Routledge 2024).

Rosenthal M and Talmor S, 'Estimating the "Legislators in Robes": Measuring Judges' Political Preferences' (2022) 43 Justice System Journal 373.

Roznai Y, 'Introduction: Constitutional Courts in a 100-Years Perspective and a Proposal for a Hybrid Model of Judicial Review' (2021) 14 ICL Journal 355.

Santaolalla F, 'El Voto de Calidad Del Presidente Del Tribunal Constitucional' [2009] Revista Española de Derecho Constitucional 201.

Schwartzberg M, 'The Arbitrariness of Supermajority Rules' (2010) 49 Social Science Information 61.

——, *Counting the Many: The Origins and Limits of Supermajority Rule* (Cambridge University Press 2013).

Shamir R, '"Landmark Cases" and the Reproduction of Legitimacy: The Case of Israel's High Court of Justice' (1990) 24 Law & Society Review 781.

Shugerman JH, 'A Six-Three Rule: Reviving Consensus and Deference on the Supreme Court' (2003) 37 Georgia Law Review 893.

Sunstein CR and others, *Are Judges Political? An Empirical Analysis of the Federal Judiciary* (Brookings Institution Press 2006).

Venice Commission, 'Preliminary Opinion 849/2016 on the Amendments to the Organic Law on the Constitutional Court and to the Law on Constitutional Legal Proceedings' (Venice Commission 2016) CDL-PI(2016)005.

——, 'Opinion No. 833/2015 On Amendments to the Act of 25 June 2015 on the Constitutional Tribunal (CDL-AD(2016)001' (Venice Commission 2016) CDL-AD(2016)001.

Vermeule A, 'Absolute Majority Rules' (2007) 37 British Journal of Political Science 643.

Vladeck SI, *The Shadow Docket: How the Supreme Court Uses Stealth Rulings to Amass Power and Undermine the Republic* (Basic Books 2023).

Waldron J, 'The Core of the Case against Judicial Review' (2006) 115 The Yale Law Journal 1346.

——, 'Five to Four: Why Do Bare Majorities Rule on Courts' (2014) 123 The Yale Law Journal 1692.

Zellmer S and Miller K, 'The Fallacy of Judicial Supermajority Clauses in State Constitutions' (2015) 47 University of Toledo Law Review 73.

The Intersection of Vulnerability, Resilience, and Antifragility in the Legal Decision-Making Process: An EU Law Perspective

*Marcel Piterman**

Abstract: Vulnerability is a critical issue in the field of law. The legal system must consider the needs of disadvantaged groups, and prioritise their rights and interests in decision-making processes. The concept of vulnerability is essential for legal professionals to develop trauma-informed approaches and understand the complex social, cultural, and economic dimensions of vulnerability. In the legal context, resilience can help individuals and communities cope with traumatic events and recover from adversity. But to enhance the solutions for vulnerability and resilience, the concept of antifragility offers a new perspective. Resilience is the ability of an individual or system to bounce back from adversity, while antifragility goes beyond resilience, referring to the ability of a system or individual to benefit from stress and grow stronger as a result. In legal decision-making, the concept of antifragility can encourage the vulnerable to identify opportunities for growth and improvement in the face of adversity, rather than simply trying to mitigate damage. This text will explore the intersection of vulnerability, resilience, and antifragility in legal decision-making. It will examine the challenges and opportunities of integrating these concepts into legal practice, as well as the potential benefits for disadvantaged groups.

Keywords: vulnerability, adversity, resilience, antifragility, trauma, legal decision-making

1. Introduction

Vulnerability is a central concern in the legal domain, demanding a thorough and compassionate approach to address the needs of marginalised groups. Beyond being a moral imperative, prioritising the rights of these groups is fundamental to the integrity of the justice system. The concept of vulnerability serves as a guiding principle for legal professionals navigating the intricate dimensions of trauma-informed practices, considering psychological, social, cultural, and economic factors.

Resilience emerges as a crucial tool in facing traumatic events within the legal arena. It involves the capacity to bounce back from hardships and move forward. However, for a more progressive approach, the exploration

* Law Faculty of the Catholic University of Portugal, Lisbon; Research Centre for the Future of Law. ORCID: 0000-0001-9127-6085.

extends to antifragility, surpassing mere resilience to embrace the potential for growth and self-improvement amid adversity. This text researches the interplay between vulnerability, resilience, and antifragility in legal decision-making, shedding light on the complexities and potential for positive transformation within the legal system.

2. Human experiences regarding vulnerability

Vulnerable individuals face elevated risks of harm or disadvantage due to diverse factors – psychological, social, economic, cultural, or political. In the legal context, these include marginalised groups like children, victims of terrorism, domestic violence, or human trafficking. Limited access to resources, discrimination, trauma, and inadequate representation contribute to their vulnerability.[1]

For the past several months, people have looked at the question of vulnerability with a new urgency, for it seems that terrorism, war, and recession of recent months have made understanding resilience and antifragility more important than ever.[2] More recently, the terror attack in southern Israel has evoked agonising memories for many Jewish people worldwide – including those in Israel who once saw the Jewish state as a refuge from violence. World leaders like the US President Joe Biden have drawn explicit parallels between the 7/10 assault and the Holocaust, when 6 million Jews were annihilated

1 For a comprehensive analysis of the purpose of providing engagement of concepts of "vulnerability" and "resilience" and the idea of a "responsive state" in constructing a universal approach to address the human condition, and the idea of human vulnerability as a critical heuristic for exploring alternative legal and political foundations, see Martha Albertson Fineman; Anna Grear, "Vulnerability: reflections on a new ethical: foundation for law and politics", Burlington, Ashgate, 2013.

2 See Igor Linkov; Jesse M Keenan, Benjamin D. Trump, "Covid-19: systemic risk and resilience", Springer, 2021. See also H. Steven Moffic *et al.*, "Anti-Semitism and psychiatry", Springer, 2020, p. V. It can be learned that "though chutzpah is not at all an everyday word used in scholarly psychiatry, it may be the best one word introduction to this edited volume. Indeed, producing this edited volume could be called an act of chutzpah. Chutzpah originally was a Hebrew word that was adapted into Yiddish, Yiddish being the common language of Jews in Eastern Europe before the Holocaust of World War II. From Yiddish, it was adopted into English and everyday usage, especially in America, in recent times. It has been variously defined, as in Merriam-Webster, as "audacity, nerve, and supreme self-confidence."

by Adolf Hitler's Nazi regime.[3] This prompts the question: What qualities define resilience in the face of adversity?

Real-world examples, such as Morgan Stanley's preparedness program post the 1993 World Trade Center attack, highlight the importance of proactive resilience. The ability to perceive reality, coupled with meaning-making, becomes paramount in constructing frameworks that imbue suffering with significance.

Maurice Vanderpol, a holocaust survivor, conducted a profound examination of Holocaust survivors, unveiling a unique phenomenon he termed the 'plastic shield'. This protective barrier was constructed from several crucial components, one of which was a sense of humour. Although the humour frequently veered into dark territory, it played an indispensable role in giving survivors a critical perspective. Also, the ability to form deep connections with others and possessing an inner psychological sanctuary that shields survivors from the intrusions of abusive individuals were central characteristics that contributed significantly to their resilience[4].

---

[3] See Marion Grenon *et al.*, "Impact of a terrorist attack on the mental health of directly exposed french adolescents: study protocol for the first step of the aval cohort study," In *Front Psychiatry*, vol. 10, no. 744, 2019. Another research on terrorism in children has concluded that "many of the effects of terrorism-induced trauma are similar to the effects of natural and man-made trauma. Children's responses include acute stress disorder, posttraumatic stress disorder, anxiety, depression, regressive behaviours, separation problems, sleep difficulties, and behavioural problems. However, several aspects of terrorist attacks result in unique stressors and reactions and pose specific challenges for treatment. The unpredictable, indefinite threat of terrorist events, the profound effect on adults and communities, and the effect of extensive terrorist-related media coverage exacerbates underlying anxieties and contributes to a continuous state of stress and anxiety. Intervention strategies include early community-based interventions, screening of children at risk, triage and referral, and trauma-loss–focused treatment programs." See Wanda P. Fremont. "Childhood reactions to terrorism-induced trauma: a review of the past 10 years", In *Journal of the American Academy of Child & Adolescent Psychiatry*, vol. 43, 2004, pp. 381–392.

[4] Maurice Vanderpol, "Resilience: a missing link in our understanding of survival", In *Harvard Review Psychiatry*, vol. 10, 2002, pp. 302–306. Born and raised in Amsterdam, Netherlands, Maurice Vanderpol experienced persecution by the Nazis and survived during the Holocaust. In 1946, he immigrated to the USA to pursue medical studies at Boston University, ultimately graduating in 1949 with a specialisation in psychiatry and psychoanalysis. He was a former president of the Boston Psychoanalytic Society and Institute and his focus was on the study of "resilience", particularly in children and holocaust survivors.

Early theories on resilience often emphasised genetics, suggesting that some individuals are inherently more resilient due to their genetic makeup[5]. While there is some validity to this notion, a growing body of empirical evidence indicates that resilience can be cultivated and developed[6]. Diane Coutu explores this, emphasising the importance of perceiving reality, deriving meaning from hardship, and the ability to improvise solutions. While it is possible to rebound from adversity with just one or two of these qualities, true resilience is attained when all three are present. These same attributes are equally applicable to resilient organisations[7].

She upholds that the ability to perceive reality is intricately linked with the second pillar of resilience: the inclination to derive meaning from traumatic circumstances. In times of adversity, some individuals tend to raise their hands in despair and exclaim, 'How can this be happening to me?' They perceive themselves as helpless victims, with the hardship they endure seemingly devoid of any lessons. In contrast, resilient individuals embark on a quest to construct frameworks that imbue their suffering with meaning, not just for themselves but also for those around them[8].

The process of making meaning from adversity is widely acknowledged by researchers as the means through which resilient individuals forge pathways from their current tribulations toward a future that is more robustly structured and promising[9]. These figurative bridges between the present and

---

5 See Kosuke Niitsu *et al*, "A concept analysis of resilience integrating genetics", In *Issues Mental Health Nursing*, vol. 38, no. 11, 2017, pp. 896–906. See also Steven M. Southwick *et al*, "Resilience definitions, theory, and challenges: interdisciplinar perspectives", In *European Journal of Psychotraumatology*, vol. 5, no. 1, 2014.

6 See Michael Neenan, "Developing resilience: a cognitive-behavioural approach", London, Routledge, 2009. See also Martin E. P. Seligman, "Building Resilience", In *Harvard Business Review*, 2011.

7 Diane Coutu, "How resilience works", In *Harvard Business Review*, no. 80, 2002, pp. 46–56. See also Daniel Goleman; Jeffrey Sonnenfeld; Shawn Achor, "Resilience", In *Harvard Business Review Press*, USA, 2017.

8 Coutu, "How resilience works", pp. 46–56.

9 Which reminds the concept of *grit*, presented as a higher-order personality trait that is highly predictive of both success and performance and distinct from other traits such as conscientiousness. The ability to sustain effort and maintain interest and determination over an extended period, even in the face of challenges, setbacks, or failures. See Angela Duckworth, "Grit: the power of passion and perseverance", Random House, UK, 2017.

an envisioned future serve a crucial role in rendering the current challenges more manageable, eliminating the sense of being overwhelmed. This concept found eloquent expression in the work of Viktor Frankl, an Austrian psychiatrist and survivor of Auschwitz.

Amidst unimaginable suffering, Frankl pioneered what he termed 'meaning therapy', a humanistic therapeutic technique aimed at guiding individuals to make decisions that give significance to their lives[10]. In his seminal work, Frankl recounted a pivotal moment in the concentration camp when the concept of meaning therapy crystallised. While on his way to work, grappling with the decision of whether to trade his last cigarette for a bowl of soup and anticipating the prospect of working under a particularly sadistic boss, he was struck by the profound sense of the triviality and meaninglessness of his existence.

It was at this moment that Frankl recognised the imperative of finding a purpose to survive. He achieved this by envisioning himself delivering a post-war lecture on the psychology of the concentration camp, intending to help outsiders comprehend the ordeals he had endured. Even though the prospect of survival remained uncertain, Frankl set concrete goals for himself, effectively transcending the immediate suffering. As he stated in his book: 'We must never forget that we may also find meaning in life even when confronted with a hopeless situation, when facing a fate that cannot be changed'.[11] In this context, it is worth noting that resilience is neither ethically good nor bad. It is merely the skill and the capacity to be robust under conditions of enormous stress and change.[12]

According to Diane Coutu, the third building block of resilience is the ability to improvise solutions. Other authors follow the lead of French

---

10 Viktor Frankl, "Man's search for meaning. an introduction to logotherapy", Beacon Press, Boston, 2006. On pursuing what is meaningful, not what is expedient, see Jordan B. Peterson, "12 rules for life, an antidote to chaos", Penguin, London, 2018, p. 161.

11 Frankl, "Man's search for meaning. an introduction to logotherapy".

12 To contrast resilience with robustness and antifragility in organisational systems, see Albert Munoz; Jon Billsberry; Véronique Ambrosini, "Resilience, robustness, and antifragility: towards an appreciation of distinct organisational responses to adversity", In *International Journal of Management Reviews*, vol. 24, 2022, pp. 181–187. For them, an antifragile organisation is enhanced by adversity, a robust organisation is untouched, and a resilient organisation is damaged, but recovers.

anthropologist Claude Levi-Strauss in calling this skill *bricolage*.[13] Intriguingly, the roots of that word are closely tied to the concept of resilience, which means 'bouncing back'.[14]

Bricolage, in a modern context, can be defined as a form of inventiveness. It is the innate ability to improvise solutions to problems when conventional tools or materials are lacking or not readily available. *Bricoleurs* are individuals who are perpetually engaged in tinkering, whether it involves constructing radios from everyday household items or repairing their vehicles. They exhibit a remarkable talent for maximising the utility of their resources by repurposing objects for unanticipated uses.[15]

An emotional example of *bricolage* emerged within the disturbing confines of concentration camps. Resilient inmates possessed the foresight to collect and save fragments of string or bits of wire whenever the opportunity presented itself. Such seemingly insignificant items held the potential to become invaluable tools for survival – perhaps for mending a pair of shoes, a task of immense significance in freezing conditions where it could determine the line between life and death.[16]

The introduction of Nassim Nicholas Taleb's concept of antifragility drives the discussion beyond resilience. Antifragility represents not just the ability to withstand stress but the capacity to thrive and improve in adversity. Understanding these concepts in the legal decision-making context opens

---

13 Claude Lévi-Strauss, "La Pensée sauvage", Paris, Plon, 1962. The author uses *bricolage* to describe the difference between the French handyman (*Monsieur Bricolage*) who uses non-specialised tools for a wide variety of purposes dealing with preconstraints and limits, and an engineer with "his" specialised tools. Also, he uses *bricolage* to describe the characteristic patterns of mythological thought. In his description, *bricolage* is opposed to the engineer's creative thinking, which proceeds from goals to means. Mythical thought, according to Lévi-Strauss, attempts to re-use available materials to solve new problems. See, Jenny Phillimore *et al*, "Bricolage: potential as a conceptual tool for understanding access to welfare in superdiverse neighbourhoods", In *IRiS Working Paper Series*, no. 14 Birmingham, 2016, pp. 3–21.

14 Lévi-Strauss, "La Pensée sauvage".

15 For a comprehensive understanding of the concept of *bricolage* as applicable not simply to traditional or residual forms of human activity, but also to the practice of modern scientific and technological development, as a universal concept, see Christopher Johnson, "Bricoleur and bricolage: from metaphor to universal concept", In *Paragraph*, vol. 35, no. 3, 2012, pp. 355–72.

16 Coutu, "How resilience works", pp. 46–56.

paths for creating systems that are not only adaptive but also equitable and antifragile. According to the Mathematical Statistician, anything that matters can be mapped or classified into three categories, what he calls 'the Triad'. The Triad classifies items in three columns along the designation 'fragile', 'robust', and 'antifragile'. The author recalls that the fragile wants tranquillity, the antifragile grows from disorder, and the robust does not care too much.[17]

In other words, the concept of antifragility represents entities that not only resist shocks and stressors but thrive and improve when exposed to volatility, randomness, and disorder. This quality surpasses mere resilience, where the system or entity remains unchanged. Antifragile systems become better under pressure. The rise of non-risk-takers who control significant aspects of people's lives has made it essential to consider the fragility of others when pursuing antifragility. Black Swans are unexpected and massive events with profound consequences.[18] Mother Nature continually destroys and regenerates, highlighting the need for systems that can benefit from random events rather than be harmed by them. Perfect robustness is unattainable, and thus, regeneration and adaptation to unpredictability are crucial for long-term survival.[19]

Besides this, politicians often focus on the concepts of resilience and solidity in their speeches and policies, rather than embracing the concept of antifragility. This approach can hinder growth and evolution. The key to understanding fragility is that it dislikes volatility, randomness, uncertainty, disorder, errors, and stressors. Fragile things require peace, predictability, and stability. Antifragility, on the other hand, not only tolerates but benefits from volatility and time. This concept is closely linked to nonlinearity, where responses are either fragile or antifragile to different sources of randomness.

---

17 Nassim Nicholas Taleb, "Antifragile: things that gain from disorder", New York, Random House, 2012, pp. 20–21.

18 See Nassim Nicholas Taleb, "The Black Swan: the impact of the highly improbable", New York, Random House, 2007. This book focuses on the extreme impact of rare and unpredictable outlier events and the human tendency to find simplistic explanations for these events, retrospectively. Taleb calls this the Black Swan theory.

19 Taleb, "Antifragile: things that gain from disorder", pp. 7–8. According to the author, "Antifragility is beyond resilience or robustness. The resilient resists shocks and stays the same; the antifragile gets better."

Also, Taleb stresses that even studies on post-traumatic growth often mistakenly use the term 'resilience' when describing the antifragile response.[20]

3. Relevant law and policy to curb vulnerability

In the complex landscape of modern challenges, legal frameworks play a pivotal role in shaping the resilience of societies, particularly within the EU. As the EU acts to address vulnerabilities and fortify the human rights of its citizens, a comprehensive collection of laws and policies has been meticulously crafted. These legal instruments, spanning civil rights, anti-discrimination measures, and social welfare policies, converge to create a resilient foundation for individuals and communities. Additionally, there may be specific legal frameworks and policies tailored to address the needs of certain vulnerable groups, such as laws protecting the rights of children or victims of violence[21].

In the EU, resilience has become an increasingly critical aspect of policy and legislation, encompassing economic, social, environmental, and crisis management dimensions. As the region faces various challenges, from economic shocks to climate change and public health crises, the EU has established a range of laws and policies designed to enhance resilience at the individual, community, and member-state levels[22].

At its core, the European Semester[23] is a fundamental tool for coordinating economic and fiscal policies across EU member states. Embedded in this process is the evaluation of national resilience to economic shocks and crises. The European Commission conducts assessments, providing recommendations to strengthen resilience, especially in terms of economic and financial stability. For instance, these assessments may result in directives promoting sustainable economic practices or recommending diversification strategies.

---

20 Taleb, "Antifragile: things that gain from disorder", p. 10.

21 The Victims' Rights Directive gives victims of crime stronger rights to support and protection across the European Union. EU Member States had to implement the rules into national law. The directive builds upon the established minimum rights and sets clearer obligations for Member States.

22 See Antonio Cortês, "Blue planet law and ecological sustainability in the twenty-first century". In Maria da Glória Garcia; Antonio Cortês (Eds.) *Blue Planet Law. Sustainable Development Goals Series*, Springer, 2023.

23 The European Semester is the EU's framework for the coordination and surveillance of economic and social policies.

Another critical aspect of EU law and policy related to resilience is the Cohesion Policy[24]. This policy framework seeks to reduce disparities in economic and social development among regions. It allocates funding and programs that specifically aim to enhance the resilience of less-developed areas. Investments under the Cohesion Policy encompass infrastructure development, education, innovation, and job creation, all with the overarching goal of bolstering the long-term resilience of regions. Noteworthy projects funded under this policy include the construction of the Baltic-Adriatic Transport Corridor. This project aims to improve transportation links between the Baltic and Adriatic Sea regions, fostering economic development and reducing disparities in infrastructure quality among EU member states. By investing in such transnational infrastructure, the EU promotes regional connectivity and resilience.

In disaster management and crisis response, the EU has put the Civil Protection Mechanism in place[25]. This mechanism adopts cooperation among member states in responding to various disasters and emergencies. Its purpose is to enhance resilience by enabling a rapid and coordinated response to both natural and man-made disasters. For instance, in the aftermath of forest fires that devastated Portugal and Spain, the Civil Protection Mechanism facilitated a joint European response and played a crucial role in facilitating cross-border cooperation. Emergency firefighting teams, aircraft, and resources from various EU member states were swiftly deployed to assist the affected regions. This coordinated effort showcased the mechanism's effectiveness in responding to large-scale natural disasters.

This is particularly important given the increasing frequency and impact of extreme weather events. Social resilience and community cohesion are addressed through initiatives like the European Solidarity Corps[26]. This program offers opportunities for young people to engage in volunteer activities

---

[24] Cohesion Policy targets all regions and cities in the EU to support: job creation, business competitiveness, economic growth, sustainable development, and improvements to citizens' quality of life.

[25] The mechanism aims to strengthen cooperation between the EU countries and 10 participating states on civil protection to improve prevention, preparedness, and response to disasters.

[26] The European Solidarity Corps funding is provided in the form of grants to organisations through a call for proposals.

that support disaster response, community resilience, and social inclusion. By participating in these activities, young volunteers contribute to building stronger and more resilient communities.

Climate change resilience is a critical concern, and the EU's climate action policies, notably the European Green Deal,[27] focus on climate adaptation and resilience-building. These policies aim to enhance the resilience of EU member states to the impacts of climate change, such as extreme weather events and rising sea levels. They emphasise the importance of climate resilience in the face of increasing environmental challenges.

The EU's commitment to digital resilience is evident through the Network and Information Security (NIS2) Directive[28]. This directive obliges critical infrastructure operators and digital service providers to ensure the security and resilience of their networks and information systems. As the digital

---

27 Climate change and environmental degradation are an existential threat to Europe and the world. To overcome these challenges, the European Green Deal will transform the EU into a modern, resource-efficient and competitive economy, ensuring: no net emissions of greenhouse gases by 2050, economic growth decoupled from resource use, and no person and no place left behind.

28 The NIS2 Directive is the EU-wide legislation on cybersecurity. It provides legal measures to boost the overall level of cybersecurity in the EU. The EU cybersecurity rules introduced in 2016 were updated by the NIS2 Directive that came into force in 2023. It modernised the existing legal framework to keep up with increased digitisation and an evolving cybersecurity threat landscape. Expanding the scope of the cybersecurity rules to new sectors and entities, further improves the resilience and incident response capacities of public and private entities, competent authorities, and the EU. The Directive on measures for a high common level of cybersecurity across the Union (the NIS2 Directive) provides legal measures to boost the overall level of cybersecurity in the EU by ensuring: Member States' preparedness, by requiring them to be appropriately equipped; cooperation among all the Member States, by setting up a Cooperation Group to support and facilitate strategic cooperation and the exchange of information among Member States; a culture of security across sectors that are vital for our economy and society and that rely heavily on ICTs, such as energy, transport, water, banking, financial market infrastructures, healthcare and digital infrastructure. Businesses identified by the Member States as operators of essential services in the above sectors will have to take appropriate security measures and notify relevant national authorities of serious incidents. Key digital service providers, such as search engines, cloud computing services and online marketplaces, will have to comply with the security and notification requirements under the Directive.

landscape becomes increasingly integral to daily life and critical infrastructure, protecting these systems is essential for societal resilience.

Furthermore, the EU's policies on sustainable finance, such as the EU Taxonomy Regulation,[29] encourage investments in environmentally and socially sustainable activities. This approach plays a role in building long-term resilience to environmental and social challenges, emphasising the interconnectedness of financial, economic, and environmental resilience.

4. Systematic assessment of gaps in law and policy

Despite existing laws and policies, there are often gaps and shortcomings in effectively addressing the vulnerabilities of marginalised and disadvantaged groups. These gaps may arise due to inadequate implementation, insufficient resources, systemic biases, or lack of awareness. For example, there might be limited access to legal aid for vulnerable individuals, or certain communities may face discrimination in law enforcement and judicial processes.

The EU and its member states have made commendable strides in recognising the significance of supporting trauma survivors, particularly those who have lived through harrowing experiences such as the Holocaust. Yet, there remain notable gaps and challenges in European laws and policies that relate to trauma survivors. Identifying and addressing these gaps is pivotal to providing comprehensive and meaningful support to those who have endured profound trauma[30].

One of the primary challenges relates to access to mental health services. While many European countries do offer mental health support, disparities persist in terms of the accessibility and quality of these services for trauma survivors. Barriers, whether geographical, financial, or cultural, impede older survivors like those of the Holocaust from accessing specialised mental

---

[29] The EU taxonomy (Regulation (EU) 2020/852) is a cornerstone of the EU's sustainable finance framework and an important market transparency tool. It helps direct investments to the economic activities most needed for the transition, in line with the European Green Deal objectives. The taxonomy is a classification system that defines criteria for economic activities that are aligned with a net zero trajectory by 2050 and broader environmental goals other than climate.

[30] See Ingo Schäfer *et al*, "Trauma and trauma care in Europe", In *European Journal of Psychotraumatology*, vol. 9, no. 1, 2018.

health care tailored to their unique needs. This discrepancy in mental health provision can leave survivors without the essential support they require to cope with the enduring impact of trauma[31].

Recognition and compensation for trauma survivors present another complex issue. Several European countries have recognised the historical trauma experienced by Holocaust survivors and have sought to provide compensation or reparations[32]. However, the eligibility criteria and the processes for seeking recognition and compensation can vary significantly from one country to another. These variations can result in disparities among survivors, with some potentially being excluded from the recognition and compensation they deserve.

Moreover, the concept of transgenerational[33] trauma poses a challenge. Where the effects of trauma resonate through generations, poses a significant challenge that European policies should address. Policies should extend support not only to survivors but also to their families, acknowledging the long-lasting impact trauma can have on familial and community dynamics. Trauma's effects can resonate through generations, impacting not only the survivors themselves but also their descendants[34]. European policies should consider the intergenerational impact of trauma, particularly concerning Holocaust survivors, and provide support to their families as well. This comprehensive approach acknowledges that trauma can have long-lasting effects on families and communities.

Persistent stigma and discrimination against Holocaust survivors, even over time, necessitate a more robust response in European policies. A fraction of survivors still encounter prejudice and discrimination, both overt and subtle[35]. European policies must do more to combat such attitudes and

---

31 For a European perspective on trauma treatment, see Evaldas Kazlauskas *et al*, "Trauma treatment across Europe: where do we stand now from a perspective of seven countries", In *European Journal of Psychotraumatology*, vol. 7, 2016.

32 See, Michael J. Bazyler; Roger P. Alford, "Holocaust Restitution: Perspectives on the Litigation and Its Legacy", New York University Press, New York, 2017.

33 See Gonçalo de Almeida Ribeiro, "O problema da tutela constitucional das gerações futuras", In *Justiça entre gerações, perspectivas interdisciplinares*, Jorge Pereira da Silva; Gonçalo de Almeida Ribeiro, (Eds.), Universidade Católica Editora, 2017, pp. 138–160.

34 See Meera Atkinson, "The poetics of transgenerational trauma", Bloomsbury, 2017.

35 See Michael Polgar, "Holocaust and human rights education: good choices and sociological perspectives", UK, Emerald Publishing Limited, 2018.

practices, ensuring that survivors can live their lives without the fear of persecution. The enduring stigmatisation of survivors can have severe mental health consequences and impede their reintegration into society. Holocaust education and remembrance are critical aspects of European policies, but there may be variations in educational initiatives across member states. While many European countries have made efforts to educate the public about the Holocaust and promote remembrance, these initiatives must be consistent and widespread. Holocaust education is not only about honouring the memory of the past but also about preventing future atrocities by imparting the lessons of history.

Moreover, legal protections are vital to ensure the rights of Holocaust survivors are upheld[36]. This is particularly relevant when it comes to issues such as restitution of property, access to social welfare, and healthcare coverage[37]. The legal protections and rights enforcement mechanisms can vary among different European countries, highlighting the need for greater consistency in safeguarding the rights and dignity of survivors. Coordination and collaboration are integral to the effective support of trauma survivors. There should be enhanced coordination among government bodies, non-governmental organisations (NGOs), and social services to provide comprehensive assistance. A more collaborative approach can streamline the provision of support and prevent survivors from falling through the gaps in the system.

Data collection and research are areas where improvement is needed. Comprehensive data on the needs, well-being, and experiences of trauma survivors, including Holocaust survivors, may be lacking in some countries. Adequate data collection and research efforts can provide insights into the specific needs of survivors and assist policymakers in tailoring policies and services accordingly. Holocaust denial and hate speech persist as concerning issues in Europe. Stricter measures and penalties against Holocaust denial and hate speech can help protect the memory and dignity of survivors.[38] A

---

36 See Johannes Morsink, "The Universal Declaration of Human Rights and the Holocaust: an endangered connection", Georgetown University Press, 2019, pp. 283–314.

37 Sidney Zabludoff, "At issue: restitution of holocaust-era assets: promises and reality", In *Jewish Political Studies Review*, vol. 19, no. 1/2, 2007, pp. 3–14.

38 Recently, Australia implemented laws prohibiting the Nazi salute as well as the display or sale of symbols linked to terrorist groups as the government responds to a rise in antisemitic incidents following the Israel–Gaza war.

more robust response to these forms of intolerance is essential to maintain the integrity of the historical record and the well-being of survivors who bear witness to the past.

As Holocaust survivors age, their needs evolve, including healthcare, long-term care, and social support. European policies should acknowledge and address the changing requirements of an aging survivor population.[39] The specific healthcare and support needs of older survivors should be factored into national and EU policies to ensure their well-being in later stages of life. It is crucial to address these challenges with a continued commitment to provide trauma survivors with the comprehensive support and recognition they deserve. By doing so, Europe can honour the resilience and dignity of these survivors and acknowledge their vital contributions to society. The dedication to rectifying these shortcomings underscores the EU's commitment to fostering a just and supportive environment for all its citizens.

The EU has made substantial strides in addressing resilience across various domains. Whether it pertains to economic shocks, environmental crises, social cohesion, or pandemic preparedness, EU laws and policies underscore the commitment to enhancing resilience and preparedness at all levels. These initiatives reflect the EU's determination to adapt and respond to an evolving landscape of challenges and crises, acknowledging the central importance of resilience in ensuring the well-being and stability of its member states and communities.

5. Embracing antifragility: a transformative approach to resilience

Adversity is an intrinsic part of the human experience, ranging from personal setbacks to global crises. What distinguishes individuals in these moments is the remarkable ability to endure and flourish in adversity, a characteristic known as resilience. Resilience is more than survival; it is the capacity to remain committed, emerge stronger, and thrive. At the core of resilience lie

---

39 Despite the reactivation of traumatic symptoms during aging and continuous mental suffering, most Holocaust survivors show good instrumental coping and preserved functioning. See Yoram Barak; Henry Szor, "Lifelong posttraumatic stress disorder: evidence from aging Holocaust survivors", In *Dialogues in Clinical Neuroscience*, vol. 2, no. 1, 2000, pp. 57–62.

psychological strength, encompassing self-efficacy, emotional regulation, and resolute optimism. Social support acts as a vital pillar, offering solace and aid during life's trials. Effective coping strategies, adaptability, and problem-solving skills are indispensable in navigating challenges[40].

However, the concept of antifragility, as articulated by Nassim Nicholas Taleb, offers a nuanced perspective on how individuals, systems, and societies respond to stress and uncertainty. Antifragility goes beyond resilience, actively seeking opportunities for growth and improvement in the face of disruption[41]. Taleb introduces the term antifragile to describe entities that gain strength and adaptability when exposed to stressors. Unlike resilient systems that maintain stability, antifragile entities actively embrace disruptions as opportunities for growth. This concept applies across various domains, including economics, technology, biology, and personal development.

For instance, in the financial world, an antifragile investment strategy does not merely seek to minimise losses during market downturns; it actively looks for opportunities in turbulent times and uses them to generate gains. Furthermore, antifragility extends to the socio-political domain. A resilient society may recover from crises, but an antifragile society anticipates and encourages a diversity of viewpoints, innovations, and adaptive mechanisms that thrive under adversity. It actively seeks to decentralise power and control to prevent single points of failure, fostering robustness and adaptability. In personal development, Taleb's concept encourages individuals to embrace uncertainty and discomfort as opportunities for growth. It challenges the conventional notion of bouncing back from setbacks and encourages thriving and becoming stronger through exposure to stress and volatility. Unlike resilient systems that merely maintain their stability or recover after disturbance, antifragile entities actively seek out and embrace disruptions as opportunities

---

40 Stating that resilience represents a distinct trajectory from the process of recovery, that resilience in the face of loss or potential trauma is more common than is often believed, and that there are multiple and sometimes unexpected pathways to resilience, George A., Bonanno, "Loss, trauma, and human resilience: have we underestimated the human capacity to thrive after extremely aversive events?" In *American Psychologist*, vol. 59, 2004, pp. 20–28.

41 For a comprehensive understanding of how antifragility can help innovative start-ups thrive, see Vicenzo Corvello *et al.*, "Betting on the future: how to build antifragility in innovative start-up companies", In *Review of Managerial Science*, 2023.

for growth and improvement. The central idea of antifragility is closely related to the concepts of fragility and robustness. Shocks easily harm a fragile system, and its performance deteriorates under stress. A robust system, on the other hand, can withstand stress without being adversely affected but does not necessarily benefit from it. In contrast, an antifragile system not only resists damage from stressors but also harnesses them to become more resilient and adaptable.

The concept of antifragility goes beyond resilience by emphasising the active pursuit of stressors and adversities as avenues for growth and improvement. It challenges the conventional notion of merely bouncing back from setbacks and encourages individuals and systems to thrive and become stronger through exposure to stress and volatility. Embracing the philosophy of antifragility can lead to more adaptable and robust responses to the unpredictable nature of the complex world[42].

The EU, recognising the needs of trauma survivors, has made commendable progress. However, gaps in laws and policies demand innovative solutions, and antifragility offers a compelling approach. Embracing antifragility means actively seeking opportunities for growth and adaptation when confronted with challenges. For the EU, applying antifragility involves designing policies that go beyond traditional resilience. This includes engaging survivors in initiatives that promote education, cultural preservation, and community building. Governance structures should be adaptable, involving continuous consultation with survivors to ensure policies remain responsive.

Learning from past mistakes and adapting is central to antifragility. In the context of European policies, this involves conducting a comprehensive review of previous compensation and recognition efforts. By identifying areas where gaps existed and survivors did not receive adequate support, this retrospective analysis can inform the development of more effective policies. Antifragility also encompasses anticipating future challenges and being proactive in addressing them. The EU can establish a dedicated task force to continuously monitor the well-being and experiences of trauma

---

42 Developing a theory of the psychological conditions, which can contribute to greater survival in complex evolving socioeconomic systems ordered by radically uncertain institutions, Brendan Markey-Towler, "Antifragility, the Black Swan and psychology", In *Evolutionary and Institutional Economics Review*, vol. 15, no. 2, Springer, 2018, pp. 367–384.

survivors, especially as they age. This proactive approach can help anticipate and address gaps in healthcare, social support, and other critical services.

By incorporating the principles of antifragility into the development and implementation of laws and policies related to trauma survivors, the EU can create a more adaptable, diverse, and responsive environment. This approach not only addresses existing gaps but also prepares for and prevents future challenges, ultimately fostering a more antifragile and supportive landscape for trauma survivors and their families. It underscores the EU's commitment to honouring the dignity of survivors and acknowledging their vital contributions to society.

6. Rethinking legal decision-making for trauma survivors

Legal decision-making within the EU regarding trauma survivors, particularly Holocaust survivors, demands a nuanced and innovative approach. The integration of antifragility into this process provides a transformative framework, urging a shift from passive resilience to active growth and adaptation. Antifragility, going beyond mere resilience, encourages legal decision-makers to actively seek opportunities for growth and support when faced with adversity. This approach aligns with the evolving needs and experiences of trauma survivors, paving the way for more comprehensive and effective policies.

To operationalise antifragility in legal decision-making, a departure from traditional resilience is proposed. Legal decisions should not be confined to compensation and recognition but should actively engage survivors and their families in initiatives promoting education, cultural preservation, and community building. This empowerment-focused approach aims to instil a sense of strength and meaning derived from their experiences. Adaptive governance is essential, urging legal frameworks to be responsive to changing survivor needs. Continuous consultation and collaboration mechanisms with survivors and participants ensure policies remain flexible, evolving to address new challenges and requirements.

Diversity and experimentation become key pillars. Legal decision-makers should explore diverse solutions, including support for initiatives like art therapy, intergenerational programs, and community engagement. The goal is to provide survivors and their families with various avenues for strength, healing, and support. Antifragility also emphasises learning from past mistakes. A comprehensive review of previous compensation and recognition efforts is crucial to identify gaps and inform the development of more effective legal decisions and policies.

Proactive anticipation of future challenges, especially as survivors age, is another critical aspect. Establishing task forces to monitor well-being ensures legal decisions remain relevant and responsive to emerging needs. Incorporating antifragility into legal decision-making reflects a commitment to providing trauma survivors with adaptable, diverse, and responsive support. This approach not only addresses existing gaps but also prepares for and prevents future challenges, fostering a more antifragile legal framework for trauma survivors and their families. It recognises the resilience and dignity of survivors and acknowledges their invaluable contributions to society.

This approach promotes more comprehensive and effective policies, acknowledging the evolving needs and experiences of survivors. It calls for legal frameworks that actively seek opportunities for growth and support in the face of adversity, aligning with the principles of antifragility.

7. Conclusion and proposals *de lege ferenda*

The integration of vulnerability, resilience, and antifragility concepts into legal decision-making processes can lead to more adaptive, equitable, and sustainable legal systems. Proposals *de lege ferenda* might involve legislative and policy changes. Prioritise the interests of vulnerable populations through legislative and policy changes that address gaps and enhance support mechanisms. Also, enhance training for legal professionals on issues related to vulnerability, equipping them with the knowledge and skills to address the unique challenges faced by trauma survivors. Foster inclusivity and diversity within the legal system to better reflect the lived experiences and needs of all members of society. This ensures a more comprehensive and empathetic approach to legal decision-making.

Moreover, embracing the concept of antifragility can significantly boost legal creative expertise. Legal professionals engaging in experimental approaches and exploring new ideas can extract innovative solutions to legal challenges, enhancing decision-making abilities, risk management, resilience, and creativity. Antifragility aids legal professionals in supporting access to justice, encouraging experimentation with novel methods, and expanding access to justice for underserved communities. Antifragile legal professionals are well-positioned to identify fresh opportunities for pro bono work and public interest lawyering, effectively expanding access to justice for those without the means to afford legal representation.

Bibliography

Barak, Yoram; Szor, Henry, Lifelong posttraumatic stress disorder: evidence from aging Holocaust survivors, In *Dialogues in Clinical Neuroscience*, vol. 2, no. 1, pp. 57–62, 2000.

Bazyler, Michael J.; Alford, Roger P., *Holocaust Restitution: Perspectives on the Litigation and Its Legacy*, New York University Press, New York, 2017.

Bonanno, George A., Loss, trauma, and human resilience: have we underestimated the human capacity to thrive after extremely aversive events? In *American Psychologist*, vol. 59, pp. 20–28, 2004.

Cortês, Antonio, Blue planet law and ecological sustainability in the twenty-first century. In Garcia, Maria da Glória; Cortês, Antonio (Eds.) *Blue Planet Law. Sustainable Development Goals Series*, Springer, 2023.

Corvello, Vicenzo *et al.*, Betting on the future: how to build antifragility in innovative start-up companies, In *Review of Managerial Science*, 2023.

Coutu, Diane, *How resilience works*, Harvard Business Review, no. 80, 2002, pp. 46–56.

Duckworth, Angela, *Grit: the power of passion and perseverance*, Random House, UK, 2017.

Fineman, Martha Albertson, Grear, Anna, *Vulnerability: reflections on a new ethical: foundation for law and politics*, Burlington, Ashgate, 2013.

Frankl, Viktor, *Man's search for meaning. an introduction to logotherapy*, Beacon Press, Boston, 2006.

Fremont, Wanda P., Childhood reactions to terrorism-induced trauma: a review of the past 10 years, In *Journal of the American Academy of Child & Adolescent Psychiatry*, vol. 43, 2004, pp. 381–392.

Goleman, Daniel; Sonnenfeld, Jeffrey; Achor, Shawn, *Resilience*, Harvard Business Review Press, USA, 2017.

Grenon, Marion *et al*, Impact of a terrorist attack on the mental health of directly exposed French adolescents: study protocol for the first step of the aval cohort study, In *Front Psychiatry*, vol. 10, no. 744, 2019.

Johnson, Christopher, Bricoleur and bricolage: from metaphor to universal concept, In *Paragraph*, vol. 35, no. 3, 2012, pp. 355–72.

Kazlauskas, Evaldas *et al*, Trauma treatment across Europe: where do we stand now from a perspective of seven countries, In *European Journal of Psychotraumatology*, vol. 7, 2016.

Lally, Katie, Meera Atkinson. The poetics of transgenerational trauma. Bloomsbury, 2017., In *Studies in 20th & 21st Century Literature*, vol. 43, no. 1, 2018.

Lévi-Strauss, Claude, *La Pensée sauvage*, Paris, Plon, 1962.

Linkov, Igor; Keenan, Jesse M., Trump, Benjamin D., *Covid-19: systemic risk and resilience*, Springer, 2021.

Markey-Towler, Brendan, Antifragility, the Black Swan and psychology, In *Evolutionary and Institutional Economics Review*, vol. 15, no. 2, Springer, 2018, pp. 367–384.

Moffic, H. Steven *et al*, *Anti-Semitism and psychiatry*, Springer, 2020.

Morsink, Johannes, *The Universal Declaration of Human Rights and the Holocaust: an endangered connection*, Georgetown University Press, 2019.

Munoz, Albert; Billsberry, Jon; Ambrosini, Véronique, Resilience, robustness, and antifragility: towards an appreciation of distinct organizational responses to adversity, In *International Journal of Management Reviews*, vol. 24, 2022, pp. 181–187.

Neenan, Michael, *Developing resilience: a cognitive-behavioural approach*, London, Routledge, 2009.

Niitsu, Kosuke *et al*, A concept analysis of resilience integrating genetics, In *Issues Mental Health Nursing*, vol. 38, no. 11, 2017, pp. 896–906.

Peterson, Jordan B., *12 rules for life, an antidote to chaos*, Penguin, London, 2018.

Phillimore, Jenny *et al*, Bricolage: potential as a conceptual tool for understanding access to welfare in superdiverse neighbourhoods, In *IRiS Working Paper Series*, no. 14 Birmingham, 2016, pp. 3–21.

Polgar, Michael, *Holocaust and human rights education: good choices and sociological perspectives*, UK, Emerald Publishing Limited, 2018.

Ribeiro, Gonçalo de Almeida, O problema da tutela constitucional das gerações futuras, In *Justiça entre gerações, perspectivas interdisciplinares*, Silva, Jorge Pereira da; Ribeiro, Gonçalo de Almeida (eds), Universidade Católica Editora, 2017, pp. 138–160.

Schäfer, Ingo *et al*, Trauma and trauma care in Europe, In *European Journal of Psychotraumatology*, vol. 9, no. 1, 2018.

Seligman, Martin E. P., Building Resilience, In *Harvard Business Review*, 2011.

Southwick, Steven M. *et al*, Resilience definitions, theory, and challenges: interdisciplinar perspectives, In *European Journal of Psychotraumatology*, vol. 5, no. 1, 2014.

Talleb, Nassim Nicholas, *Antifragile: things that gain from disorder*, New York, Random House, 2012.

Taleb, Nassim Nicholas, *The Black Swan: the impact of the highly improbable*, New York, Random House, 2007.

Vanderpol, Maurice, Resilience: A missing link in our understanding of survival, In *Harvard Review Psychiatry*, vol. 10, 2002, pp. 302–306.

Zabludoff, Sidney, At issue: restitution of holocaust-era assets: promises and reality, In *Jewish Political Studies Review*, vol. 19, no. 1/2, 2007, pp. 3–14.

PART II

Powerlessness

Machine-Learning Transparency for the Vulnerable: An International Human Rights Law Perspective

Dominika Iwan-Sojka[*,1]

Abstract: The chapter explores how transparency impacts individuals in vulnerable situations in the context of machine learning (ML) processes. It assumes that the increasing digitalisation of private and civil services leads to new forms of vulnerability in which the digital identity of individuals is created by using, selling and distributing data collected or generated by ML systems. ML systems are understood as relying on big data and training algorithms to augment or replace human decision-making. Due to difficulties in determining the reasons behind a particular decision concerning individuals, known as the black-box problem, apart from the international human rights framework, no rules have yet been adopted that directly refer to digital vulnerability in the context of ML. Transparency in ML would ideally cover input (training and testing) data and the outcomes of decision-making. However, for the time being, transparency in accounting for the vulnerable embraced in the terms above is opposed to trade secrecy and public interests. Here, commercial and public interests seem to precede human rights. Commercial interests protect financial security and a company's good name, whereas public interests aim to secure collectives from the unfair distribution of goods or threats to national security. Last but not least, the chapter determines the contexts in which the private and public sectors should account for vulnerability in developing and deploying ML processes. Second, the transparency of ML processes is located in the wider sweep of a human-centric approach to technology. Here, transparency in the input and outcomes of ML processes would contribute to decreasing the vulnerability of individuals.

Keywords: inclusiveness, machine learning processes, transparency, vulnerability, digital identity

1. Introduction

Individuals are being more and more active in and through cyberspace. Therefore, cyberspace presents unique opportunities to develop, test, and deploy various technologies that interact with those individuals. ML models

* Ph.D., Assistant Professor, Faculty of Law and Administration of the University of Silesia in Katowice, Poland ORCID: 0000-0001-8666-1667.

1 The paper was prepared as part of research project No. 2020/37/N/HS5/01483 "The prohibition of discrimination in algorithmic decision-making" financed by the National Science Centre (Poland)

are an example of technology that works to reduce the human input to accommodate decision-making processes to the specific profile of an individual. ML tools, which are trained and tested on data collected and generated from cyberspace, have contributed to organising and easing our lives, during the COVID-19 pandemic in particular. Therefore, ML technologies offering varying degrees of accuracy and transparency are attracting interest from both private and public sectors. Big-tech companies in particular are investing heavily to increase their significance on the global markets (healthcare, education, social benefits, elections, surveillance, justice, migration, detention, etc.). Likewise, increasing opportunities to reduce human input and use apparently neutral technologies have attracted interest at state level. Accordingly, digitalisation creates the potential for services and products that facilitate work practices and, along with digitisation, opens the way for digital transformation where new business concepts are created.

However, the outcomes of automation and autonomy have led to mixed results. Private companies trying to adapt their policies to sustainability are not able to predict all the social outcomes their products and services reveal. For example, during the pandemic, YouTube replaced human moderators with ML systems to remove content that violated the platform's policies on hate speech and misinformation. This move led to a significant increase in content removal, with the removal of any critical comments that contained the words Chinese Communist Party.[2] At the same time, the big-tech sector makes human rights risk assessments voluntarily and can easily shield themselves behind the argument that any regulation impedes progress.[3] Similarly, by falling into algocracy,[4] states are naturally operationalising the promising benefits of privately-driven digitalisation, including the use of algorithmic

---

2 James Vincent, "YouTube Brings Back More Human Moderators after AI Systems Over-Censor," The Verge, 21 September 2020, <https://www.theverge.com/2020/9/21/21448916/youtube-automated-moderation-ai-machine-learning-increased-errors-takedowns>.

3 The Office of the High Commissioner for Human Rights, "World Stumbling Zombie-like into a Digital Welfare Dystopia, Warns UN Human Rights Expert," OCHR, 17 October 2019, <https://www.ohchr.org/EN/NewsEvents/Pages/DisplayNews.aspx?NewsID=25156>.

4 John Danaher, "The Threat of Algocracy: Reality, Resistance and Accommodation," *Philosophy and Technology* 29, no. 3 (2016): 245–68, <https://doi.org/10.1007/s13347-015-0211-1>.

decision-making,[5] and can amplify existing vulnerabilities.[6] Welfare recipients can easily be named as outliers rather than right holders in the sense that they are prone to be denied of welfare service by a state.[7]

The chapter addresses two forms of vulnerability –– vulnerable *groups* and vulnerable *contexts* – where individuals are subject to machine learning decision-making (MLDM) processes, and looks at how a lack of transparency of these processes impacts information asymmetries between agent and recipients in vulnerable situations in order to access remedies. For clarity, the term MLDM processes will be used instead of MLDM systems to catch the specific nature of the relation between an agent and the vulnerable in legal protection schemes. Contextualised in the university admissions decision-making processes, Tetyana (Tanya) Krupiy has suggested using the term AI[8] decision-making processes rather than decision-making systems. She argues that it is more productive in terms of inclusion, since it captures a broad range of processes that gives a better understanding of how the system is structured and operates rather than focusing on technical and changing explanations of the term 'AI'.[9] In this sense, decision-making processes also

5 Algorithmic decision-making refers to an output of a computational procedure that uses computer code in instructions (an algorithm) to translate data into a specific outcome.

6 The notion of vulnerability has been widely discussed. See Paolo De Stefani, "Conceptualizing 'Vulnerability' in the European Legal Space: Mixed Migration Flows and Human Trafficking as a Test," *Frontiers in Human Dynamics* 4 (2022), <https://www.frontiersin.org/articles/10.3389/fhumd.2022.861178>; Martha Albertson Fineman, "'Elderly' as Vulnerable: Rethinking the Nature of Individual and Societal Responsibility," *The Elder Law Journal* 20 (2012): 71, <https://doi.org/10.2139/ssrn.2088159>.

7 Terry Carney, "Artificial Intelligence in Welfare: Striking the Vulnerability Balance?," *Monash University Law Review* 46, no. 2 (2021): 25, <https://doi.org/10.26180/13370369.v2>.

8 Artificial Intelligence (AI) is an umbrella term that captures a wide range of technologies that aim at providing an artificial agent that performs functions previously connoted with a human intelligence. In technical terms, machine learning involves technologies representing the actual learning ability of the model. Therefore, in the paper, I will use the term 'machine learning' rather than AI.

9 Tetyana (Tanya) Krupiy, "A Vulnerability Analysis: Theorising the Impact of Artificial Intelligence Decision-Making Processes on Individuals, Society and Human Diversity from a Social Justice Perspective," *Computer Law & Security Review* 38 (2020): 5–8, <https://doi.org/10.1016/j.clsr.2020.105429>.

account for prior stages of designing the ML model,[10] namely determining what, for whom, and how the model should be developed and deployed. The broader perspective is particularly needed when individuals receive an outcome that shapes their factual or legal situation.

The topic of vulnerability resulting from MLDM processes has not yet been analysed among scholars, unlike the areas of discriminatory and privacy-breaching algorithms.[11] The following questions lead the discussion in this chapter. What does vulnerability mean in the context of MLDM processes? How should the transparency of these processes be structured to decrease the situation of vulnerability? The chapter is structured in three parts. First, the paper decodes two forms of vulnerability in the context of MLDM processes, namely when certain groups or individuals become vulnerable. Second, to ensure the consistency of debate around transparency, the chapter presents the current state of public MLDM processes as they directly shape the individual's situation. The final section concludes and proposes recommendations for deploying MLDM processes.

---

10 Along with collecting, generating, cleaning, labelling, aggregating, analysing, manipulating and processing of data to create the ML model. Krupiy, 7.

11 Solon Barocas, "Data Mining and the Discourse on Discrimination," CS Yale, 2014, <https://www.cs.yale.edu/homes/jf/Barocas-Taxonomy.pdf>; Solon Barocas and Andrew D. Selbst, "Big Data's Disparate Impact" 104 (2016): 671, <https://doi.org/10.2139/ssrn.2477899>; Stephanie Bornstein, "Antidiscriminatory Algorithms," *Alabama Law Review* 70 (2019): 519; Amanda Bower et al., "Fair Pipelines," *arXiv:1707.00391 [Cs, Stat]*, 2 July 2017, <http://arxiv.org/abs/1707.00391>; Kate Crawford, "Think Again: Big Data," *Foreign Policy* (blog), accessed on 27 October 2021, <https://foreignpolicy.com/2013/05/10/think-again-big-data/>; Jenni Hakkarainen, "Naming Something Collective Does Not Make It so: Algorithmic Discrimination and Access to Justice," *Internet Policy Review* 10, no. 4 (7 December 2021), <https://doi.org/10.14763/2021.4.1600>; Carsten Orwat, *Risks of Discrimination through the Use of Algorithms* (Berlin: Federal Anti-Discrimination Agency, 2020), <https://doi.org/10.5445/IR/1000123477>; Frederik J. Zuiderveen Borgesius, "Strengthening Legal Protection against Discrimination by Algorithms and Artificial Intelligence," *The International Journal of Human Rights* 24,no. 10 (25 November 2020): 1572–93, <https://doi.org/10.1080/13642987.2020.1743976>; F. Zuiderveen Borgesius, "Discrimination, Artificial Intelligence, and Algorithmic Decision-Making" (Strasbourg: Council of Europe, Directorate General of Democracy, 2018), <https://dare.uva.nl/search?identifier=7bdabff5-c1d9-484f-81f2-e469e03e2360>.

2. Encoding vulnerability into ML

When Australia deployed Robodebt – an automated (and not ML) system – to detect welfare fraud, it turned out to be problematic because the reported overpayments in many cases wrongly identified individuals that, given the scale of deployment, led to systematic errors in calculations. Once the vulnerable groups were subjected to reporting, the system aggravated their situation. It was demonstrated that the model disproportionately impacted indigenous people, older people and people with disabilities. All of these groups belonged to the category of those usually more dependent on welfare care. The Australian Ombudsman reported an increased number of mental health issues, including suicide attempts, as a result of being on the red list.[12] In this case, the scale of deployment as well as the lack of understanding and transparency played a pivotal role in Robodebt's failure, since individuals were not able to access and understand information on how the system calculated them as at-risk individuals. In terms of transparency in particular, publicly available error rates in the applied calculating method were not available.[13]

There are social and legal implications of automated and MLDM processes that open up the vulnerabilities box. Poor design and limited understanding of individual vulnerabilities are common flaws when deploying MLDM in the public sector. Accounting for vulnerability is more challenging as the impacts that MLDM systems have on an individual's situation become more immediate. ML models are further able to find connections between attributes and information about individual data subjects and to use it for profiling.[14] These proxy attributes can be identified by ML models during the training phase, leading to misuse or the misinterpretation of specific categories of data (and

---

[12] Katherine Prygodicz and Others v Commonwealth of Australia (No. 2) FCA 634, No. VID 1252 of 2019 (Federal Court of Australia 11 June 2021).

[13] Yee-Fui Ng, Maria O'Sullivan, and Moira Paterson, "Revitalising Public Law in a Technological Era: Rights, Transparency and Administrative Justice," *UNSW Law Journal* 43, no. 3 (2020): 1068–69, <https://www.unswlawjournal.unsw.edu.au/wp-content/uploads/2020/09/11-NG-ET-AL.pdf>.

[14] COMPAS deployed in the United States is an example of such a model used in criminal justice with a direct consequences on individuals' sentence.

individuals) by the model.[15] Adjusted to MLDM processes, vulnerability is reflected in the asymmetry of power when individuals entrust ML systems' providers with certain kinds of information and become vulnerable to the scale and consequence of this power.

Paolo De Stefani has argued that, 'compared with the human rights language, "vulnerability" better articulates the relationship between legal categories and rapidly changing social and ecological landscapes.'[16] Vulnerability is translated into several forms, with Terry Carney understanding it in three ways, namely inherent to a person, context-specific and pathogenic. The first notion of vulnerability is used to describe a feature inherent to an individual. Based on their individual characteristics, such as age, gender, religion, race, sexual orientation or economic status, individuals become vulnerable to worsening their situation because of someone else's (a state or a private company's) decision made through MLDM processes. The context-specific vulnerability describes a situation when an individual is affected by personal, social, political, economic or environmental circumstances. Finally, there is the notion of pathogenic vulnerability, which is exacerbated by defective state policies. The additional harm results from the state's action or inaction.[17]

Tetyana Krupiy argues that focusing on the vulnerability theory in the context of AI in general opens the way towards analysing the impacts of MLDM processes, forming part of social institutions and relationships between individuals and society.[18] The vulnerability theory serves here only as a justification to ensure the transparency of MLDM processes in terms of how these processes operate in the given contexts. This theory does not create a new legal entitlement, such as a human right to transparent MLDM. However, the notion of vulnerability is particularly useful with supplementing inadequacies of intersectional discrimination, when a person experiences various forms of discrimination at once (for example, simultaneously on grounds

---

15 Vitor Bernardo, "EDPS TechDsipatch on Explainable Artificial Intelligence" (Technology and Privacy Unit of the European Data Protection Supervisor, 2023), 10, <https://edps.europa.eu/system/files/2023-11/23-11-16_techdispatch_xai_en.pdf>.

16 De Stefani, "Conceptualizing 'Vulnerability' in the European Legal Space."

17 Carney, "Artificial Intelligence in Welfare," 34.

18 Krupiy, "A Vulnerability Analysis," 9.

of gender, ethnic origin, and age), and limits on privacy when information does not necessarily belong to the category of personal data.

In the context of MLDM processes, I extract two types of vulnerability that are not mutually exclusive. The first category embraces vulnerable *groups*. In the equality and non-discrimination discourse, treaty bodies sometimes implicitly refer to the notion of vulnerability by mentioning substantive equality and thus creating positive obligations to protect and fulfil.[19] For example, the African Commission on Human and Peoples Rights has stated that 'substantive equality requires that groups who have suffered previous disadvantages or continue to suffer within a state are entitled to some advantageous treatment.'[20] When determining state obligations concerning vulnerability, there are various notions of which type of vulnerability should be protected by law, in other words – which vulnerability should a state protect with proactive measures. The ECtHR case law provides an extensive description on what vulnerabilities should be accounted for (such as children, gender minorities, people with disabilities, detainees, ethnic, and linguistic minorities, as well as individuals who find themselves in economic poverty or dependent on state allowances).[21] The notion of vulnerability appears as context-dependant and impacting the proportionality test towards assessing the performance of obligations by the state concerned (something that amounts to due diligence by a State). De Stafani has noted that the notion of vulnerability is a weak

[19] Nesa Zimmermann, "Legislating for the Vulnerable? Special Duties under the European Convention on Human Rights," *Swiss Revue of International and European Law* 25 (1 January 2015): 553; Mikaela Heikkilà and Maija Mustaniemi-Laakso, "Vulnerability as a Human Rights Variable: African and European Developments," *African Human Rights Law Journal* 20, no. 2 (2020): 791, <https://doi.org/10.17159/1996-2096/2020/v20n2a19>; Heikkilà and Mustaniemi-Laakso, 793; Oddný Mjöll Arnardóttir, "Vulnerability under Article 14 of the European Convention on Human Rights," *Oslo Law Review* 4, no. 3 (2017): 150–71, <https://doi.org/10.18261/issn.2387-3299-2017-03-03>.

[20] Front for the Liberation of the State of Cabinda v Republic of Angola, No. Communication 328/06 (African Commission on Human and Peoples Rights 5 November 2013).

[21] Chapman vs the United Kingdom, No. 29133/03 (ECtHR [GC] 18 January 2001); Mariavittoria Catanzariti, "The Juridification of Vulnerability in the European Legal Culture," *Oñati Socio-Legal Series* 12, no. 6 (1 December 2022): 1391–1416; De Stefani, "Conceptualizing 'Vulnerability' in the European Legal Space," 9; Heikkilà and Mustaniemi-Laakso, "Vulnerability as a Human Rights Variable," 780–81.

dispositive. It performs as a gate keeper for the inclusion of aliens in a state, but depends on the actual multi-layered practice of that state. De Stefani has concluded that 'at the end of the day, a vulnerable person is the one the state wishes to include and integrate'.[22]

The second category of vulnerability relates to individuals who do not necessarily fall into a vulnerable group, but who find themselves in a vulnerable *situation*. There are several reasons why individual end up in vulnerable situations in the analysed context. First, in the context of large language models (such as ChatGPT and Bard), the models find correlations between words, but do not understand the causation and societal links that may be attached to them. Second, individuals are confronted with choosing a particular type of behaviour for which they need specific skills. They have to adapt to the way they understand ML models and outcomes. Replicating existing social inequalities is another commonly mentioned factor for emerging vulnerability situations. Finally, along with creating relationships between the decision-maker and the individual who is the subject of a decision, a new relationship occurs – between individuals who are all subjected to the same MLDM processes. These processes depend on the classifying factors when an individual becomes a cluster of quantifiable characteristics.[23]

Both types of vulnerability cover those who are affected by inequalities resulting from the digital and AI divide.[24] For years, the digital divide has been defined as the gap between those who have access to information and communication technologies (ICTs) and those who do not, with this asymmetry giving an advantage to those who already had access to other

---

22 De Stefani, "Conceptualizing 'Vulnerability' in the European Legal Space," 9.

23 Krupiy, "A Vulnerability Analysis," 13–15.

24 Mitchel Ondili, "The Impact of the AI Divide on Vulnerable Groups - Centre for Intellectual Property and Information Technology Law," *Strathmore University Centre for Intellectual Property and Information Technology Law* (blog), January 21, 2021, <https://cipit.strathmore.edu/the-impact-of-the-ai-divide-on-vulnerable-groups/>, <https://cipit.strathmore.edu/the-impact-of-the-ai-divide-on-vulnerable-groups/>.

resources, but not necessarily improving the lives of those who did not.[25] The understanding of the digital divide has been evolving towards other layers of access to ICTs, from the usage gap, production gap, and digital differentiation to digital inclusion.[26] The latter means that ICTs, including MLDM processes, are democratised to include also those affected by ICTs, by empowering the vulnerable with skills to use ICTs, participate in and benefit from the information society. When applied to our context, increasing the accessibility of ML models requires additional skills that, when lacking, lower the individual possibilities to improve one's lives compared to others that have the required skills.

In the broader sweep of the digital divide, Mitchel Ondili has extracted ML-based vulnerability that operates in the following domains, namely the use divide, the literacy gap and bias problems. The use divide resulting from the lack of necessary infrastructure to promote ICTs, leading to gaps between those who possess the necessary skills to use ML tools and those who do not. The data used to train and test ML models is also collected or generated from the vulnerable (which, according to Ondili, consist mainly of African, Latin American, and Asian societies) and then these ML models are sold back to these vulnerable. The literacy gap focuses on language and digital literacy barriers. The accessibility of services based on ML models

---

25 However, David Nemer has criticised the term for being reductionist in appealing to technological determinism. According to Nemer, using the term of digital divide would mean that technology is unapproachable and it impacts the whole way of human thinking, feeling and acting, both as individuals and whole societies. Therefore, a way of changing this narrative from digital divide to digital inclusion would be achieved through transparency in ML models among other things. Nemer has indicated that increasing access to ICTs is not enough to detach from the technological determinism encoded from the digital divide. David Nemer, "From Digital Divide to Digital Inclusion and Beyond," *The Journal of Community Informatics* 11 (14 April 2015): 1, <https://doi.org/10.15353/joci.v11i1.2857>.

26 The usage gap is based on mental and material access to ICTs (skills to operate computers, usage access to search, select, process and apply information from various sources, as well as to strategically use the information to improve one's life). The production gap indicates the gap between those who consume and who produce the content. Digital differentiation occurs when characteristics of internet users are more important in shaping and using the internet than the characteristics of the internet networks. Here, the internet serves as the medium for political and social influence. Nemer, 2–3.

mainly developed through English-speaking communities. This situation is evolving, however, as more and more languages are being used to create natural language processing models or generative pre-trained models. However, accessibility of ML models to people with disabilities, for example, is still a challenge. Second, the consent-based approach to ML models is based on either entering or withdrawing from the service or product. In time, given the evolution of MLDM, individuals should be able to improve not only their digital skills, but progressively adapt their soft skills such as analytical thinking, creativity, flexibility, and openness towards the changing working environment to collaborate with the assistance of MLDM.[27] Thirdly, algorithmic bias challenges equal access to products and services, as ML models are trained and tested on sets of data of specific origins and it is hard to ensure diversity in the data. ML models are further developed by a specific type of individuals (mostly males from the Global North), and are used in a variety of (sometimes dubious) contexts.[28]

Given the widely under-regulated and embryonic legal nature of vulnerability[29] in the human rights context,[30] there is a two-fold approach to vulnerability origins in ontological vulnerability, meaning that, given the circumstances and the personal characteristics, every human being is exposed to some kind of vulnerability. In the context of the human rights paradigm, the notion of vulnerability performs as a functional notion and not as the classification of an individual as such. It follows from examining the causes and conditions of exposure to human rights violations and not who is exposed.[31] However, given some criticism over ontological (universal) vulnerability, it might be difficult to determine those who are actually in need of special care

---

27 There are jobs that are highly substitutable by ML and are at high risk of being replaced; others, such as in medicine or childcare will have to adjust; and there are some that cannot be replaced by ML models, namely jobs that require making creative decisions, such as potential investors and managers.

28 Ondili, "The Impact of the AI Divide on Vulnerable Groups – Centre for Intellectual Property and Information Technology Law."

29 Vulnerability is the product of jurisprudential and institutional practice rather than legal documents such as treaties.

30 Heikkilà and Mustaniemi-Laakso, "Vulnerability as a Human Rights Variable."

31 Elena Pariotti, "Vulnerability and Human Rights: Which Compatibility?," *International Journal for the Semiotics of Law* 36, no. 4 (1 August 2023): 1404, <https://doi.org/10.1007/s11196-023-09977-y>.

due to potential human rights violations, as well as avoiding paternalism or stigmatisation in human rights language.

While analysing the notion of vulnerability in the context of migration flows, De Stefani has stressed the role of a proper vulnerability assessment.[32] When accommodated to an MLDM environment, the vulnerability assessment should be performed when the group of users of cyberspace are all exposed to various extents of differential treatment (such as pricing discrimination, targeted advertising, profiling, targeted state policies concerning the detection of social fraud, or preventing pregnancies among teenagers), as differentiation risks additional victimisation. There are categories of users in cyberspace that require additional support in some contexts. Such support is particularly needed in relation to cybersecurity. It requires special care given to those users who are not familiar with the challenges occurring in cyberspace, as their lack of awareness may result in extortion or sharing personal data for malicious purposes. ML systems amplify the relatively low level of knowledge on what data is gathered or generated about the users, for what purposes and what the outcomes are. As a result, an individual may be unable to see specific job adverts because the ML-supported platform extracts data about them and trains the algorithms to adapt to 'their' profile as a candidate for specific types of positions exclusively. In the public domain, as will be described below, the low quality of MLDM processes concerning transparency, respect for privacy, and non-discrimination significantly impacts the quality of trust between the agent and recipients of MLDM and the resulting lack of access to necessary remedies.

The significance of transparency in accounting for vulnerability in MLDM processes cannot, therefore, be overstated. I will now take a look at what transparency means and whether it can be applied to the process of increasing protection for vulnerable groups and individuals in vulnerable situations.

3. Role of ML transparency in vulnerability language

Lawyers seek to address the social effects of digitalisation through sectorial regulation, treaties, soft law, or ethics. There are legal frameworks, municipal

---

32 De Stefani, "Conceptualizing 'Vulnerability' in the European Legal Space," 4.

laws, treaties and policies, all of which are either ML-specific[33] or concerned with data protection,[34] consumer protection, human rights treaties, and so on.[35] Regulations of MLDM processes that should account for the vulnerable groups and contexts are no exception here.[36] The human rights framework strongly connects vulnerability with transparency, since this framework is equipped with tools to inhibit the social impacts of innovations and ensure access to remedies. Operationalised in the human rights framework, the concept of vulnerability allows for a focus on specific groups or identities that are more prone to harm (and human rights violations) than others. Hence, the groups and identities require special (additional) measures to ensure

[33] For example, in the EU context, the Digital Services Act introduced the requirements concerning transparency and explainability of ML models used in online platforms. "Regulation (EU) 2022/2065 of the European Parliament and of the Council of 19 October 2022 on a Single Market For Digital Services and Amending Directive 2000/31/EC (Digital Services Act) (Text with EEA Relevance)," 277 OJ L § (2022), <http://data.europa.eu/eli/reg/2022/2065/oj/eng>.

[34] "Regulation (EU) 2016/679 of the European Parliament and of the Council on the protection of natural persons with regard to the processing of personal data and on the free movement of such data, and repealing Directive 95/46/EC (General Data Protection Regulation)," Pub. L. No. Official Journal of the European Union L 119/1 (2016), <https://eur-lex.europa.eu/eli/reg/2016/679/oj>.

[35] The EU framework consists of a wide range of EU secondary law sources that apply to selected issues related to ML. For example, the European Parliament and the Council adopted the Accessibility Directive that, starting from 28 June 2025, harmonises the EU internal market by introducing harmonised rules for accessible products and services. "Directive (EU) 2019/882 of the European Parliament and of the Council of 17 April 2019 on the Accessibility Requirements for Products and Services (Text with EEA Relevance)," 151 OJ L § (2019), <http://data.europa.eu/eli/dir/2019/882/oj/eng>. Other acts relate to products safety, platform providers, anti-discrimination directives, unfair commercial practices, product liability, sale of goods, digital content, and so on. The UNESCO has proposed an AI competence framework for students and teachers as well as recommendations to set a minimum age limit for using generative ML models. UNESCO, "AI Competency Frameworks for School Students and Teachers," UNESCO, 4 December 2023, <https://www.unesco.org/en/digital-education/ai-future-learning/competency-frameworks>; Yonah Welker, "Can Emerging AI Strategies Protect Vulnerable Groups?," euronews, 22 November 2023, <https://www.euronews.com/next/2023/11/22/can-emerging-ai-strategies-protect-people-with-disabilities-and-other-vulnerable-groups>.

[36] The EU AI Act risk-based approach is a good example of it.

their full enjoyment of human rights.[37] In the context of specific groups, vulnerability is partly connected with the rights of non-discrimination and equality. It acts as a lens through which those who apply international human rights law in practice should interpret a specific case.[38] However, the human rights framework does not apply equally to states and private companies, since only states can be parties to human rights treaties. Therefore, a clear distinction must also be drawn between duty-bearers and right-holders with regards to the transparency of MLDM processes that account for vulnerability. In this chapter, I will focus solely on the required standards of transparency at state level.

In general, transparency relates to insights on the structure of MLDM systems, including input and output data, the technology applied, the way the model has been trained, variables, and parameters.[39] Due to difficulties in determining the reason for a particular decision concerning individuals, known as the black-box problem, outside of the international human rights framework, rules that would directly account for ML-related vulnerability

---

37 Heikkilà and Mustaniemi-Laakso, "Vulnerability as a Human Rights Variable," 778.

38 Vulnerability to some extent overlaps with, but also goes beyond, the right to equality, the latter on the other hand supplements the right to non-discrimination. Vulnerability will not be used as substituting any human rights principle here but as a lens through which the interpretation of human rights and related concepts in specific cases should be applied. In the rights-holders' and duty-bearers' language, vulnerability is therefore not helpful, since it does not create a foundation for rights. Pariotti, "Vulnerability and Human Rights," 1406–7; Heikkilà and Mustaniemi-Laakso, "Vulnerability as a Human Rights Variable," 790–791.

39 The Impact Assessment Fundamental Rights and Algorithms prepared by the Dutch Ministry of Interior and Kingdom Relations in 2022 further distinguishes internal and external transparency. Internal transparency relates to insights within an organisation, including for the purpose of internal and external control. External transparency is aimed at the general public. Notably, transparency is considered there as an element of the procedural fundamental right to good administration Janneke Gerards *et al.*, "Impact Assessment Fundamental Rights and Algorithms - Report - Government.Nl" (Ministry of the Interior and Kingdom Relations, 31 March 2022), 45, 93, <https://www.government.nl/documents/reports/2022/03/31/impact-assessment-fundamental-rights-and-algorithms>.

and establish the required standards of transparency are still only evolving.[40] Depending on the technology applied, there are black-box and white-box ML models. The use of the black-box terminology indicates that it involves a system that regular individuals are unable to understand. Even though the inputs and outputs of the ML system can be observed, there is no access to the inside causation and correlation methodologies (not to mention an understanding of it[41]). Once a state decides to deploy a black-box model, it does not necessarily produce risks as long as transparency is put in place. Transparency plays a crucial role in explaining MLDM processes and possibly opening access to remedies should the outcome be flawed. A special risk assessment is therefore needed. In contrast, white-box models are suggested for law enforcement and criminal justice decisions, healthcare, banking, urban planning, self-driving cars, and administrative justice.[42]

In a relational vein, Sunstein's concept of input and output transparency in state-to-individual relationships plays a pivotal role to determining the scope of transparency, which may improve the situation of the vulnerable. Outputs are defined as facts that are associated with certain activity or policy, whereas inputs present the views of stakeholders involved in decision-making processes. His welfarist approach helps identify which trade-offs are at stake when discussing transparency, namely benefits and costs on both sides of the transparency relationship. While output transparency can serve a disinfectant role by increasing accountability and performance, what the recipients will do with the information is relatively unpredictable once it is revealed. With regard to output transparency concerning high-value data sets, Sunstein has appealed for answers to the following: (1). Could recipients benefit from

---

[40] For example, the risk-based approach incorporated in the EU AI Act adapts to the vulnerability discussion. Likewise, the Government of Canada has introduced the Algorithmic Impact Assessment Tool for the government agencies. Treasury Board of Canada Secretariat, "Algorithmic Impact Assessment Tool," guidance, Government of Canada, 22 March 2021, <https://www.canada.ca/en/government/system/digital-government/digital-government-innovations/responsible-use-ai/algorithmic-impact-assessment.html>.

[41] Meredith Broussard, *More than a Glitch: Confronting Race, Gender, and Ability Bias in Tech* (Cambridge, Massachusetts: The MIT Press, 2023), 171.

[42] John Burke, "Unlocking the Potential of White Box Machine Learning Algorithms | TechTarget," *TechTarget* (blog), 7 December 2022, <https://www.techtarget.com/searchenterpriseai/tip/Unlocking-the-potential-of-white-box-machine-learning-algorithms>.

information? (2) Could disclosure promote accountability that would improve the performance of the (public/private) agent?[43] Since information covered by input transparency relates to illegitimate or illicit conduct, or reveals the mistakes of predecessors, the trade-offs of input transparency are different to those prescribed to output transparency. The costs of input transparency are usually higher and do not necessarily lead to the expected outcomes (for example, an improvement of actions or of the recipients' situation). At the same time, the classification of what is input and output depends on whether and how the recipient would benefit from the disclosure. Sunstein has noted that:

'A central reason is that government often has information that people can actually use, perhaps to make life more navigable, perhaps to avoid serious risks. It should not keep that information to itself. Another reason is that sunlight can operate as a disinfectant. And whether the information involves the government's own performance or the performance of the private sector, disclosure can spur better performance'[44]

I will now look at how transparency can be adjusted to the MLDM processes. Since ML models are trained on inputs to produce outputs, the idea of the transparency of inputs and outputs performs as an interesting framework to reduce vulnerability. This transparency corresponds with notions of white (i.e. self-interpretable) and black boxes.[45] In contrast to a black box[46]

---

[43] Cass R. Sunstein, "Output Transparency vs. Input Transparency," *SSRN Electronic Journal*, 1 January 2016, 9, <https://doi.org/10.2139/ssrn.2826009>.

[44] Sunstein, 14–15.

[45] The concepts of white and black boxes are different from white- and black-box testing methods. The latter are used in software testing to evaluate the quality of the model. Black-box (data-driven, or closed box) testing is a method that assesses the external behaviour of the system, namely the inputs received by the system and the outputs the system produces. White box (clear, code-based, structural, or transparent) testing examines the structure of the product and requires an extensive knowledge of the used technology. "Black Box Vs White Box Testing," PractiTest, accessed 30 January 2024, <https://www.practitest.com/resource-center/article/black-box-vs-white-box-testing/>; Deven R. Desai and Joshua A. Kroll, "Trust But Verify: A Guide to Algorithms and the Law," *Harvard Journal of Law & Technology* 31, no. 7 (2017): 37–39.

[46] Black-box models (such as deep learning, boosting, and random forests) are deployed in complex scenarios with not necessarily linear interactions between pieces of data.Thanks to their ability to account for complexities in behaviours, black-box models achieve a better predictive accuracy rate and are more effective in sorting large data sets. The cost of these advantages is that black-box models are non-transparent and difficult to interpret.

(examples of which include Chat GPT-3 and Dall-E), a white box ML allows individuals to interpret the ML decision by analysing the inputs and outputs.[47] Self-interpretable models consist of easy understandable algorithms in terms of finding connections between input data and outcomes or target variables. Given the benefits of deploying black-box models, more attention has been paid to ensuring that these models are also more transparent. This post-hoc approach can be applied by providing either a local or global explanation of the ML model. A *post-hoc* global explanation should ideally result in an overall understanding of the decision-making processes, for example, by revealing information on the general trends of the model or how it arrives at a decision.[48] The local explanation is provided by programs[49] that produce information after the ML model reached a decision. The programs enable more explainability of black-box models through observing and interpreting the model's behaviour, as well as the ability to manipulate input data and interpret the change in outcomes.[50]

Likewise, instead of focusing on the accessibility of the black box, Anupam Chander has proposed a narrower understanding of transparency – transparency of inputs and outputs. This idea compromises calls for transparency of design[51] with algorithmic affirmative action. Thanks to this approach, those

---

[47] The following methods are considered white box models: linear, decision, and regression trees. Although these methods are recommended for risk assessment or autonomous vehicles, they are criticised for lower accuracy in more complex relationships. Daisy Tsang, "White Box vs. Black Box Algorithms in Machine Learning," *ActiveState* (blog), 19 July 2023, <https://www.activestate.com/blog/white-box-vs-black-box-algorithms-in-machine-learning/>.

[48] Bernardo, "EDPS TechDsipatch on Explainable Artificial Intelligence," 6–7.

[49] Such programs are Local Interpretable Model-agnostic Explanation (LIME) and Shapley Additive Explanations (SHAP).

[50] Tsang, "White Box vs. Black Box Algorithms in Machine Learning."

[51] Transparency *of* design is challenging for those who invest in developing or deploying ML models. If regulated, it would open up a Pandora's box by enabling external users to manipulate algorithms. There is yet another concept of transparency *by* design, which, like privacy by design, relates to incorporating the value of transparency ex ante – while conceptualising the ML design. See: Heike Felzmann *et al.*, "Towards Transparency by Design for Artificial Intelligence," *Science and Engineering Ethics* 26, no. 6 (1 December 2020): 3335, <https://doi.org/10.1007/s11948-020-00276-4>.

who deploy ML models would not be obliged to publicise the models, given trade secrecy or collective interests protecting the model. At the same time the recipients of MLDM processes would have a better understanding how a decision or prediction is reached by the model. Transparency would ideally cover inputs and outputs of MLDM processes. Whereas transparency of inputs relies on training and testing data used for MLDM processes, transparency of outputs assist in revealing in which situations ML models produce or contribute to the situation of vulnerability, including discrimination.[52] In the broader sweep of algorithmic affirmative action, transparency would require more scrutiny in reporting a vulnerability situation resulting from the ML deployment. The price of such transparency would be that, when attached to the vulnerability discussions, transparency of inputs and outputs would contribute to reducing ML-related vulnerability, while not necessarily taking into account the cause of it.

Two forms of transparency have been discussed, namely transparency *of* design and transparency *by* design. Transparency by design differs from transparency of design because the former is an ex ante assessment during the design process. In relational transparency, the exclusive delivery of information is insufficient to ensure an equal relation between an agent and a recipient of that information, with researchers pointing to the relevance of the recipient's understanding of information in this regard. An informational approach to transparency aims to reduce information asymmetries between the agent and the recipient. Therefore, in public domains, transparency would require the full disclosure of relevant information related to the processes within an organisation that applies an ML model in decision-making processes. Those who are involved in decision-making processes should have prior access to information concerning the quality and aims of deploying MLDM processes, as well as ex post access to MLDM outcomes. According to Felzmann et al., an outcome of accounting for transparency would be a trust understood as embracing acceptance of vulnerability occurring from the MLDM.[53]

---

52 Anupam Chander, "The Racist Algorithm?," *Michigan Law Review*, no. 115.6 (2017): 1039–43, <https://doi.org/10.36644/mlr.115.6.racist>.

53 Felzmann et al. (n 51) 3337–3338.

Transparency in MLDM processes does have its shortcomings. Felzmann et al. have demonstrated significant tensions between transparency in theory and in practice during an ML model's life-cycle. In theory, however, as a normative ideal, transparency constitutes a value with vague practical applications. Translated into practical applications, transparency performs as an actual tool for measuring an ML model's legal, social and economic influence.[54] This influence differs depending on the area in which the model is applied. Those systems that produce legal effects, or significantly impact an individual's situation, require a higher standard of transparency than ML models recommending, for example, the next movie to watch.[55] Felzmann have further extracted three meanings of transparency, namely normative, relational and systemic. Normative transparency describes transparency as an ideal and value with unclear practical meaning. Relational transparency constitutes an equal relationship between an agent and the recipient of information. Systemic transparency relates to social implementation of transparency, which is guaranteed through measures that allow for accountability of those who should reveal information.[56]

In practical terms, transparency is gradual, as it may affect the scope of understanding of the entire model, its individual components or the particular training algorithm. A model is transparent if information about it enables the decision-making to be validated and audited by relevant stakeholders through the prism of legal requirements. Vitor Bernardo has demonstrated possible pathways to trust-building with regard to ML models. Transparency alone is insufficient without providing the model's predictability and explainability. The latter is particularly important in critical applications of MLDM processes when sensitive information is at stake.[57] However, Bernardo has stressed the challenges of implementing transparency, including misinterpretation, risks to personal data (including that of vulnerable data subjects), risks to trade secrecy and an over-reliance on models when users place too much trust in the MLDM processes. He opts for balance between various values, such as privacy, transparency and secrecy protected by law, indicating

---

54 Felzmann et al. (n 51) 3335–3336.

55 Bernardo, "EDPS TechDsipatch on Explainable Artificial Intelligence," 2.

56 Felzmann et al. (n 51) 3335–3336.

57 Bernardo, "EDPS TechDsipatch on Explainable Artificial Intelligence," 4.

also that a human factor is important in these processes.[58] This balancing requires prior political decisions, however, rather than legal ones.

Transparency in MLDM processes require making several trade-offs between accuracy and explainability; between transparency and respect for vulnerability; or between trade/state secrecy and access to remedies. ML models vary in terms of accuracy and explainability. Usually, the more accurate the model is, the less explainable it becomes. Tensions between transparency and respect for the vulnerable are visible in the sense that the transparency of input data may require revealing information about data holders, including vulnerable ones. Therefore, transparency is one factor among others and, given the specific contexts or individual situations, it may turn from a positive to negative outcome.[59] While transparency constitutes a promising change to accounting for the vulnerable in the public sphere, administrative justice in particular, the explainable AI (XAI) approach has been criticised for entrenching problematic AI decision-making. The XAI approach would narrow the reasons for the particular decision, which would further limit the grounds to contest these decisions. Therefore, mechanisms like impact assessment or multi-layered explanations used in the EU General Data Protection Regulation,[60] for instance, would remedy risks in fostering AI in administrative justice.[61] An example can be found in the guide into human rights impact assessment adopted by the Dutch Ministry of Interior

---

58 Bernardo, 11–15.

59 To describe these tensions, Felzmann *et al.* give an example of content moderation algorithms. Transparency on an individual level means that an individual whose content has been removed from the social platform can receive a proper explanation of how and why a decision was made. Systemic transparency means that the general public receives information on how, how many, why, in what cases, and who made the decision. Relational transparency would require measures to ensure an equal relation between users and content moderators. However, for the time being, transparency reports produced by platform providers are often in contrast with their broader policies. As a result, users do not trust platform providers, since they are given insufficient influence over the platform policies. Felzmann *et al.* (n 51) 3339–42.

60 Regulation (EU) 2016/679 of the European Parliament and of the Council on the protection of natural persons with regard to the processing of personal data and on the free movement of such data, and repealing Directive 95/46/EC (General Data Protection Regulation).

61 Carney, "Artificial Intelligence in Welfare," 45–48.

and Kingdom Relations in 2022, which considers respect for vulnerable groups as a public value that should be considered when assessing why ML models development and use are necessary.[62]

My reflection is that the transparency of MLDM processes does not require an absolute approach in which the owner of the model reveals all the information about the model, but that the recipient, an individual in a vulnerable situation, receives and understands what, how, and why the model was applied, as well as the consequences of that for their individual situation. Therefore, in the context of state deployment, interior transparency for supervisory bodies is out of question, as it corresponds with the right to an effective remedy. External or systemic transparency is more problematic, since it relies on the general public receiving and being able to understand information provided by the owner of the ML model. There, ensuring that the public understands information becomes challenging, as it may require revealing intellectual property rights. For the time being, transparency in accounting for the vulnerable embraced in the terms above is opposed to trade secrecy and public interests. Here, commercial and public interests overshadow human rights protection. The commercial interests protect financial security and a company's good name, whereas public interests aim at securing collectives from the unfair distribution of goods or threats to national security that may provide a proportionate justification to using the model

Out of several challenges to deploying ML by states is that providing adequate reasons for a decision made by state officials is understood as the standard of legal review required by law. Terry Carney has suggested that ML can merely be explainable, but does not provide reasoned justification in a particular case. Explainability embraces the system, the rules applied and the algorithms behind it, but does not reflect the proper justification of a particular decision. Even if such explainability was sufficient for legal review, MLDM is associated with a lack of public information behind the logic of the decision, compared to the decision made by a human. In this context, the lack of transparency severely impacts the scope of information an individual can obtain from the state.[63] In a similar vein, Yee-Fui Ng, Maria O'Sullivan, and Moira Paterson have argued that the lack of understanding of

---

62 Gerards *et al.* (n 39) 14.

63 Carney, "Artificial Intelligence in Welfare," 41–43.

MLDM process applied to an individual situation and the black box problem deepens the opaqueness of the models in public applications in particular.[64]

To address the challenges of building trust in the public deployment of MLDM processes, along with accounting for the vulnerable *groups* and *situations*, controversies around low-quality development and deployment of ML are approached from the principle of beneficence. To remedy the risk of untrustworthiness in Australia, some governmental departments have started to use what is known as the golden rule in any automated decision-making. This rule assumes that automation can be applied to decisions resulting in positive outcomes for the addressees, namely, when the field in which automated decision-making is applied results in creating the beneficial situation for an individual. On the other hand, when the decision creates potentially harmful outcomes for an individual, human intervention is required.[65] Terry Carney has further suggested progressing dialogue between those deploying and the final recipients of MLDM, as well as flexibility and an openness to changing the model once it is reported to have worsened the situation of recipients. He concludes that: 'AI continued to be a top-down bureaucratically controlled and driven process' instead of the appropriate governmental design, which he has called the 'agile co-design' as a possible venue to pursue digital welfare states in the area of administrative justice.[66]

4. Conclusions

The contexts in which private and public sectors account for vulnerability in developing and deploying MLDM processes vary. In public domains, the transparency of MLDM processes can be achieved by focusing on the right to receive reasons for a decision when an individual should be given reasons as to their individual situation determined by an MLDM process, along with access to remedies should the decision be flawed and unexplainable. Furthering the right to information focused on ML specificities would be a good step forward. ML-related information should embrace information about the

64 Ng, O'Sullivan, and Paterson, "Revitalising Public Law in a Technological Era: Rights, Transparency and Administrative Justice," 1052.
65 Ng, O'Sullivan, and Paterson, 1050.
66 Carney, "Artificial Intelligence in Welfare," 43–44.

software used to train an ML model, anonymised data used to train and test the model, as well as the factual circumstances surrounding the decisions behind the development and deployment of the model.[67] The human rights framework is central to these processes when MLDM processes are applied towards individuals. Designing these processes is a crucial moment when the risk assessment should take place. In terms of vulnerable groups, such as those with disabilities, the elderly, those with a specific socio-economic status or gender, these should be considered during the design phase. This could take forms of consultations, feedback from potential users or active participation in this phase.

For individuals in vulnerable situations, bias mitigation algorithms, regular audits, and feedback would enhance an understanding of the data used to train and test models, and thereby reduce algorithmic bias. However, trust towards MLDM processes is most important and that cannot be achieved without transparency towards the explainability of the processes. Giving up some trade secrecy to help ensure explainability constitutes an important factor for building trust from vulnerable groups and from individuals in vulnerable situations, since it would assist them in adjusting themselves to the increasing amount of MLDM processes deployed by states. Ensuring transparency is a value that should be protected, because it not only acts as a technical safeguard, but most importantly as a social and legal one to build trust between a state and individuals.

Accounting for vulnerability in MLDM processes through ensuring transparency is only one step in the many complex processes around human-centric ML models. Further steps require building the categories of contexts in which MLDM processes can pose a risk to individuals in vulnerable situations, improving digital skills and increasing access to ICTs conducting risk assessment specific to social and historical factors behind these processes, as well as diversity-oriented oversight and participation at the development, deployment and assessment stages.[68]

---

67 Ng, O'Sullivan, and Paterson, "Revitalising Public Law in a Technological Era: Rights, Transparency and Administrative Justice," 1053.

68 Welker, "Can Emerging AI Strategies Protect Vulnerable Groups?"

Bibliography

Legal documents

Chapman vs the United Kingdom [2001] ECtHR [GC] 29133/03.

Directive (EU) 2019/882 of the European Parliament and of the Council of 17 April 2019 on the accessibility requirements for products and services (Text with EEA relevance) 2019.

Front for the Liberation of the State of Cabinda vs Republic of Angola [2013] African Commission on Human and Peoples Rights Communication 328/06.

Katherine Prygodicz and Others vs Commonwealth of Australia (No 2) FCA 634 [2021] Federal Court of Australia VID 1252 of 2019.

Regulation (EU) 2016/679 of the European Parliament and of the Council on the protection of natural persons with regard to the processing of personal data and on the free movement of such data, and repealing Directive 95/46/EC (General Data Protection Regulation) 2016 [Official Journal of the European Union L 119/1].

Regulation (EU) 2022/2065 of the European Parliament and of the Council of 19 October 2022 on a Single Market For Digital Services and amending Directive 2000/31/EC (Digital Services Act) (Text with EEA relevance) 2022 (OJ L).

Secretariat TB of Canada, 'Algorithmic Impact Assessment Tool' (*Government of Canada*, 22 March 2021) <https://www.canada.ca/en/government/system/digital-government/digital-government-innovations/responsible-use-ai/algorithmic-impact-assessment.html> accessed 23 December 2021.

References

Barocas, Solon. "Data Mining and the Discourse on Discrimination." CS Yale, 2014. <https://www.cs.yale.edu/homes/jf/Barocas-Taxonomy.pdf>.

Barocas, Solon, and Andrew D. Selbst. "Big Data's Disparate Impact" 104 (2016): 671. <https://doi.org/10.2139/ssrn.2477899>.

Bernardo, Vitor. "EDPS TechDsipatch on Explainable Artificial Intelligence." Technology and Privacy Unit of the European Data Protection Supervisor, 2023. <https://edps.europa.eu/system/files/2023-11/23-11-16_techdispatch_xai_en.pdf>.

Bornstein, Stephanie. "Antidiscriminatory Algorithms." *Alabama Law Review* 70 (2019): 519.

Bower, Amanda, Sarah N. Kitchen, Laura Niss, Martin J. Strauss, Alexander Vargas, and Suresh Venkatasubramanian. "Fair Pipelines." *arXiv:1707.00391 [Cs, Stat]*, 2 July 2017. <http://arxiv.org/abs/1707.00391>.

Broussard, Meredith. *More than a Glitch: Confronting Race, Gender, and Ability Bias in Tech*. Cambridge, Massachusetts: The MIT Press, 2023.

Burke, John. "Unlocking the Potential of White Box Machine Learning Algorithms | TechTarget." *TechTarget* (blog), 7 December 2022. <https://www.techtarget.com/searchenterpriseai/tip/Unlocking-the-potential-of-white-box-machine-learning-algorithms>.

Carney, Terry. "Artificial Intelligence in Welfare: Striking the Vulnerability Balance?" *Monash University Law Review* 46, no. 2 (2021). <https://doi.org/10.26180/13370369.v2>.

Catanzariti, Mariavittoria. "The Juridification of Vulnerability in the European Legal Culture." *Oñati Socio-Legal Series* 12, no. 6 (December 1, 2022): 1391–1416.

Chander, Anupam. "The Racist Algorithm?" *Michigan Law Review*, no. 115.6 (2017): 1023. <https://doi.org/10.36644/mlr.115.6.racist>.

Chapman v. the United Kingdom, No. 29133/03 (ECtHR [GC] 18 January 2001).

Crawford, Kate. "Think Again: Big Data." *Foreign Policy* (blog) (accessed on 27 October 2021). <https://foreignpolicy.com/2013/05/10/think-again-big-data/>.

Danaher, John. "The Threat of Algocracy: Reality, Resistance and Accommodation." *Philosophy and Technology* 29, no. 3 (2016): 245–68. <https://doi.org/10.1007/s13347-015-0211-1>.

De Stefani, Paolo. "Conceptualizing 'Vulnerability' in the European Legal Space: Mixed Migration Flows and Human Trafficking as a Test." *Frontiers in Human Dynamics* 4 (2022). <https://www.frontiersin.org/articles/10.3389/fhumd.2022.861178>.

Desai, Deven R., and Joshua A. Kroll. "Trust But Verify: A Guide to Algorithms and the Law." *Harvard Journal of Law & Technology* 31, no. 7 (2017): 1–66.

Directive (EU) 2019/882 of the European Parliament and of the Council of 17 April 2019 on the accessibility requirements for products and services

(Text with EEA relevance), 151 OJ L § (2019). <http://data.europa.eu/eli/dir/2019/882/oj/eng>.

Felzmann, Heike, Eduard Fosch-Villaronga, Christoph Lutz, and Aurelia Tamò-Larrieux. "Towards Transparency by Design for Artificial Intelligence." *Science and Engineering Ethics* 26, no. 6 (1 December 2020): 3333–61. <https://doi.org/10.1007/s11948-020-00276-4>.

Fineman, Martha Albertson. "'Elderly' as Vulnerable: Rethinking the Nature of Individual and Societal Responsibility." *The Elder Law Journal* 20 (2012): 71–111. <https://doi.org/10.2139/ssrn.2088159>.

Front for the Liberation of the State of Cabinda vs Republic of Angola, No. Communication 328/06 (African Commission on Human and Peoples Rights November 5, 2013).

Gerards, Janneke, Schafer, Arthur Vankan, and Iris Muis. "Impact Assessment Fundamental Rights and Algorithms - Report - Government.Nl." Ministry of the Interior and Kingdom Relations, 31 March 2022. <https://www.government.nl/documents/reports/2022/03/31/impact-assessment-fundamental-rights-and-algorithms>.

Hakkarainen, Jenni. "Naming Something Collective Does Not Make It so: Algorithmic Discrimination and Access to Justice." *Internet Policy Review* 10, no. 4 (7 December 2021). <https://doi.org/10.14763/2021.4.1600>.

Heikkilà, Mikaela, and Maija Mustaniemi-Laakso. "Vulnerability as a Human Rights Variable: African and European Developments." *African Human Rights Law Journal* 20, no. 2 (2020): 777–98. <https://doi.org/10.17159/1996-2096/2020/v20n2a19>.

Katherine Prygodicz and Others vs Commonwealth of Australia (No 2) FCA 634, No. VID 1252 of 2019 (Federal Court of Australia, 11 June 2021).

Krupiy, Tetyana (Tanya). "A Vulnerability Analysis: Theorising the Impact of Artificial Intelligence Decision-Making Processes on Individuals, Society and Human Diversity from a Social Justice Perspective." *Computer Law & Security Review* 38 (2020): 105429. <https://doi.org/10.1016/j.clsr.2020.105429>.

Mjöll Arnardóttir, Oddný. "Vulnerability under Article 14 of the European Convention on Human Rights." *Oslo Law Review* 4, no. 3 (2017): 150–71. <https://doi.org/10.18261/issn.2387-3299-2017-03-03>.

Nemer, David. "From Digital Divide to Digital Inclusion and Beyond." *The Journal of Community Informatics* 11 (14 April 2015). <https://doi.org/10.15353/joci.v11i1.2857>.

Ng, Yee-Fui, Maria O'Sullivan, and Moira Paterson. "Revitalising Public Law in a Technological Era: Rights, Transparency and Administrative Justice." *UNSW Law Journal* 43, no. 3 (2020). <https://www.unswlawjournal.unsw.edu.au/wp-content/uploads/2020/09/11-NG-ET-AL.pdf>.

Office of the High Commissioner for Human Rights. "World Stumbling Zombie-like into a Digital Welfare Dystopia, Warns UN Human Rights Expert." OCHR, 17 October 2019. <https://www.ohchr.org/EN/NewsEvents/Pages/DisplayNews.aspx?NewsID=25156>.

Ondili, Mitchel. "The Impact of the AI Divide on Vulnerable Groups - Centre for Intellectual Property and Information Technology Law." *Strathmore University Centre for Intellectual Property and Information Technology Law* (blog), 21 January 2021. <https://cipit.strathmore.edu/the-impact-of-the-ai-divide-on-vulnerable-groups/>.

Orwat, Carsten. *Risks of Discrimination through the Use of Algorithms*. Berlin: Federal Anti-Discrimination Agency, 2020. <https://doi.org/10.5445/IR/1000123477>.

Pariotti, Elena. "Vulnerability and Human Rights: Which Compatibility?" *International Journal for the Semiotics of Law* 36, no. 4 (1 August 2023): 1401–13. <https://doi.org/10.1007/s11196-023-09977-y>.

PractiTest. "Black Box Vs White Box Testing." (accessed on 30 January 2024). <https://www.practitest.com/resource-center/article/black-box-vs-white-box-testing/>.

Regulation (EU) 2016/679 of the European Parliament and of the Council on the protection of natural persons with regard to the processing of personal data and on the free movement of such data, and repealing Directive 95/46/EC (General Data Protection Regulation), Pub. L. No. Official Journal of the European Union L 119/1 (2016). <https://eur-lex.europa.eu/eli/reg/2016/679/oj>.

Regulation (EU) 2022/2065 of the European Parliament and of the Council of 19 October 2022 on a Single Market For Digital Services and amending Directive 2000/31/EC (Digital Services Act) (Text with EEA relevance), 277 OJ L § (2022). <http://data.europa.eu/eli/reg/2022/2065/oj/eng>.

Secretariat, Treasury Board of Canada. "Algorithmic Impact Assessment Tool." Guidance. Government of Canada, 22 March 2021. <https://www.canada.ca/en/government/system/digital-government/digital-government-innovations/responsible-use-ai/algorithmic-impact-assessment.html>.

Sunstein, Cass R. “Output Transparency vs. Input Transparency.” *SSRN Electronic Journal*, 1 January 2016. <https://doi.org/10.2139/ssrn.2826009>.

Tsang, Daisy. “White Box vs. Black Box Algorithms in Machine Learning.” *ActiveState* (blog), 19 July 2023. <https://www.activestate.com/blog/white-box-vs-black-box-algorithms-in-machine-learning/>.

UNESCO. “AI Competency Frameworks for School Students and Teachers.” UNESCO, 4 December 2023. <https://www.unesco.org/en/digital-education/ai-future-learning/competency-frameworks>.

Vincent, James. “YouTube Brings Back More Human Moderators after AI Systems Over-Censor.” The Verge, 21 September 2020. <https://www.theverge.com/2020/9/21/21448916/youtube-automated-moderation-ai-machine-learning-increased-errors-takedowns>.

Welker, Yonah. “Can Emerging AI Strategies Protect Vulnerable Groups?” euronews, 22 November 2023. <https://www.euronews.com/next/2023/11/22/can-emerging-ai-strategies-protect-people-with-disabilities-and-other-vulnerable-groups>.

Zimmermann, Nesa. “Legislating for the Vulnerable? Special Duties under the European Convention on Human Rights.” *Swiss Revue of International and European Law* 25 (1 January 2015): 539.

Zuiderveen Borgesius, F. “Discrimination, Artificial Intelligence, and Algorithmic Decision-Making.” Strasbourg: Council of Europe, Directorate General of Democracy, 2018. <https://dare.uva.nl/search?identifier=7bdabff5-c1d9-484f-81f2-e469e03e2360>.

Zuiderveen Borgesius, Frederik J. “Strengthening Legal Protection against Discrimination by Algorithms and Artificial Intelligence.” *The International Journal of Human Rights* 24, no. 10 (25 November 2020): 1572–93. <https://doi.org/10.1080/13642987.2020.1743976>.

A Person Injured by an AI System vs an AI Operator: Non-Contractual Civil Liability from the EU Legislation Perspective

Iwona Gredka-Ligarska[*,1]

Abstract: Considerations on vulnerability and law are connected with the question of human vulnerability towards AI. However, it is not humans who are vulnerable to AI technology; rather the weak points come from insufficient legal provisions that do not offer adequate protection. In many cases, harm or damage will occur due to an operator's misuse. If there is no contractual relationship between the operator and the injured person, it becomes a situation of tort liability based on fault. A comparison of the legal position of a victim with the legal position of an AI operator reveals the injured party's vulnerability and the difficulties they face. The first threat is that the injured party will often lack the knowledge about the actual cause of harm or damage: whether it was the operator's improper use of an AI system or a defect in the AI system itself. The second difficulty will relate to the need to demonstrate that the operator of the AI system failed to exercise due diligence when using the system. It will also be challenging for the claimant to prove that the damage occurred due to negligence or intentional harmful actions or omissions by the defendant. The European legislator has recognised these risks and is seeking to counteract them. This is confirmed by the European Commission's Proposal for a Directive of the European Parliament and of the Council on Adapting Non-contractual Civil Liability Rules to Artificial Intelligence (AI Liability Directive).

This chapter aims to analyse the legal instruments proposed by the European legislator to address the existing problems. The analysis will allow for an assessment of whether the legislative reforms of non-contractual civil liability, as proposed at the EU level, are adequate and sufficient to eliminate the vulnerability currently faced by victims. The summary will also offer proposals *de lege ferenda*.

Keywords: vulnerability, artificial intelligence, AI operator, non-contractual civil liability, EU legislation

* PhD, Assistant Professor at the Faculty of Law and Administration of the University of Silesia in Katowice, Poland ORCID: 0000-0002-9243-3158.

1 This chapter presents the results of research project no. 2021/41/B/HS5/01001 "The use of autonomous AI in the labour process and employer's civil liability towards third parties," fully financed by the National Science Centre, Poland

1. Introduction

Under the current legal framework, the basis of liability for damage caused with the involvement of an AI system is inextricably linked to the cause of damage. If the source of damage is a defect in an AI system, liability for the resulting damage will be imposed on the manufacturer of the system. Under the European Commission's Proposal for a Directive of the European Parliament and of the Council on Liability for Defective Products,[2] AI systems are clearly qualified as a product.[3] A claimant is required to prove the defectiveness of the product, the damage suffered and the causal link between the defectiveness and the damage.[4] Both under the currently applicable Directive 85/374/EEC[5] and under the proposed PLD, liability for a defective product is risk-based, which means that the claimant does not have to prove the manufacturer's fault.[6]

However, if the cause of damage is not a defect in an AI system, then the liability basis is different. In such situations, the party responsible for the occurrence of damage will no longer be the manufacturer of the AI system. If the AI system was not operated directly by the consumer (the person who suffered damage), but was used by a professional operator, then it becomes necessary to establish whether the AI system's operator is liable for the damage caused. Under the current legislative framework, the basis for such liability is – in principle – the operator's fault. Already at this stage, the vulnerability of the injured person is exposed. This is the case since, under

---

2 Brussels, 28 September 2022, COM(2022) 495 final, 2022/0302(COD). <https://eur-lex.europa.eu/legal-content/EN/TXT/?uri=CELEX%3A52022PC0495>. (Hereinafter: the PLD proposal) (accessed on 29 February 2024).

3 See Art. 4(1–4) of the PLD proposal.

4 See Art. 9(1) of the PLD proposal.

5 The Council Directive 85/374/EEC of 25 July 1985 on the approximation of the laws, regulations and administrative provisions of the Member States concerning liability for defective products, [1985] OJ L210/85. <https://eur-lex.europa.eu/legal-content/EN/TXT/?uri=celex%3A31985L0374>. (Hereinafter: Directive 85/374/EEC) (accessed on 29 February 2024).

6 For more on products liability in Austria, the Czech Republic, Denmark, England and Wales, France, Germany, Italy, the Netherlands, Norway, Poland, Spain, Switzerland, Canada, Israel, South Africa and the United States of America, see: Piotr Machnikowski ed., *European Product Liability: An Analysis of the State of the Art in the Era of New Technologies*, (Cambridge, Antwerp, Portland: Intersentia, 2016), 111–616.

the applicable laws, the injured party bears the burden of establishing what the cause of damage was (either a defect in the AI system or the wrongful behaviour of the system's operator). Determining this is necessary in order to specify who the addressee of a claim for damages should be (either the manufacturer or the operator of an AI system). However, determining the cause of the damage requires expert knowledge (often from multiple different specialists), while the injured person most often does not have this knowledge. As a result, it becomes necessary to prepare expensive expert reports without any certainty as to whether it is even possible to establish the cause of damage at all in a given situation. In this regard, the injured person is faced with vulnerability, though this is not due to the operation of 'soulless' artificial intelligence, but rather to the applicable legal provisions, which are not appropriate to deal with AI technology. If the cause of damage is possible to determine and, in the circumstances of a given case, the addressee of the claim for damages is the professional operator of an AI system, then the injured person is confronted with another challenge. Namely, in order for the injured person to bring an action to court, they must prove that the damage was caused by the fault of the defendant (the operator of the AI system).

This chapter focuses on situations in which the cause of the damage is not a defect in an AI system and, therefore, the responsible party is not the manufacturer of the system. The analysis relates to situations in which the damage is caused with the involvement of an AI system used by the operator[7] and there is no preexisting legal relationship between the injured person (natural person) and the operator of that system. In the present analysis, first of all, the current legislative framework is presented, including an identification of the existing vulnerabilities affecting persons injured by AI systems used by professional operators. The second stage concentrates on the proposals for legislative reforms through which the Union legislator intends to solve problems relating to – fault-based – liability for damages caused with the involvement of AI systems. The following part of the considerations offers an answer to the question of whether the proposed legal solutions are

---

[7] The term "operator" – for the purposes of this chapter – should be understood as a professional party using an AI system in pursuance of their professional or economic purposes and profiting from the above.

appropriate and sufficient to guarantee effective legal protection to injured parties, which involves removing the currently existing vulnerabilities. The final part of this study contains considerations *de lege ferenda*.

2. The current legal provisions and identification of an injured person's vulnerability

A consumer (natural person) may suffer damage caused by a professional operator of an AI system who inappropriately uses the system. If, in such situation, the injured person was not in any legal relationship with the operator of the AI system causing damage, then, as a rule, non-contractual civil liability based on fault will apply.

At the same time, it must be emphasised that, in the analysed situations, according to the legislative framework applicable in particular Member States of the EU, the main basis of liability is fault. There is no tortious liability model that would be uniform and common for all Member States of the EU. This is a result of the fact that the harmonisation of law at the Union level has not covered tortious law. In addition, the European legislator is not planning any comprehensive harmonisation of tortious law on the Union level in the near future.[8] A partial harmonisation was introduced under Directive 85/374/EEC. However, this directive does not apply to operators of AI systems since, as mentioned above, it is addressed exclusively to manufacturers. Although the traditions of tortious law and the provisions of the law of torts are different in particular Member States of the EU, the main basis of non-contractual liability is still fault. This is also the case with such dissimilar systems of tortious law as the German and French ones.[9]

---

[8] Jonas Knetsch, "Are Existing Tort Theories Ready for AI? A Continental European Perspective", in *The Cambridge Handbook of Artificial Intelligence: Global Perspectives on Law and Ethics*, ed. Larry A. DiMatteo, Cristina Poncibò and Michel Cannarsa, (Cambridge: Cambridge University Press, 2022), 101.

[9] According to § 823(1) BGB: "A person who, intentionally or negligently, unlawfully injures the life, body, health, freedom, property or another right of another person is liable to make compensation to the other party for the damage arising from this." According to Art. 1240 of the French Civil Code: "Any human action whatsoever which causes harm to another creates an obligation in the person by whose fault it occurred to make reparation for it."

This chapter does not investigate specific regimes of tortious law applicable in particular Member States of the EU. In the contrary, the object of the present considerations is the main basis of liability in situations when the damage suffered by a natural person (consumer) is caused with the involvement of an AI system used by a professional operator. This basis, as pointed out above, is fault. On the other hand, strict liability in the Member States of the EU is, in principle, limited to selected activities or objects that have been qualified by national legislators as particularly hazardous.[10] By way of example, one can point to '[s]trict liability for aircraft owners, nuclear power stations, environmental pollution, railway operators, and car owners and/or keepers'.[11] In certain jurisdictions (e.g. in France), strict liability for material objects is defined in more general terms,[12] by using a 'general clause' to allow judicial policymaking to define strict liability.[13] For the time being, artificial intelligence is generally not considered to be particularly dangerous. So far, Member States of the EU have not qualified as particularly hazardous either activities using the AI technology or AI-embedded devices or systems. This means that strict liability does not currently apply to such activities, devices and systems. However, it can be assumed that exceptions will relate to traditional objects covered by the strict liability regime that, over time, will be replaced by AI-embedded devices or systems. An example of this can be seen with motor vehicles. Currently, in most Member States of the EU, a keeper and/or owner of a motor vehicle incurs strict liability for damages caused to a third party.[14]

---

10 Francesco D. Busnelli *et al.*, "Strict Liability", in *Principles of European Tort Law: Text and Commentary*, European Group on Tort Law, (Vienna, New York: Springer, 2005), 103–104.

11 Erdem Büyüksagis and Willem H. Van Boom, "Strict Liability in Contemporary European Codification: Torn between Objects, Activities, and Their Risks", *Georgetown Journal of International Law* 44, No. 2 (2013): 614.

12 Eric Tjong Tjin Tai, "Liability for AI Decision-Making" in *The Cambridge Handbook of Artificial Intelligence: Global Perspectives on Law and Ethics*, Ed. Larry A. DiMatteo, Cristina Poncibò and Michel Cannarsa, (Cambridge: Cambridge University Press, 2022), 125.

13 Büyüksagis and Van Boom, "Strict Liability in Contemporary European Codification", 610–611.

14 Christiane Wendehorst, "Strict Liability for AI and other Emerging Technologies", *Journal of European Tort Law* 11, No. 2 (2020): 174–175.

Therefore, it seems reasonable to maintain strict liability also with regard to autonomous vehicles.

In the case of fault-based non-contractual liability, the burden of proof is, in principle, with the injured person, who must demonstrate not only the damage, but also the fault of the defendant and a causal link between the damage and the fault.[15] In practice, the last two elements, from the point of view of the claimant, will often be an insurmountable barrier. A claimant who is not a professional and does not have knowledge about the operation of a complex AI system may face serious difficulties in determining what actions (or omissions) of the defendant in relation to the AI system have caused the damage. The required standard of care of an operator in relation to specific AI systems remains unspecified. Opinions of forensic expert witnesses, prepared for the purposes of pending court proceedings, may also prove insufficient to evidence the fault of the defendant (the operator of an AI system). This is due to the fact that the development of algorithms is based on cooperation between many expert panels (analysts, knowledge engineers, programmers, program designers, developers, algorithm's testers). In this connection, an individual expert witness does not have comprehensive knowledge about the working principles of the entire AI system. Serious difficulties in establishing and evidencing fault of an AI system's operator come down to the inherent characteristics of artificial intelligence, such as complexity, opaqueness, autonomy, a capacity to learn and interact with the environment, including with humans. As often highlighted in academic publications, those features

---

[15] For more on fault-based liability, see Anna Beckers and Gunther Teubner, *Three Liability Regimes for Artificial Intelligence: Algorithmic Actants, Hybrids, Crowds*, 1st ed. (Oxford-London-New York-New Delhi-Sydney: Hart Publishing, 2021), 72–73; Mark A. Geistfeld, Ernst Karner, Bernhard A. Koch and Christiane Wendehorst (Eds.), Civil Liability for Artificial Intelligence and Software: Tort and Insurance Law, European Centre of Tort and Insurance Law, Vol. 37, (Berlin, Boston: Walter de Gruyter, 2023), 44–60.

may lead, in practice, to the emergence of a 'black-box effect'.[16] This means that we cannot follow the entire decision-making process of the AI system. We can only observe the result of an AI system's activity, but without full knowledge on how it was generated. In the literature on this topic, attention is paid to the fact that '[t]he potential of fault-based liability depends heavily on the degree of autonomy of the device using AI, which means that the more control is shifted from the user to the autonomous system, the less a claimant will be able to establish a wrongful behaviour on behalf of the user'.[17] Therefore, fault-based liability is more favourable to professional operators of AI systems, and not to their victims.

Apart from the vulnerabilities indicated above, which relate to anyone injured by AI systems, attention should be drawn to another shortcoming of fault-based liability. Namely, a professional operator of an AI system incurs liability for its own acts or omissions and for the acts and omissions of its employees. Such a professional operator of an AI system is liable, among other things, for inappropriate use, monitoring or supervision of the system, however, this is not liability for the outcome, but for the lack of due diligence.[18] On the other hand, an operator does not incur the risk relating to the capacity of artificial intelligence to inflict damage when the operator itself has exercised a level of diligence expected of it as a professional. By contrast, the capacity of AI systems to learn is correlated to their unpredictability and this capacity opens up the way for a given system to be transformed into dangerous artificial intelligence.[19] In practice, it may be the case that a

---

[16] For more on the "black-box effect," see Bartosz Brożek *et al.*, "The Black Box Problem Revisited: Real and Imaginary Challenges for Automated Legal Decision Making", *Artificial Intelligence and Law*, (2023), online version, <https://doi.org/10.1007/s10506-023-09356-9>, accessed on 29 February 2024;

[17] Davide Castelvecchi, "Can We Open the Black Box of AI?", *Nature* 538(7623), 2026, 20–23; Carlos Zednik, "Solving the Black Box Problem: a Normative Framework for Explainable Artificial Intelligence", *Philosophy & Technology* 34, No. 2 (2021): 265–288; Paulo H. Padovan, Clarice M. Martins and Chris Reed, "Black is the New Orange: How to Determine AI Liability", *Artificial Intelligence and Law* 31, No. 1 (2023): 133–167.

[18] Knetsch, "Are Existing Tort Theories Ready for AI?", 104.

[19] See: Greg Swanson, "Non-Autonomous Artificial Intelligence Programs and Products Liability: How New Al Products Challenge Existing Liability Models and Pose New Financial Burdens", *Seattle University Law Review* 42, No. 3 (2019): 1201–1222.

self-modifying system causes damage and no specific defect of the system can be determined, and on top of that the operator exercises due diligence. As a result, in the context of AI systems, we are dealing with residual risk, which is '[r]isk that is not eliminated even when one takes reasonable care'[20] Accidents arising out of residual risk are considered 'inevitable' in the sense that human acts cannot entirely prevent such accidents. As emphasised by Erdem Büyüksagis and Willem H. van Boom: '[w]hen accidents occur from residual risk, fault-based liability does not allow the compensation and deterrence mechanisms to work'.[21]

3. How does the EU legislator plan to solve the existing problems?

Currently, the Union legislator intends to remove the problems relating to fault-based liability through the legal instruments provided for in the European Commission's Proposal for a Directive of the European Parliament and of the Council on Adapting Non-contractual Civil Liability Rules to Artificial Intelligence (AI Liability Directive).[22] The regulatory scope of this directive would cover also the liability of professional operators of AI systems for any damage caused to a natural person when the parties had not been in any contractual relationship, as analysed in this chapter. The legal solutions proposed in the AILD proposal are intended to improve the legal situation of anyone injured by AI systems. However, the reform will not affect the basis of liability, which will still be fault. For the purposes of coherence of the system of legal protection, the AILD proposal was correlated to the AI Act,[23] among other things, by consolidating the terminology ('AI system',

---

20 Büyüksagis and Van Boom, "Strict Liability in Contemporary European Codification", 612.

21 Ibid., p. 613.

22 COM (2022) 496 final. <https://eur-lex.europa.eu/legal-content/EN/TXT/?uri=CELEX%3A52022PC0496>. (Hereinafter: the AILD proposal) (accessed on 29 February 2024).

23 The European Commission Proposal for a Regulation of the European Parliament and of the Council Laying Down Harmonised Rules on Artificial Intelligence (Artificial Intelligence Act) and Amending Certain Union Legislative Acts. <https://eur-lex.europa.eu/legal-content/EN/TXT/?uri=celex%3A52021PC0206>. (Hereinafter: the AI Act). (accessed on 29 February 2024).

'high-risk AI system', 'provider', and 'user').[24] In the AILD proposal, the Union legislator also used the division into high-risk AI systems and non-high-risk AI systems, which was introduced in the AI Act. Each of the two types of AI systems was correlated to a different level of legal protection.

The key legal solutions proposed in the AILD proposal focus on: 1. relaxing the burden of proof at the pre-trial and trial stage, and the related presumption of breaching the duty of care; and 2. presuming a causal link between the defendant's fault and the output produced by the AI system, or the failure to produce an output. However, facilitation in obtaining evidence was unfortunately provided only for high-risk AI-systems. Rights in this regard have been afforded both to claimants[25] and potential claimants.[26] At the pre-trial stage, a potential claimant may request the manufacturer or user of a high-risk AI system to disclose relevant evidence about the system suspected of having caused damage. If the request is not complied with and the potential claimant substantiates their claim, then the potential claimant may request the court to order the disclosure of relevant evidence by the party that has failed to comply with the request for information.[27] An analogous right was afforded to a claimant at the stage of judicial procedures, but to exercise this right, the claimant must already have undertaken all proportionate attempts at gathering the relevant evidence from the defendant.[28] If the defendant fails to comply with the court's order to disclose or preserve evidence at the defendant's disposal, it will result in the court applying a rebuttable presumption. In other words, the court will presume that the defendant has not complied with the obligation to exercise due diligence, in particular, with regard to those circumstances that were supposed to be demonstrated through the requested pieces of evidence, which the defendant failed to disclose.[29]

At the same time, the AILD proposal introduces a rebuttable presumption of causal link "between the fault of the defendant and the output produced by the AI system, or the failure of the AI system to produce an output, where all of the following conditions are met:

---

24 Article 2(1–4) of the AILD proposal.
25 Art. 2(6) of the AILD proposal.
26 Art. 2(7) of the AILD proposal.
27 Art. (1) of the AILD proposal.
28 Art. 3(2) of the AILD proposal.
29 Art. 3(5) of the AILD proposal.

(a) the claimant has demonstrated, or the court has presumed pursuant to Article 3(5), the fault of the defendant, or of a person for whose behaviour the defendant is responsible, consisting in non-compliance with a duty of care laid down in EU or national law directly intended to protect against the damage that occurred;
(b) it can be considered reasonably likely, based on the circumstances of the case, that the fault has influenced the output produced by the AI system or the failure of the AI system to produce an output;
(c) the claimant has demonstrated that the output produced by the AI system or the failure of the AI system to produce an output gave rise to the damage."[30]

As clearly follows from the above-cited Article 4(1) of the AILD proposal, all the three prerequisites must be jointly met. The EU legislator has correlated the application of the presumption of a causal link with the observance of safety requirements laid down in the AI Act. In case of a claim for damages asserted against a user of a high-risk AI system, which is subject to appropriate requirements laid down in the AI Act, the prerequisite of proving the fault of the defendant or a person for whom the defendant is responsible will be met if the claimant demonstrates that the user: "a) did not comply with its obligations to use or monitor the AI system in accordance with the accompanying instructions of use or, where appropriate, suspend or interrupt its use pursuant to [Article 29 of the AI Act]; or (b) exposed the AI system to input data under its control which is not relevant in view of the system's intended purpose pursuant to [Article 29(3) of the Act]'.[31] This means that compliance by users of high-risk AI systems with the requirements provided for such systems, as laid down in the AI Act, will protect the users against the presumption under Article 4(1) of the AILD proposal.

In the case of a claim for damages relating to a high-risk AI system, however, a national court will not apply the presumption of a causal link if the defendant demonstrates that the claimant is in a position to obtain relatively easy access to evidence and expert knowledge that are sufficient to prove a causal link between the fault of the defendant or a person for which the defendant is responsible and the output produced by the AI system or

30 Art. 4(1) of the AILD proposal.
31 Art. 4(3) of the AILD proposal.

failure to produce an output by the system.[32] Although the presumption of a causal link is dedicated both to high-risk AI systems and to non-high-risk AI systems, with regard to the latter, the EU legislator has planned a serious restriction. Namely, when it comes to a claim for damages asserted in respect to a non-high-risk AI system, the presumption under Article 4(1) of the AILD proposal will only apply if the court reaches a conclusion that that it is excessively difficult for the claimant to prove the causal link.[33] The presumption of a causal link will not apply in the case of a claim for damages against a defendant who used the AI system in the course of a personal, non-professional activity. An exception was provided for a situation where: 'the defendant materially interfered with the conditions of the operation of the AI system or if the defendant was required and able to determine the conditions of operation of the AI system and failed to do so'.[34]

4. Are the EU's legislative proposals sufficient to eliminate the vulnerability of a person injured by an AI system?

The above overview of the legal solutions included in the AILD proposal demonstrates that the proposed legislative reforms are not sufficient to meaningfully increase the standard of protecting anyone injured by AI systems and to remove the existing vulnerabilities. This conclusion follows primarily from the fact that facilitation in obtaining evidence was only offered to those injured by high-risk AI systems. Moreover, it does not seem that, in practice, the proposed facilities can materially improve the situation of those injured. This is the case because easier access to evidence is not tantamount to the actual ability of injured parties to take advantage of such pieces of evidence. Specialist information about a particular AI system, provided at the request of a claimant or potential claimant, needs to be processed and understood and, within the framework of court proceedings, used in order to prove the defendant's fault. An injured person will not be in a position to do that

32 Art. 4(4) of the AILD proposal.
33 Art. 4(5) of the AILD proposal.
34 Art. 4(6) of the AILD proposal.

independently, and – as has been the case so far – already at the pre-trial stage, the injured person will need to use the assistance of experts.

Second, and most importantly, the EU legislator did not decide to introduce a presumption of the defendant's fault directly. Under the statutory regime proposed in the AILD proposal, a claimant will still have to prove the fault of the defendant (or of a person for whose acts the defendant is responsible). This refers in full to people injured by AI systems that do not qualify as high-risk systems, but also concerns people injured by high-risk AI systems. This is the case since, in respect of the latter, one can expect that professional users of such systems will, most often, provide data at the request of a claimant or a potential claimant to guard themselves against a presumption of fault. As a result, it can be assumed that, in practice, the presumption of breaching the duty of care will not be frequently used by the courts. At the same time, the circumstance as to whether the provided information really amounts to relevant evidence – in my opinion – will be very difficult to verify in practice.

Thirdly, the presumption of a causal link between the defendant's fault and the output produced by the AI system, or failure to produce an output by the AI system, was correlated to multiple and not entirely clear requirements that must be jointly fulfilled.[35] In the context of AI systems that do not qualify as high-risk systems, the possibility to apply the presumption was additionally made dependant on the level of complication of the case and was left to the discretion of the adjudicating court. If the analysed directive was to be adopted, those injured by such systems would be uncertain about their legal situation.

5. Reflections *de lege ferenda*

The EU legislator is of the opinion that it is still too early to introduce risk as grounds for liability for damages caused by AI systems applied by professional

---

[35] For more opinions on the AILD proposal, see Piotr Machnikowski (Ed.), *Prawo deliktowe wobec nowych technologii*, (Warsaw: Wolters Kluwer, 2023), 565–571; Miriam Buiten, Alexandre de Streel and Martin Peitz, "The Law and Economics of AI Liability", *Computer Law & Security Review* 48, (2023): 5, 17–19.

users.[36] However, with a view to guaranteeing real legal protection to injured persons already at the current stage, it would be justified to relieve them from the burden of proof and to shift that burden to the defendants. Such a solution, consisting in the reversal of the burden of proving fault and the causal link between the fault and the damage caused, was proposed, for example, in the NTF Report.[37] In this context, if a professional operator of an AI system would like to be exempt from liability for the damage caused, the operator would have to prove before the court that they complied with their duty of care. If the professional operator failed to maintain due care, the operator would have to demonstrate that there was no causal link between the operator's fault and the damage, which means that the damage would have occurred one way or another, even if the defendant had not breached their duty of care. In my opinion, reversing the burden of proof should relate to all AI systems, not only those qualifying as high-risk AI systems.

In the long run, however, it seems that the optimal solution would be to change the liability model to depart from the basis of fault and instead adopt the basis of risk. However, this would mean that a prerequisite of liability should be the active involvement of an AI system in the event causing damage, rather than a causal link between the damage and the operation of the AI system, which must be proven by the claimant.

If the EU decides not to introduce a legal regime reaching beyond what was proposed in the AILD, then solutions to the current problems should be sought in national legislations. For example, one such solution could be to qualify particular objects or activities powered by AI as particularly hazardous. This would imply an extension of the legal regimes currently applicable in particular Member States of the European also to objects or activities based

---

36 In the Explanatory Memorandum to the AILD proposal, it was emphasised that: "[t]he proposal takes into account [...] the fact that the kind of products and services equipped with AI systems that could affect the public at large and put at risk important legal rights, such as the right to life, health and property, and therefore could be subject to a strict liability regime, are not yet widely available on the market." See the Explanatory Memorandum to the AILD proposal, p. 14.

37 "Liability for Artificial Intelligence and other emerging digital technologies", Report from the Expert Group on Liability and New Technologies – New Technologies Formation. Luxembourg: Publications Office of the European Union, 2019, p. 48. <https://op.europa.eu/en/publication-detail/-/publication/1c5e30be-1197-11ea-8c1f-01aa75ed71a1/language-en> (accessed on 29 February 2024).

on AI. As a result of this change, damage caused with the involvement of AI-embedded systems or devices would be covered by strict liability.[38] In fact, the social consequences of algorithmic activities are already so extensive that such activities might be qualified as hazardous. In light of the above, attention should be paid to the opinion of researchers who consider the introduction of strict liability with regard to AI-embedded devices and for that liability model to also cover professional front-end operators of AI systems.[39]

6. Conclusion

The standard of protection afforded to anyone injured by an AI system used by a professional operator should certainly be increased in the EU. Currently – at least in the context of applicable legislation – the standard is at a comparable level in Member States of the EU and in China.[40] This is not very optimistic since, thus far, the EU has been in the vanguard when it came to the development of legal solutions with the human being at the centre, protecting human rights and European values. To achieve that purpose, in the subject area analysed in this chapter, it is necessary to introduce more far-reaching legal solutions than the ones proposed in the AILD proposal.

In order to improve the, currently very weak, legal position of anyone injured by an AI system applied by a professional operator, the legal solutions

---

38 A tendency to expand strict liability to also cover new technologies, including AI, is apparent. For example, in France, strict liability applies not only to road traffic accidents but also "[t]he French Conseil d'État has acknowledged strict liability for operators of medical devices used in public hospitals, even though they do not fall under the framework of the 1985 directive." Additionally, "[t]he French civil courts have acknowledged a general principle of strict liability for 'guardians' (gardiens) of things, regardless of whether they are defective and have caused harm to another individual." See Knetsch, "Are Existing Tort Theories Ready for AI?", 105–106. See also Jonas Knetsch, "The Role of Liability without Fault", in *French Civil Liability in Comparative Perspective*, (Eds.) Jean-Sébastien Borghetti and Simon Whittaker, (London: Hart, 2019), 123–142.

39 See: Wendehorst, "Strict Liability for AI and other Emerging Technologies", 174.

40 For more, see: Iwona Gredka-Ligarska, "Employer as an AI system operator and non-contractual civil liability for damage caused by AI systems: the EU and Chinese perspectives" in *Law – Commerce – Economy XII. Collection of Scientific Works*, (Eds.) Jozef Suchoža, Ján Husár and Regina Hučková (Košice: Vydavateľstvo ŠafárikPress, 2023), 115–129.

that seem much more efficient are the ones proposed in the European Parliament Resolution of 20 October 2020 with recommendations to the Commission on a civil liability regime for artificial intelligence.[41] This draft proposal was not, finally, met with approval as it was considered too severe from the point of view of users of AI systems. It seems, however, that the legislative proposals included in the draft set a good course. For the time being, however, there is a serious disturbance in the balance between the legal situation of professional operators of AI systems and the legal situation of people injured by such systems. By contrast, a natural person suffering damage – as a consumer – is by definition the weaker party when confronted with an operator of an AI system, who is a professional and profits from the use of the system.

Bibliography

Beckers Anna and Gunther Teubner, *Three Liability Regimes for Artificial Intelligence: Algorithmic Actants, Hybrids, Crowds*, 1st ed. (Oxford-London-New York-New Delhi-Sydney: Hart Publishing, 2021).

Bosek Leszek, "Perspectives on Development of Civil Liability for Intelligent Robots", *Forum Prawnicze* 52, No. 2 (2019): 15.

Brożek Bartosz *et al.*, "The Black Box Problem Revisited: Real and Imaginary Challenges for Automated Legal Decision Making", *Artificial Intelligence and Law*, (2023), online version, <https://doi.org/10.1007/s10506-023-09356-9>.

Buiten Miriam, Alexandre de Streel and Martin Peitz, "The Law and Economics of AI Liability", *Computer Law & Security Review* 48 (2023): 5, 17–19.

Busnelli Francesco D. *et al.*, "Strict Liability", in *Principles of European Tort Law: Text and Commentary*, European Group on Tort Law (Vienna, New York: Springer, 2005).

Büyüksagis Erdem and Willem H. Van Boom, "Strict Liability in Contemporary European Codification: Torn between Objects, Activities, and Their Risks", *Georgetown Journal of International Law* 44, No. 2 (2013): 614.

---

[41] (2020/2014(INL)), <https://www.europarl.europa.eu/doceo/document/TA-9-2020-0276_EN.html> (accessed on 29 February 2024).

Castelvecchi Davide, “Can We Open the Black Box of AI?”, *Nature* 538(7623), 2026, 20–23.

Council Directive 85/374/EEC of 25 July 1985 on the approximation of the laws, regulations and administrative provisions of the Member States concerning liability for defective products, OJ L210/85, <https://eur-lex.europa.eu/legal-content/EN/TXT/?uri=celex%3A31985L0374>.

European Commission's ‘Proposal for a Directive of the European Parliament and of the Council on Adapting Non-contractual Civil Liability Rules to Artificial Intelligence (AI Liability Directive)’, COM (2022) 496 final, <https://eur-lex.europa.eu/legal-content/EN/TXT/?uri=CELEX%3A52022PC0496>.

European Commission's ‘Proposal for a Directive of the European Parliament and of the Council on Liability for Defective Products’, COM (2022) 495 final, <https://eur-lex.europa.eu/legal-content/EN/TXT/?uri=CELEX%3A52022PC0495>.

European Commission's ‘Proposal for a Regulation of the European Parliament and of the Council Laying Down Harmonized Rules on Artificial Intelligence (Artificial Intelligence Act) and Amending Certain Union Legislative Acts’, COM (2021) 206 final, <https://eur-lex.europa.eu/legal-content/EN/TXT/?uri=celex%3A52021PC0206>.

European Parliament Resolution of 20 October 2020 with recommendations to the Commission on a civil liability regime for artificial intelligence (2020/2014(INL)), <https://www.europarl.europa.eu/doceo/document/TA-9-2020-0276_EN.html|>.

Geistfeld Mark A., Ernst Karner, Bernhard A. Koch and Christiane Wendehorst eds., Civil Liability for Artificial Intelligence and Software: Tort and Insurance Law, European Centre of Tort and Insurance Law, Vol. 37 (Berlin, Boston: Walter de Gruyter, 2023).

Gredka-Ligarska Iwona, “Employer as an AI system operator and non-contractual civil liability for damage caused by AI systems: the EU and Chinese perspectives” in *Law – Commerce – Economy XII. Collection of Scientific Works*, (Eds.) Jozef Suchoža, Ján Husár and Regina Hučková (Košice: Vydavateľstvo ŠafárikPress, 2023).

Knetsch Jonas, “Are Existing Tort Theories Ready for AI? A Continental European Perspective”, in *The Cambridge Handbook of Artificial Intelligence: Global Perspectives on Law and Ethics* (Ed.) Larry A. DiMatteo, Cristina

Poncibò and Michel Cannarsa (Cambridge: Cambridge University Press, 2022).

Knetsch Jonas, "The Role of Liability without Fault", in *French Civil Liability in Comparative Perspective*, (Eds.) Jean-Sébastien Borghetti and Simon Whittaker (London: Hart, 2019).

Machnikowski Piotr (Ed.), *European Product Liability: An Analysis of the State of the Art in the Era of New Technologies* (Cambridge, Antwerp, Portland: Intersentia, 2016).

Machnikowski Piotr (Ed.), *Prawo deliktowe wobec nowych technologii* (Warsaw: Wolters Kluwer, 2023).

Padovan Paulo H., Clarice M. Martins and Chris Reed, "Black is the New Orange: How to Determine AI Liability", *Artificial Intelligence and Law* 31, No. 1 (2023): 133–167.

Report from the Expert Group on Liability and New Technologies – New Technologies Formation, 'Liability for Artificial Intelligence and other emerging digital technologies', Luxembourg: Publications Office of the European Union, 2019, p. 48. <https://op.europa.eu/en/publication-detail/-/publication/1c5e30be-1197-11ea-8c1f-01aa75ed71a1/language-en>.

Swanson Greg, "Non-Autonomous Artificial Intelligence Programs and Products Liability: How New AI Products Challenge Existing Liability Models and Pose New Financial Burdens", *Seattle University Law Review* 42, No. 3 (2019): 1201–1222.

Tjong Tjin Tai Eric, "Liability for AI Decision-Making" in *The Cambridge Handbook of Artificial Intelligence: Global Perspectives on Law and Ethics*, ed. Larry A. DiMatteo, Cristina Poncibò and Michel Cannarsa (Cambridge: Cambridge University Press, 2022).

Wendehorst Christiane, "Strict Liability for AI and other Emerging Technologies", *Journal of European Tort Law* 11, No. 2 (2020): 174–175.

Zednik Carlos, "Solving the Black Box Problem: a Normative Framework for Explainable Artificial Intelligence", *Philosophy & Technology* 34, No. 2 (2021): 265–288.

A New Poverty Law? Addressing the Inadequacies of International and European Law and Filling the Gaps Identified at a National Level

*Maria d'Oliveira Martins**

Abstract: People experiencing poverty are a vulnerable group in our societies, subject to the prejudices of others. Poverty is still associated with several prejudices that create a social fear of people experiencing poverty ('aporophobia', as Adela Cortina calls it) and justify an attitude of rejection towards them. This feeling of rejection is clearly expressed in the defensive and even repressive laws throughout history.

This text will offer a panoramic view of the main elements of contemporary poverty law, pointing out the shortcomings of international law, EU interventions, and national laws that leave the poorest vulnerable and exposed despite the many legal instruments that address their problems.

The main idea is to affirm that no entity can replace the States (despite all the shortcomings of their intervention) in the fight against poverty. It proposes that the States take a step forward by making a more significant commitment to eradicating poverty and unconditional respect for the rights of the poorest.

This text proposes demanding respect for the freedom of expression of the poorest, a more significant commitment to a minimum income as a directly enforceable right, and the adoption of a minimum content of social rights based on a priority for those most in need.

Keywords: poverty law, discrimination, aporophobia, minimum income, freedom of expression, receptive need

1. The feeling of rejection that places the poor in a situation of vulnerability

Society rejects the poorest, based on the most basic feelings of disgust and fear. This sense of rejection can be seen in the formulation of myths – which are nothing more than prejudices without any connection to reality – about poverty. It is believed, for example, that the poor take advantage of the welfare

* Associate Professor at the Law Faculty of the Catholic University of Portugal, Lisbon; Research Centre for the Future of Law. ORCID: 0000-0003-2352-2736.

system, using all sorts of schemes and tricks to unduly obtain benefits and use up the available funds. It is assumed that the poor do not pay taxes or contribute to the common good. It is believed that those who live on the minimum income are living well.[1]

This rejection deepens when the poorest are foreigners, as this feeling is mixed with racism and xenophobia. In more extreme cases, this feeling of rejection takes the form of crimes against the poorest: physical attacks, harassment and, in some cases, even attempted murder.[2]

The aversion to the poorest is so internalised that large cities unconsciously and uncritically accept hostile architecture. This architecture is characterised by the existence of urban elements that prevent the homeless from occupying public spaces.[3] It is also evident in the growing number of countries that criminalise begging or regulate it in such a way as to condition both the places where the poorest can be and the discourse they can have in public space.

The Spanish philosopher Adela Cortina has addressed and analysed this feeling of aversion towards the poorest. In an attempt to give a name to this aversion, she called it *aporophobia.*[4]

In law, this phobia was often translated into a commitment to punitive solutions, based on the assumption that poverty corresponds to a character flaw.

The first Poor Laws (the English version of which is the best known, dating from the 14th century) were based on the condemnation of idleness and the obligation to work. The laws showed tolerance only for the poor who were

---

1 From a French perspective: ATD Quart Monde - *En finir avec des idées fausses sur les pauvres et la pauvreté.* Paros: Éditions Quart Monde, 2020.

2 Take the shocking case in 2022 of a homeless man who was burned by a passer-by in Portugal (see the news item of 22 September 2022 - <https://rr.sapo.pt/noticia/pais/2022/09/22/sem-abrigo-queimado-no-porto-instituicoes-chocadas-com-violencia-consideram-caso-alarmante/300732/>.

3 For some examples of hostile architecture: <https://www.vivadecora.com.br/pro/arquitetura-hostil/>.

4 Adela Cortina - *Aporophobia: Why We Reject the Poor Instead of Helping Them*. Princeton and Oxford: Princeton University Press, 2022, (digital version without page number), chapter i.

unable to work.[5] The aim of these first Poor Laws was to eliminate beggars by forcing people to work, even if it meant accepting lower wages than they might have expected. Anyone who refused to do so would be punished. An example of this is the condemnation of idlers in the English *Vagabonds and Beggars Act of* 1494, which stated that that 'vagabonds, idle and suspected persons shall be set in the stocks for three days and three nights and have none other sustenance but bread and water and then shall be put out of town'

All the countries of Europe adopted this punitive approach to poverty, which was reflected in many criminal laws that were in force in the 20th century.

An example of this can be found in the French Penal Code of 1810 (repealed only in 1994), which prohibited 'vagrancy' and repressed begging in its Articles 269 et seq. In Switzerland, in the second half of the 19th century, all the cantons similarly made begging a punishable offence, 'either in their penal codes or in their police laws and regulations'.[6] The same was true of Germany, which criminalised begging in its *Reichsstrafgesetzbuch* (Imperial Penal Code) of 1871. The same policy was also followed in Austria, where the 'vagrancy' law was enacted in 1885.[7] The same model was also adopted by all the states of the United States of America,[8] many of which were still enforced until the 1970s, mirroring the English *Poor Laws* as legal remnants of the colonial period. In Portugal, under the Penal Code of 1852, anyone who did who not have a fixed place of residence or profession could be declared 'vagrant', according to Articles 256 and 260. The declaration of being a vagrant was accompanied by a prison sentence of up to six months, with

---

5 Also with the same logic, in 1388, the *Statute of Cambridge*, which was considered in England to be the first Poor Law, prohibited begging, making communities responsible only for the poor who were unable to work.

6 Daniel Moeckli. "Bettelverbote: einige rechtsvergleichende Überlegungen zur Grundrechtskonformität", 2010 (available at Zurich Open Repository and Archive, University of Zurich:, p. 4.

7 Daniel Moeckli, p. 5.

8 Daniel Moeckli, pp. 4 and 5. A clear influence of English law is recognised in the US Supreme Court ruling: Papachristou v. City of Jacksonville, 405 U.S. 156 (1972) <https://supreme.justia.com/cases/federal/us/405/156/>: "Jacksonville's ordinance and Florida's statute were 'derived' from early English law."

their subsequent delivery to the government to provide them with labour for the appropriate period.[9,10]

While times have changed, the aversion to the poor persists, as reflected in the current anti-poverty law, as it will be shown.

At a European level, this text will analyse the permanence of a poverty law that continues to allow the development of a culture that violates equality and that, even today, leaves the poorest unprotected and vulnerable to the prejudices of their fellow citizens. By recognising and identifying the shortcoming in the current law, the intention is to propose ways forward.

2. The main elements of the current anti-poverty law

2.1. Human rights and the European social model

The current poverty law can be characterised on two different levels. The first is the international level (with particular reference to EU law, as this is written in a European context); the second is the national level.

At the international level, the fight against poverty is primarily about recognising human rights. The first instrument to mention poverty was the United Nations Charter (1945). On the one hand, Article 55 recognises the right to development. On the other hand, Article 56 affirms the principle of international cooperation for the realisation of human rights.[11] Three years later, the United Nations Universal Declaration of Human Rights also addressed this issue (see Articles 3, 22, 23, and 25).

However, it was not until 1966, with the International Covenant on Economic, Social and Cultural Rights, that the Universal Declaration was followed by the development of a body of human rights specifically aimed at combating poverty. Among the most important rights in this area is the recognition of the right to housing, food, clothing and an adequate standard of living (Article 11).

---

9 See Articles 256 and 261.

10 The Penal Code of 1886 maintained these solutions in Articles 256 and 262, which remained in force until 1982.

11 Ahmed Aoued. "The right to food: the significance of the United Nations Special Rapporteur" *in* Lucy Williams (Ed.) – *International Poverty Law*. London/New York: Zed Books, 2013, kindle edition.

Today, in the EU, concern about poverty goes beyond the affirmation of human rights. Not only because the social matrix stems from the founding texts of the European Economic Community (cf. Articles 123 et seq. of the Treaty of Rome, which already provided for the creation of the European Social Fund[12]) and from the European Social Charter (which as early as 1961 took on a social concern in the rights it recognised), but also because, since the European Council summit on 22 July 1975, 'we can observe the beginning of explicit community action to combat poverty'.[13]

In this context, the Commission has launched poverty programmes,[14] including the EU Food Distribution programme for the Most Deprived Persons of the Community (1987–2013), renamed the Fund for European Aid to the Most Deprived (FEAD) in 2014. The Commission also provides financial support to a number of anti-poverty organisations, including the European Anti-Poverty Network, the European Federation of National Organisations Working with the Homeless and Eurochild.

---

12 The references to caring for poverty have been expanded over time:

- the first explicit reference to the term *poverty* appeared in the treaties in 1992 with the signing of the Treaty on European Union (Maastricht Treaty) in Article 130-u (1) (signalling this commitment, the Protocol on Economic and Social Cohesion was annexed to the Treaty on European Union).
- the Treaty of Amsterdam, signed in 1997, introduced into the Treaty on European Union a commitment to the social rights recognised in the European Social Charter of 1961 and the Charter of the Social Rights of Workers (see Article 136), particularly with regard to promoting employment, improving living and working conditions, social protection and combating social exclusion. Article 137 makes the first reference to the aim of combating social exclusion (the reference to combating poverty is still only in relation to developing countries; see Article 177, formerly 130u).
- In the current version of the Treaty on the Functioning of the European Union (after the Lisbon Treaty), there is a commitment to fight social exclusion in Articles 9 and 153. In Article 208, the commitment to eradicate poverty remains within the scope of development co-operation.

13 Helmut P. Gaisbauer. "Absolute poverty and the EU Social Policy Agenda" *in* Helmut p. Gaisbauer, Gottfried Schweiger and Clemens Sedmak (Eds.) - *Absolute poverty in Europe: Interdisciplinary Perspectives on a Hidden Phenomenon*. Bristol: Policy Press, 2019, p. 289. This concern was part of the process of enlargement to the northern countries (Denmark, Ireland, and the United Kingdom) and gave rise to the first anti-poverty programme, as mentioned below (*ibid.*, p. 295).

14 <https://www.eapn.eu/key-events-3-eu-anti-poverty-programmes-1975-1993/>.

Since the Lisbon Extraordinary European Council (2000), the EU has established the Open Method of Coordination as a model for action.[15] According to this method, the Commission defines strategic lines and objectives for the fight against poverty and social exclusion to be pursued by the Member States.

From 2021, the European Social Fund has been strengthened and renamed 'European Social Fund Plus', bringing together four funding instruments: the European Social Fund, the FEAD, the Youth Employment Initiative, and the EU Programme for Employment and Social Innovation.

2.2. Social rights

At the national level, in terms of the fight against poverty, it is possible to highlight the commitment of European states to the right to social security, health, and education, as a means of preventing and alleviating poverty; the recognition of the duty to work; and the recognition of the right to a minimum income.

In most European countries, the introduction of the social security system does not mean that individuals do not have to contribute to their own support. In this sense, most social security systems are, on the one hand, essentially based on welfare systems designed to replace earned income in situations where workers are unable to perform their duties. On the other hand, it is also based on activation policies. In other words, policies designed to promote the integration of all those who use the labour market, whether through vocational training or the obligation to register with employment offices. In many cases, registration becomes essential for access to certain social benefits.

The strong link between social security and work can be understood from the idea of 'making the beneficiary responsible [...] in the active job search

[15] Maurizio Ferrera, Manos Matsaganis and Stefano Sacchi. "Open coordination against poverty: the new EU 'social inclusion process' " *in* Journal of European Social Policy 2002, London, Thousand Oaks and New Delhi: SAGE Publications, Vol 12 (3) (227–239), p. 230

process'[16] (in a process that can be reduced to three main ideas: training, self-responsibility of individuals, and (re)integration into the labour market[17]).

In some European Member States, the centrality of work is expressed in their constitutional text as a fundamental obligation to work (see Article 35 of the Spanish Constitution, Article 4 of the Italian Constitution, the preamble to the French Constitution of 1946 and Article XII of the Hungarian Constitution). Other European constitutions prefer to assume a right to work among social rights (see, for example, Article 11 of the Luxembourg Constitution, Article 22 of the Greek Constitution and Article 67 of the Polish Constitution).

In addition to social security, public spending based on health and education social rights plays a fundamental role in the fight against poverty. It plays a preventive role by contributing both to a healthy, active life and to access to training that ensures entry into the labour market. It also plays an intervention role by promoting the equality of access to these goods.

Still at a national level, it is worth highlighting the emergence – albeit only at the end of the 20th century – of the concept of minimum income. This recognises the 'obligation of a social state to control the risks resulting from the problem of poverty that cannot be attributed to the individuals themselves, and to restore a minimum *status for the* satisfaction of personal needs'.[18]

The minimum income is a last resort to resolve situations of severe poverty identified by the authorities that cannot be resolved by other instruments of social intervention. As the German Constitutional Court recognised in BVerfGE 125, 175: If a person does not have the material means to guarantee an existence that is in line with human dignity, because he or she is unable to obtain it either out of his or her gainful employment, or from own property or by benefits from third parties, the state is obliged within its mandate to

---

16 João Carlos Loureiro. *Adeus ao Estado Social? A Segurança Social entre o crocodilo da economia e a medusa da ideologia dos "direitos adquiridos"*. Coimbra: Wolters Kluwer/ Coimbra Editora, 2010, p. 96 (author's translation).

17 João Carlos Loureiro. *Adeus ao Estado Social?...*, p. 97 (author's translation).

18 Andreas Krell. "Controle judicial dos serviços públicos básicos na base dos direitos fundamentais sociais". In: Ingo Wolfgang Sarlet (org.) - *A Constituição Concretizada. Construindo pontes entre o público e o privado*. Porto Alegre: Livraria do Advogado, 2000, p. 42 (author's translation).

protect human dignity and to ensure, in the implementation of its social welfare state mandate, that the material prerequisites for this are at the disposal of the person in need of assistance.

The minimum income has been adopted in all European Member States, although, as Frazer and Marlier show,[19] its implementation is not uniform.

The novelty of the minimum income approach to poverty law is that it introduces a complement to the eminently preventive approach to poverty and opens up a perspective that moves away from the classical one. The focus is no longer exclusively on whether people are willing to work or not, but rather on whether their income is sufficient or not, formulating an obligation for the state to examine the conditions of each individual in order to guarantee everyone the protection of minimum subsistence conditions.

3. The current law of fighting poverty does not solve the problem of poverty

3.1. International law: when law is little more than the expression of a certain morality

It is true that, 'in qualitative terms, the current human rights regime provides the rights necessary to resolve the structural obstacles faced by people living in poverty'.[20] Indeed, the very recognition of human rights at an international level can only be a significant step forward in terms of the right to fight poverty.

However, merely enshrining human rights cannot address the specific problems of poverty. To a large extent, the international norms and human rights recognised by the United Nations are only an expression of morality

---

19 Hugh Frazer and Eric Marlier – "Minimum Income Schemes in Europe: A study of national policies 2015". Brussels: European Commission, 2016 <https://www.researchgate.net/publication/299652131_Minimum_income_schemes_in_Europe_A_study_of_national_policies>, p. 7.

20 Sigrun I. Skogly: "Is there right not to be poor?" *in* Human Rights Law Review, 2(1), 2002, pp. 59–80, p. 64.

on this issue, as there are no mechanisms to defend the rights of those who most need to invoke them.[21]

Since the recognition of social rights in the International Covenant of 1966, there has been a noticeable lack of implementation mechanisms at an international level. It was only in 2013 that the Optional Protocol to the Covenant on Economic, Social and Cultural Rights entered into force in the international order, providing for a Committee on Economic, Social and Cultural Rights that seeks to parallel the provisions of the International Covenant on Civil and Political Rights.[22] Despite the progress made in 2013, the realisation of human rights related to poverty remains challenging, largely due to the vagueness of the norms contained in the Covenant on Social and Cultural Rights. To address these problems, 'several commentators share the view that a reformulation of economic, social and cultural rights in more specific terms would improve their realisation and their justiciability'.[23]

The inadequacy of human rights – due to the lack of any international implementation mechanism – places the responsibility for implementing the results of international instruments at the national level. The Committee on Economic, Social and Cultural Rights has also expressed this concern in its successive reports: if the first steps towards the promotion and protection

21 "Human rights could end up being no more than empty rhetoric that raises the hopes of the poor without giving them the practical tools to better their lives." - Asuncion Lera St Clair – "How Can Human Rights Contribute To Poverty Reduction? A Philosophical Assessment Of The Human Development Report 2000" *In* Lucy Williams (Ed.) – International Poverty Law – An Emerging Discourse. London /New York: Zed Books, 2013, kindle edition.

22 A proposal to this effect was even formulated in the 1990s, as a guarantee of the effectiveness of these rights, but it did not materialise at the time. – Philip Alston – "No right to complain about being boor: the need for an optional protocol to the economic rights covenant" in Eide, Asborn e Helgesen, Jan (Eds.) – "The future of human rights protection in a changing world. Fifty years since the four freedoms address. Essays in honour of Torkel Opsahl. Oslo: Norwegian University Press, 1991, p. 86.

23 Eva Brems. *Human Rights: Universality and Diversity*. The Hague, Boston, London: Martinus Nijhoff Publishers, 2001, p. 468.

of human rights are not taken at a national level, it is difficult to implement the morality expressed at the human rights level.[24]

3.2. EU dependent on the Member States' intervention in social policy

The difficulties experienced at the level of international law are also felt at the level of the EU, albeit on a different scale, because the existing level of integration allows, as we have seen, the launching of targeted social programmes with a significant impact on people's lives.

Despite the important impetus that the EU institutions have given to the fight against poverty and social exclusion, we must also point out their weaknesses.

These weaknesses are largely the result of the Open Method of Coordination. Since this method does not go much further than defining strategic lines and objectives for combating poverty and social exclusion, its implementation depends on the goodwill of the states.

The EU does not have the power to act on the issues most relevant to solving the problem of poverty. Nor does it have sufficient budgetary resources. 'In quantitative terms, the EU's budget is hardly more than 1% of the GDP of

---

[24] The Committee on Economic, Social and Cultural Rights fixes the responsibility of the ombudsman with regard to the right to food: "any person or group who is a victim of a violation of the right to adequate food should have access to effective judicial or other appropriate remedies at both national and international levels. All victims of such violations are entitled to adequate reparation, which may take the form of restitution, compensation, satisfaction or guarantees of non-repetition. National ombudsmen and human rights commissions should address violations of the right to food" - Committee On Economic, Social And Cultural Rights - General Comment No. 12 (Twentieth Session, 1999) The Right to Adequate Food (Art. 11) <https://tbinternet.ohchr.org/_layouts/15/treatybodyexternal/download.aspx?symbolno=e%2fc.12%2f1999%2f5&lang=en>.

The same says in relation to the right to water: "all victims of violations of the right to water should be entitled to adequate reparation, including restitution, compensation, satisfaction or guarantees of non-repetition. National ombudsmen, human rights commissions, and similar institutions should be permitted to address violations of the right" - Committee On Economic, Social And Cultural Rights - General Comment No. 15 (2002) - The Right To Water (Arts 11 And 12 Of The International Covenant On Economic, Social And Cultural Rights) <https://tbinternet.ohchr.org/_layouts/15/treatybodyexternal/download.aspx?symbolno=e%2fc.12%2f2002%2f11&lang=en>.

all its member countries. This also creates a limitation in terms of spending decisions, since it cannot include an anti-cyclical component'.[25] In any case, it always depends on the intervention of the Member States.

This excessive dependence on the Member States in the implementation of the European social model also creates difficulties concerning the sharing of social resources. There are well-known dysfunctions in the coordination of social security mechanisms at a European level (provided for in Regulation (EC) no. 883/2004)[26] as well as fears of 'social tourism' and related issues.[27] The problem of refugees and the question of the distribution of social resources that they raise is not insignificant either, if states are to meet their obligations to ensure a minimum of dignity for people waiting for their situation to be resolved.

3.3. National law and its flaws

The model of social rights protection that prevails in Europe, and which was built to respond to the problems of poverty, also faces certain problems.

The chosen model falls short of the objective of eradicating poverty, because the rights – social security, health and education social rights – on which it is based are subject to 'weakened justiciability'.[28] The constitutional response is, therefore, ultimately characterised by the indeterminacy inherent in these rights (since they are by nature open to legislative clarification)

By their very nature, social rights (since achieving them depends on the intervention of the legislator) prevent the courts from pre-empting or

---

25 Maria d'Oliveira Martins. *Lições de Finanças Públicas e Direito Financeiro*. Coimbra: Almedina, 2019, p. 234 (author's translation).

26 Sofia Pais draws attention to Article 7 of Directive 2004/38, which makes the right to reside in the European Union conditional on having sufficient resources and health insurance – Sofia Pais – "Todos os cidadãos da União Europeia têm direito de circular e residir livremente no território dos Estados-Membros, mas uns têm mais direitos do que outros…" *in* Scientia Juridica, 253, 2010 (467–496).

27 Rui Lanceiro. "Dano and Alimanovic: the recent evolution of CJEU caselaw on EU citizenship and cross-border access to social benefits" *in* Unio - Eu Law Journal, Vol. 3, No. 1, January 2017, pp. 63–77.

28 Jorge Reis Novais. *Direitos Sociais - Teoria Jurídica dos Direitos Sociais enquanto Direitos Fundamentais*. Lisboa: AAFDL Editora, 2016, p. 140 (author´s translation).

correcting the legislator's hand.[29] Furthermore, achieving social rights is also dependent on the existence of available resources (the reservation of the financially possible or in its original formulation *Vorbehalt des Möglichen*). In this context, the fight against poverty is reduced to a budgetary decision, which is also exempt from judicial control.

The reservation of the financially possible is a concept born from the jurisprudence of the German Federal Constitutional Court (*Bundesverfassungsgericht*).[30] As defined by this Court, the reservation of the financially possible requires recognition of the limitation of resources in the realisation of rights to benefits to be demanded from the state. Only benefits that could reasonably be demanded from the state could be asserted against it. This reservation therefore corresponds to the idea that at any given moment the state – taking into account its possibilities – has a maximum limit for social intervention, which it cannot exceed when it comes to realising social rights.[31]

Faced with the reservation of the financially possible, understood in this way, the judiciary is therefore limited in its action by the principle of the separation of powers: it is not up to the courts to set priorities and determine the optimal allocation of resources. Courts cannot define determine when, how and to what extent social rights should be implemented.

The political-legislative freedom granted by the Constitution in the implementation of indeterminate rules, in light of this reservation, is such that, in most cases, there is no need for concrete proof of the impossibility of action on the part of the budgetary decision-maker. In other words, in principle, the allegation of a legal scarcity is enough to justify a decision not to intervene. The judiciary is paralysed by this allegation, since in the absence of budgetary decision-making powers, it is not up to the courts to allocate the available resources or to define the priorities to which they should be allocated.[32]

---

29 As Reis Novais explains, the courts are only reserved for monitoring "compliance with the other constitutional principles, namely the principle of the prohibition of excess, in the case of restrictive state action, and the principle of the prohibition of deficit in the case of any constitutional omission" – Jorge Reis Novais, p. 123 (author's translation).

30 BVerfGE 33, 303, 18 July 1972 (Numerus Clausus I) <https://www.servat.unibe.ch/dfr/bv033303.html#Opinion>.

31 Maria d'Oliveira Martins. *A despesa pública justa – Uma análise jurídico-constitucional do tema da Justiça na despesa pública*. Coimbra: Almedina, 2016, pp. 316–317.

32 Maria d'Oliveira Martins. *A despesa pública justa*..., pp. 318–319.

In addition to this general problem, there are specific problems that social security – the linchpin in the fight against poverty – is currently facing: funding problems and problems of access to already established benefits.

Problems with access to social benefits have been analysed in some states, such as France, the UK,[33] and Germany.[34] In these states, attention has been drawn to the 'poverty that escapes social protection systems', given the high percentage of non-recourse to social benefits, which can exceed 50%, even in the case of minimum benefits.[35] This invisibility of some poor is due to factors such as the complexity of accessing social security, the digitalisation of social security, which affects the possibility of accessing information (often only available online), or even the invasive nature of many forms of assistance and the fear of stigmatisation.

In addition, it is very important to mention that the problems of financing social security are linked to various factors (demographic factors, migration, and labour problems). Taken together, these problems are responsible for the reduction in the resources available for social purposes and, more specifically, for the fight against poverty.

---

33 "This is the case in the United Kingdom, the only country where official data are produced by the statistical departments of the two main ministries responsible for social protection. They form part of the social policy monitoring indicators published each year to report on the effectiveness of public policies"." – Céline Marc, Mickaël Portela, Cyrine Hannafi, Rémi Le Gall, Antoine Rode and Stéphanie Laguérodie - "Quantifier le non-recours aux minima sociaux en Europe. Un phénomène d'ampleur qui peine à susciter le débat" *in* Les dossiers de la Drees, n° 94, mars 2022, p. 9 <https://drees.solidarites-sante.gouv.fr/sites/default/files/2022-03/DD94.pdf>, p. 9 (author's translation).

34 "(...) the main studies on the non-use of welfare benefits in Germany agree that this is a 'serious social problem' (Harnisch, 2019, 29), as the phenomenon is statistically frequent, with some of the highest rates among the countries we observe." – Antoine Rode - La quantification du non-recours en Europe. Historique et principales «scènes de production» des mesures réalisées dans 5 pays européens. 12 | 2022|Working Paper # 34 - Odenore (Observatoire des non-recours aux droits et services) <https://odenore.msh-alpes.fr/sites/odenore/files/Mediatheque/quantification_du_non-recours_rode_wp_34_odenore.pdf>, p. 18 (author's translation).

35 Céline Marc, Mickaël Portela, Cyrine Hannafi, Rémi Le Gall, Antoine Rode and Stéphanie Laguérodie. "Quantifier le non-recours aux minima sociaux en Europe. Un phénomène d'ampleur qui peine à susciter le débat" *in* Les dossiers de la Drees, no. 94, mars 2022, p. 9 (available at <https://drees.solidarites-sante.gouv.fr/sites/default/files/2022-03/DD94.pdf>).

The decline in the numbers of the working population means that financing social security is becoming increasingly dependent on general government revenue, which leads to a tendency to reduce expenditure in order to guarantee stability (for example, by capping pensions). The exponential increase in the freedom of movement, with the inevitable link to various legal systems, is forcing social security to find answers in terms of coordination with systems in a number of countries to meet the increase in demand for social support.[36]

The problem of insufficient labour income is not insignificant either. Increasingly, labour income is not sufficient to meet the needs of daily life (house payments and basic expenses – electricity, water, heating, and food). In this context, the social security system is forced to set minimum levels of social benefits (often requiring an increase in public spending on social transfers)[37] and to set up complementary systems. With regard to this last point in particular (labour problems creating problems for social security), it should be noted that this could be the trigger for the collapse of a model that implies the obligation to work,[38] undermining what seemed to be the most solid pillar of the Poverty Law of all times. The erosion of this pillar is exacerbated by the realisation that the problem of poverty is much more complex than previously thought and that its causes are not necessarily related to idleness (think of child poverty or disability poverty to get a good idea that idleness does not really explain everything).

The idea of an unconditional basic income was developed in the 1980s, based on the erosion of the concept of work, largely due to the problems of

---

36 "(In)sustentabilidade da segurança/ seguridade social: entre as 'brumas da memória' e as 'brumas do futuro' em tempos de neoglobalização e neognosticismo(s): tópicos de um roteiro/ Social Security (Un)Sustainability: Between the Mist of Memory and the Mist of the Future in Time(s) of Neoglobalization and Neognosticism. Topics for a Roadmap"

37 "There are several mechanisms in comparative law that aim to minimise this issue, from the minimum value of pensions (for example, the Portuguese case, where the social supplement is not subject to a means test) to the existence of a basic pension (with a uniform or variable amount), to systems that apply a means test." - Loureiro João Carlos – "A Segurança Social, o Seguro Social: Novos Perímetros e Universalidade", *in* Boletim da Faculdade de Direito da Universidade de Coimbra, no. 94, tomo 1, 2018 (693–706), p. 680 (author's translation).

38 Frank Vandenbroucke and Koen Vleminckx – "Disappointing poverty trends: is the social investment state to blame?" in Journal of European Social Policy, Vol. 21(5), 2011, (450–471), p. 456.

social security mentioned above. This income corresponds to a sum of money to be given to everyone, regardless of other sources of income and without verification of current or past work.[39] Van Parijs, one of the main advocates of this measure, even argues that it would be a profound moral advance for the welfare state, on a par with the abolition of slavery and the introduction of universal suffrage.[40]

Although we have highlighted the minimum income as a decisive step in the fight against poverty, it must be recognised that in many European states the level of minimum income provided is also considered woefully inadequate.[41] The minimum income even ends up being below the various poverty thresholds in some countries.[42] As a result, its impact on poverty reduction is limited (often 'very limited').[43] Only in four European countries does it meet the objective of alleviating poverty (Ireland, Iceland, the Netherlands, and the United Kingdom). In the remaining cases, it only serves to reduce the severity of poverty.

---

39 "An unconditional basic income, or, as I shall usually call it, a basic income, is a grant paid to every citizen, irrespective of his or her occupational situation and marital status, and irrespective of his or her work performance or availability for work. It is, in other words, an individual guaranteed minimum income without either a means test or a (willingness to) work condition" – P. Van Parijs – "Why surfers should be fed: the liberal case for an unconditional basic income", in Philosophy and Public Affairs, no. 20, 1991 (101–131) <https://family.piercespace.com/wp-content/uploads/2020/09/Philippe-Van-Parijs-Why-Surfers-Should-be-Fed-The-Liberal-Case-for-an-Unconditional-Basic-Income.-Philosophy-Public-Affairs-Vol.-20-No.-2-Spring-1991-.pdf>, p. 102.

40 P. Van Parijs – "Competing justifications of basic income". *In* PARIJS, P. Van (ed.) - *Introduction to Arguing for Basic Income*. London: Verso, 1992, 3–43 <https://www.uclouvain.be/cps/ucl/doc/etes/documents/1992.Verso_-_Intro__Competing_.final.pdf>, p. 5

41 "In terms of the generosity of MI benefits to ensure a decent life, only a few schemes (CH, CY, IS, LI, NL) achieve a largely adequate level of income support. A significant number fall somewhat short of an adequate level of support (AT, BE, DK, CZ, ES, FI, IE, IT [Bolzano, Trento], LT, LU, MT, NO, PL, SE, SI, UK) and in fourteen countries (BG, DE, EE, EL, FR, HR, HU, IT [Basilicata, Friuli Venezia Giulia, Molise, New Social Card, Puglia, Sardegna, Sicilia, Valle d'Aosta], LV, MK, PT, RO, RS, SK) the level is very inadequate" - Hugh Frazer and Eric Marlier, p. 8.

42 "[…] in most countries, the levels of MI benefits fall below the at-risk-of-poverty (AROP) threshold" - Hugh Frazer and Eric Marlier, p. 8.

43 FRAZER E MARLIER (2016), p. 8.

3.4. Consequences of the inadequacies of the present poverty law

The shortcomings identified mean that the phenomenon of poverty persists with no end in sight. Because of these shortcomings, poverty in many countries continues to be dealt with according to the political winds, the availability of budgets and the good or bad will of political communities. In times of plenty, it is treated more generously. In times of scarcity, the fight against poverty inevitably loses resources.

This reality leaves the poorest vulnerable and exposed to the political will of the moment. It also leaves them exposed to voluntary charity, with all the problems that entails. Because it is based on charity rather than rights, it provides aid that is not only stigmatising and a source of social shame, but also creates dependency among its beneficiaries (for instance, food distribution is not usually linked to measures to break the cycle of poverty). As Onora O'Neill puts it 'failure to make beneficience do the task of justice is no failure of the beneficent. Voluntary and charitable organisations do not fail in beneficience if they cannot meet all fundamental material needs, so leaving some still in desperate poverty'.[44]

It also exposes them to the prejudices of society. It should be noted that although the policy of criminalising begging was abandoned in the 1960s, it was resumed in many states from the 1990s onwards. As the ECtHR stated in 2021: of the thirty-eight countries that make up the Council of Europe, only nine do not criminalise begging (Portugal, Albania, Andorra, Finland, Georgia, Greece, Moldova, Slovakia, and Ukraine).[45,46] Linking this new trend to prejudice is the theory known as 'Broken Windows', which is responsible in many cases, particularly in the United States, for the return of policies that criminalise begging. It was described in an article in The Atlantic magazine in March 1982[47] and was formulated by a specialist in municipal policing, George Kelling. 'Professor Kelling hypothesised that the unchecked proliferation of low-level crime, such as open drug use, public intoxication, graffiti,

---

[44] O'NEILL (1986), p. 162.

[45] Case Lacatus vs Switzerland (2021) https://hudoc.echr.coe.int/eng#{%22itemid%22:[%22001-207377%22]}.

[46] On the subject, see MARTINS (2023).

[47] WILSON and KELLING (1982).

panhandling, and prostitution causes fear and leads to the abandonment of public places. Such crime leads to a further increase in the level of a neighbourhood's disorder, and finally results in significant demoralisation among residents'.[48]

4. What solutions are there to the problem of poverty?

4.1. The constitutional recognition of a public duty to unconditionally respect the rights of the poorest

The inadequacies of the legal instruments for combating poverty make it necessary to rethink the issue. From above, and given the limitations found in international and European law, no entity can replace the Member States (in spite of the many problems they have, as pointed out above) when it comes to fulfilling this objective.

To propose a greater commitment on the part of the state to its duties towards the poorest, one of the possible solutions is to make a commitment at a national level to unconditional respect for the rights of the poorest and to the total eradication of poverty.

This commitment must be assumed in the Constitution of each State. It must therefore be a long-term engagement made to be respected and promoted by successive governments over time. A commitment to the eradication of poverty, in order to remove its effect of placing people in situations of violence, oppression, repression, exploitation, or extreme need, on the assumption that this is a denial of human dignity.

4.2. Respect for the rights of freedom of expression and the presence of the poorest in the public space

One of the demands resulting from the above-mentioned greater commitment on the part of the state to its duties towards the poorest is the recognition of the state's protection of the most basic rights: the recognition of freedom of expression and the recognition of the fundamental right of the poorest to be present in the public space.

As far as freedom of expression is concerned, we can benefit from the lessons of the 1991 Case of *Loper vs New York City Police Department* and

---

48 LEOUSSIS (1995) - p. 531.

of the 30 June 2012 decision of the Austrian Constitutional Court, which recognises that freedom of expression is a crucial element to be taken into account when considering public policies to prohibit and criminalise begging.

Recognising that the protection of the poorest means giving constitutional backing to the instruments they have at their disposal to get out of the situation of need in which they find themselves. The right to beg should be understood as 'one of the most profound demands of the human person (...) the free spiritual communication of one's thoughts to others'.[49]

At the same time, the protection of the rights of the poor is also a matter of refusing to typify repressive measures that are an expression of aporophobia or prejudice against them. Full respect for the fundamental rights of the poor means restricting any kind of criminal action based not on the commission of acts that harm third parties, but on a certain type of discourse, a discourse that is nothing but the fruit of extreme vulnerability. From this point of view, all types of criminalisation of begging should be reconsidered, given the discursive basis on which they are based.

From this point of view, even the criminalisation of aggressive begging should be considered inappropriate, since it compresses a discourse that should enjoy the protection of freedom of expression.[50] 'The lack of objectivity of the prohibition without exception is also demonstrated by the fact that the legislator tolerates a number of other forms of use in public places where people are approached, for example, with the aim of making a donation for charitable purposes, buying newspapers or magazines or visiting certain entertainment or hospitality establishments', as expressly stated by the Austrian Constitutional Court in its Judgement of 30 June 2012.

When it comes to recognising the fundamental right to move and be present in public spaces, the recognition of a special duty to protect the poorest implies a treatment that respects the equality and dignity of all, preventing the police authorities from simply taking action to chase away or even arbitrarily detain beggars and homeless people so as not to disturb others with their requests or life stories.[51]

---

49 ALEXANDRINO (2017), p. 615 (our translation).

50 MARTINS (2023).

51 On the idea of neutrality and the understanding that has been developing around the US Supreme Court judgement Reed v. Town of Gilbert (2015) see LAURIELLO (2016).

4.3. Rethinking the concept of minimum income questioning the absoluteness of budgetary powers

The protection of the poorest also forces us to rethink the concept of minimum income in the light of a right to have basic survival needs met by the State. It is possible to take the existential minimum as a directly invocable right, questioning the absoluteness of budgetary powers. It is worth remembering that not even some libertarian authors refuse to recognise a survival minimum.[52] The poorest should benefit from the consensus around this minimum: 'Every society develops a certain social consensus on how to balance market efficiency and social compassion'.[53]

Taking the minimum income as a state obligation seriously should be seen as part of the re-foundation of the right to poverty (especially when labour income is insufficient and social security is unable to solve all the problems). Since universal preventive instruments do not fulfil their mission of eradicating poverty, it is necessary to develop support that meets people's needs.

The formulation of a constitutional obligation to give priority to the poorest and to respect their fundamental rights unconditionally can only suggest a reversal of the logic of social rights on which the poverty law of the 20th century was based. This reversal should be inspired by Karl Popper's formula for minimising suffering,[54] opening itself up to judicial review. Once based on a universalist logic of preventing poverty, it is now based on a personalised logic of solving specific problems. It calls on all people to maintain humanity, as the principle of human dignity demands.

In this sense this view supports specifically:

- a demanding definition of the universe, based on a line drawn according to the poverty threshold or, at least, to a basket of essential goods, so that the state can reach out to all those who are clearly in a situation of extreme poverty;

---

52 HAYEK, F. A., 2013, pos. 6935-43 (versão kindle): "A system which relies on the spontaneous ordering forces of the market, once it has reached a certain level of wealth, is also by no means incompatible with government providing, outside the market, some security against severe deprivation".

53 HAQ, Mahbub ul, 1995, p. 143.

54 POPPER (2003), pp. 255–256, note 6.

- the unconditional allocation of the minimum income to those within the universe of those identified as being in a situation of extreme poverty (abandoning other eligibility criteria), according to a simple and comprehensive scheme;
- the adoption of mechanisms for annually updating the value of the minimum income, according to an objective criterion that allows the basic needs of a minimally decent life to be covered.

4.4. Designing the minimum content of social rights based on prioritising the poorest and meeting their needs

Once this special obligation to protect the poorest is established in the sense of the recognition of a constitutional obligation to respect their fundamental rights unconditionally and to give priority to their needs, it will be clear the need for a scrupulous understanding of social rights as well.

The concept of *receptive need* that was formulated in the author's doctoral thesis 'Fair Public Expenditure' (*'A Despesa Pública Justa'*) can bring light in this matter, in an attempt to impose limits on the legislator when it comes to implementing social rights that, for the most part, are indeterminable and subject to setting out what is financially possible.

In the light of the *receptive need* concept, it should be considered as incompatible with human dignity to defend, even in the name of solidarity, the idea that everyone should pay the same tax, just as it as it is to argue the obligation to provide all the goods provided for in the Constitution in an undifferentiated way.

The combination of the social rights with the special consideration given to the situation of the poorest clears the idea of a priority to those who, because of their situation of need, do not have the goods covered by these rights.

Those who already have access to goods that are also the subject of public provision should not be prioritised when it comes to defining public spending obligations. Expenditure should be prioritised, first and foremost, in relation to those who can demonstrate either an inability to do so or that without these benefits they would be in a situation of vulnerability.[55] This priority should be assumed as the minimum content of every social right.

---

[55] MARTINS (2016), p. 414.

5. Conclusions

The problem of poverty is tackled at different levels: international, European, and national. However, there are shortcomings at all levels. The fight against poverty cannot be done without national intervention, although it needs to be reformulated. The fight against poverty, more than a human rights issue, is an issue that should be approached from the perspective of civil and political rights. Without the full recognition by each State of an approach based on the recognition of human dignity and equality, there are no magic formulas for the fight against poverty.

Eradicating poverty means overcoming the prejudices that have historically been associated with it, starting from an approach that is necessarily based on unconditional respect for everyone's rights, starting with respect for freedom of expression and presence in the public sphere. The protection of the poorest, based on the human dignity of all, also forces us to rethink the concept of minimum income (and even the minimum content of social rights) in the light of a right to have basic survival needs met by the State. This should be redefined in terms of directly enforceable rights, challenging the absoluteness of budgetary powers.

Bibliography

Ackerman Bruce and Alstot, Anne. *The Stakeholder State*. New Haven & London: Yale University Press, 1980.

Alston, Philip. "No right to complain about being boor: the need for an optional protocol to the economic rights covenant" in EIDE, Asborn e HELGESEN, Jan (eds.) – "The future of human rights protection in a changing world. fifty years since the four freedoms address. Essays in honour of Torkel Opsahl. Oslo: Norwegian University Press, 1991.

Alexandrino, José de Melo *in* MIRANDA, Jorge e MEDEIROS, Rui – Constituição Portuguesa Anotada. Coimbra: Coimbra Editora, vol. I, 2017.

Aoued, Ahmed. "The right to food: the significance of the United Nations Special Rapporteur" in Lucy Williams (Ed.) – *International Poverty Law*. London/New York: Zed Books, 2013.

ATD Quart Monde. *En finir avec des idées fausses sur les pauvres et la pauvreté.* Paros: Éditions Quart Monde, 2020.

Brems, Eva. *Human Rights: Universality and Diversity*. The Hague, Boston, London: Martinus Nijhoff Publishers, 2001.

Committee On Economic, Social And Cultural Rights. General Comment No. 12 (Twentieth Session, 1999) The Right to Adequate Food (Art. 11) (available at <https://tbinternet.ohchr.org/_layouts/15/treatybodyexternal/download.aspx?symbolno=e%2fc.12%2f1999%2f5&lang=en>).

Committee On Economic, Social And Cultural Rights. General Comment No. 15 (2002) - The Right To Water (Arts 11 and 12 of the International Covenant On Economic, Social And Cultural Rights) (available at <https://tbinternet.ohchr.org/_layouts/15/treatybodyexternal/download.aspx?symbolno=e%2fc.12%2f2002%2f11&lang=en>).

Cortina, Adela. *Aporophobia: Why We Reject the Poor Instead of Helping Them*. Princeton and Oxford: Princeton University Press, 2022 (digital version without page number).

Ferrera Maurizio, Matsaganis Manos and Sacchi, Steffano – "Open coordination against poverty: the new EU 'social inclusion process'" *in* Journal of European Social Policy 2002, London, Thousand Oaks and New Delhi: SAGE Publications, Vol 12 (3) (227–239).

Frazer, Hugh and Marlier, Eric. "Minimum Income Schemes in Europe: A study of national policies 2015". Brussels: European Commission, 2016 (available at <https://www.researchgate.net/publication/299652131_Minimum_income_schemes_in_Europe_A_study_of_national_policies>).

Gaisbauer Helmut P. – "Absolute poverty and the EU Social Policy Agenda" in Helmut P. Gaisbauer, Gottfried Schweiger and Clemens Sedmak (Eds.) - *Absolute poverty in Europe: Interdisciplinary Perspectives on a Hidden Phenomenon*. Bristol: Policy Press, 2019.

Haq, Mahbub ul – *Reflections on Human Development*. Oxford: Oxford University Press, 1995.

Hayek, F.A., *Law, Legislation and Liberty*. London and New York: Routledge, 2013 (kindle edition).

Krell Andreas, Controle judicial dos serviços públicos básicos na base dos direitos fundamentais sociais. In: Ingo Wolfgang SARLET (org.). A Constituição Concretizada. Construindo pontes entre o público e o privado. Porto Alegre: Livraria do Advogado, 2000.

Lanceiro, Rui, "Dano and Alimanovic: the recent evolution of CJEU caselaw on EU citizenship and cross-border access to social benefits" *in* Unio - Eu Law Journal, Vol. 3, No. 1, January 2017, pp. 63–77.

Lauriello, Anthony D., "Panhandling Regulation after Reed v. Town of Gilbert", in Columbia Law Review, vol. 116, 2016 (disponível em <https://columbialawreview.org/content/panhandling-regulation-after-reed-v-town-of-gilbert/|>).

Loureiro, João Carlos. *Adeus ao Estado Social? A Segurança Social entre o crocodilo da economia e a medusa da ideologia dos "direitos adquiridos"*. Coimbra: Wolters Kluwer/Coimbra Editora, 2010.

Loureiro, João Carlos, "A Segurança Social, o Seguro Social: Novos Perímetros e Universalidade", *in* Boletim da Faculdade de Direito da Universidade de Coimbra, no. 94, tomo 1, 2018 (693–706).

Loureiro, João Carlos, "(In)Sustentabilidade Da Segurança/Seguridade Social: Entre as 'Brumas Da Memória' e as 'Brumas Do Futuro' em Tempos de Neoglobalização e Neognosticismo (S)" in Boletim da Faculdade de Direito da Universidade de Coimbra no. 94, tomo 2, 2018 (1031–1052).

Marc, Céline, PORTELA, Portela, Mickaël, Hannafi, Cyrine, Le Gall, Rémi, RODE, Rode, Antoine and Laguerodie, Stéphanie, "Quantifier le non-recours aux minima sociaux en Europe. Un phénomène d'ampleur qui peine à susciter le débat" *in* Les dossiers de la Drees, n° 94, mars 2022, p. 9 (available at <https://drees.solidarites-sante.gouv.fr/sites/default/files/2022-03/DD94.pdf>).

Martins, Maria d'Oliveira, *A despesa pública justa – Uma análise jurídico-constitucional do tema da Justiça na despesa pública*. Coimbra: Almedina, 2016.

Martins, Maria d'Oliveira, *Lições de Finanças Públicas e Direito Financeiro*. Coimbra: Almedina, 2019.

Martins, Maria d'Oliveira, "A criminalização da mendicância e o Acórdão Lacatus c. Suíça do TEDH tomado como uma oportunidade perdida numa defesa intransigente da dignidade dos mais pobres", *in Homenagem à Professora Doutora Maria da Glória Garcia*, Lisboa: Universidade Católica Editora: Lisboa: UCEditora, 2023.

Leoussis Fay, "The New Constitutional Right to Beg – Is begging really protected speech?" (1995) (available at <https://popcenter.asu.edu/sites/default/files/problems/panhandling/PDFs/Leoussis_1995.pdf>).

Moeckli, Daniel. "Bettelverbote: einige rechtsvergleichende Überlegungen zur Grundrechtskonformität", 2010 (available at Zurich Open Repository and Archive, University of Zurich: <https://doi.org/10.5167/uzh-36269>).

Novais, Jorge Reis. *Direitos Sociais - Teoria Jurídica dos Direitos Sociais enquanto Direitos Fundamentais*. Lisboa: AAFDL Editora, 2016.

O'Neill, Onora – *Faces of Hunger: An Essay on Poverty, Justice and Development*. London: Allen & Unwin, 1986.

Pais Sofia. "Todos os cidadãos da União Europeia têm direito de circular e residir livremente no território dos Estados-Membros, mas uns têm mais direitos do que outros…" *in* Scientia Juridica, 253, 2010 (467–496).

Popper, Karl. *The Open Society and Its Enemies. Volume One: The Spell of Plato*. London: Routledge, 2003.

Rode, Antoine. La quantification du non-recours en Europe. Historique et principales «scènes de production» des mesures réalisées dans 5 pays européens. 12 | 2022|Working Paper # 34 - ODENORE (Observatoire des non-recours aux droits et services) (available at <https://odenore.msh-alpes.fr/sites/odenore/files/Mediatheque/quantification_du_non-recours_rode_wp_34_odenore.pdf>).

Skogly, Sigrun I.: "Is there right not to be poor?" *in* Human Rights Law Review, 2(1), 2002, pp. 59–80.

St Clair Asuncion Lera. "How Can Human Rights Contribute To Poverty Reduction? A Philosophical Assessment Of The Human Development Report 2000" *In* LUCY WILLIAMS (Ed.) – International Poverty Law – An Emerging Discourse. London /New York: Zed Books, 2013, Kindle Edition.

Van Parijas, Philippe. "Why surfers should be fed: the liberal case for an unconditional basic income". In Philosophy and Public Affairs, no. 20, 1991, pp. 101-131 (available in <https://family.piercespace.com/wp-content/uploads/2020/09/Philippe-Van-Parijs-Why-Surfers-Should-be-Fed-The-Liberal-Case-for-an-Unconditional-Basic-Income.-Philosophy-Public-Affairs-Vol.-20-No.-2-Spring-1991-.pdf>).

Van Parijas, Philippe. "Competing justifications of basic income". *In* PARIJS, P. Van (ed.) - *Introduction to Arguing for Basic Income*. London: Verso, 1992, 3–43 (available in PDF at <https://www.uclouvain.be/cps/ucl/doc/etes/documents/1992.Verso_Intro__Competing_.final.pdf>).

Vanderbroucke Frank and Fleminckx, Koen. "Disappointing poverty trends: is the social investment state to blame?" in Journal of European Social Policy, Vol. 21(5), 2011.

Wilson, James Q. and Kelling, George, "Broken Windows", in *The Atlantic*, de março de 1982 (available at <http://faculty.washington.edu/matsueda/courses/371/Readings/Wilson%20and%20Kelling%20(1982).pdf>).

Case law cited

BVerfGE 33, 303, 18 july 1972 (Numerus Clausus I) (available at <https://www.servat.unibe.ch/dfr/bv033303.html#Opinion>).

BVerfGE 125, 175 of 20 October 2009 (Hartz IV) (available at <https://www.servat.unibe.ch/dfr/bv125175.html>).

Judgement of the Supreme Court of the United States, Papachristou v. City of Jacksonville, 405 U.S. 156 of 1972 (available at <https://supreme.justia.com/cases/federal/us/405/156/>).

Case of Lacatus v. Switzerland (2021) (available at <https://hudoc.echr.coe.int/eng#{%22itemid%22:[%22001-207377%22]}>).

Loper v. New York City Police Department 1991 available at <https://law.justia.com/cases/federal/district-courts/FSupp/766/1280/1647335/>).

Judgement of 30 June 2012 of the Austrian Constitutional Court (available at <https://www.ris.bka.gv.at/VfghEntscheidung.wxe?Abfrage=Vfgh&Dokumentnummer=JFT_09879370_10G00155_00&IncludeSelf=True>).

PART III

In Clash with Legal Systems

The Protection of Vulnerable Victims Through Substantive Criminal Law: Some Insights from the European Context

Dyango Bonsignore[*,1]

Abstract: In Criminal Law, the protection of the vulnerable has followed two main approaches: protecting vulnerable groups against discrimination and protecting vulnerable victims of specific crimes. This paper draws, among others, on the Spanish Criminal Code as a salient example to highlight some issues related to the protection of vulnerable victims.

Keywords: vulnerability, victims, criminal law, discrimination, crime policy

1. Introduction

The notion of vulnerability has received an increasing amount of attention by scholars across disciplines over the last few years. Although the reasons for this rise in interest are complex and may need systematic scrutiny, perhaps it is not too outlandish to place the work of scholars like Fineman,[2] Butler[3] and Nussbaum[4] as central when thinking about this renewed interrogation on what it means to be vulnerable. Broadly speaking, efforts have been made to

* Lecturer in Criminology and Criminal Policy at the University of Alicante, Spain. ORCID: 0000-0002-4282-8995.

1 This work has been written as a part of the research projects: "La vulnerabilidad victimal en el Sistema de justicia penal" (ref. GRE21-14A) funded by the University of Alicante, and "Agravantes y subtipos agravados. Una propuesta de racionalización del Código Penal desde la economía legislativa" (GRAVITAS) (ref. PID2022-136847NB-I00), funded by the Spanish Ministry of Science and Innovation.

2 Martha Albertson Fineman, 'The Vulnerable Subject: Anchoring Equality in the Human Condition', *Yale Journal of Law and Feminism* 20, no. 1 (2008): 1–23; Martha Albertson Fineman, 'Equality, Autonomy, and the Vulnerable Subject in Law and Politics', in *Vulnerability. Reflections on a New Ethical Foundation for Law and Politics*, ed. Martha Albertson Fineman and Anna Grear (Routledge, 2013), 13–28.

3 Judith Butler, *Vida Precaria: El Poder Del Duelo y La Violencia* (Paidós, 2006).

4 Martha C. Nussbaum, *El Ocultamiento de Lo Humano. Repugnancia, Vergüenza y Ley* (Katz, 2006).

bring the 'human' back to the centre of philosophical reflection and public policy, in part as a response to the limitations attributed to the rhetoric of the liberal-autonomous subject. The abstraction inherent in this blueprint of the average man, although in many ways necessary from a historical and political point of view, could have contributed to a fundamental misunderstanding of what human nature is, while forgetting the unavoidable fragility and interdependency that characterises human existence. It has been argued that, in hiding the multiple limitations faced by the liberal subject, the political framework operates on inadequate premises while drawing a distinction between those able to fit themselves into the abstract citizen's clothes, and those who struggle to blend in. On the flipside, it is also argued that, while recognising the universal vulnerability that unites the human condition makes it important to avoid the stereotyping and marginalisation of many, one should be wary of generalising too much, this time under the umbrella of vulnerability. Distinction is necessary, from a social and political standpoint, as different human beings find themselves exposed to different sources of vulnerability, to which they may have also different resources of protection. An intersectional and 'layered' view on vulnerability, with due consideration of protective factors, social and personal capital, are necessary to deal with individual needs while fostering a (realistic) conception of autonomy and agency.[5]

Although these are discussions that could have profound legal implications, I am under the impression that the penetration of the vulnerability debate in legal scholarship has been slow, fragmented and fundamentally pragmatic in nature. Nevertheless, there might be room to argue that vulnerability has long had a firm position within juridical consciousness, even if it was not always explicitly stated. After all, the ongoing struggle for the

---

[5] Kimberle Crenshaw, 'Demarginalizing the Intersection of Race and Sex: A Black Feminist Critique of Antidiscrimination Doctrine, Feminist Theory and Antiracist Politics', *The University of Chicago Legal Forum*, no. 140 (1989): 139–67; Kimberle Crenshaw, 'Mapping the Margins: Intersectionality, Identity Politics, and Violence against Women of Color', *Source: Stanford Law Review* 43, no. 6 (1991): 1241–99; Florencia Luna, 'Elucidating the Concept of Vulnerability : Layers Not Labels', *International Journal of Feminist Approaches to Bioethics* 2, no. 1 (2009): 128; Wendy Rogers, Catriona MacKenzie, and Susan Dodds, 'Why Bioethics Needs a Concept of Vulnerability', *International Journal of Feminist Approaches to Bioethics* 5, no. 2 (2012): 16, <https://doi.org/10.1353/ijf.2012.0024>.

effective protection and even expansion of human, social and political rights may owe much to the effort of shielding humanity from its 'bare' conditions of existence, namely from vulnerability[6]. Nevertheless, as previously stated, this paper has a much narrower focus and must leave the examination of these questions as contextual and cursory.

Instead, the analysis deployed in this chapter will only address the situation from the point of view of substantive criminal law and criminal policy. Although examples will be drawn from various national contexts within the EU, and from Spanish criminal law in particular, discourse will be kept at a higher level of generality for the sake of clarity and usefulness within international conversation.

With this in mind, the chapter is organised as follows: the next section starts with a panoramic examination of the relationship between vulnerability and criminal law, paying particular attention to this relationship under several European legal systems, with France, Belgium, and Spain providing the most salient examples. The subsequent section offers a deeper examination of the current state of vulnerability protection by Spanish criminal law, although observations are highly relevant to the European observer, with significant similarities with other countries where a wide regulation has been put in place. This examination will consider an important distinction between two different approaches: the group-centric framework applied to the protection of vulnerable groups against discrimination and hate crime, and the individual-centric framework applied to 'particularly vulnerable victims'. As we will see, both approaches differ significantly and should be considered as responding to distinct aims, methods and even representations of the vulnerable. Finally, section four will outline some of the most salient issues and critiques that have been raised, particularly in areas most relevant to the European observer. Special attention will be given to the material implications of the issues raised and the effects these might have on the protection of vulnerable populations.

---

6 Bryan S. Turner, *Vulnerability and Human Rights*, *Vulnerability and Human Rights* (Pennsylvania State University Press, 2006), 6.

2. Protecting vulnerable victims through criminal law. A European perspective

In a sense, there is ample room to argue that a notion of vulnerability has been at the core of criminal law, although often in an implicit manner. Broadly speaking, vulnerability can be found as the shared condition of humanity that energised Hobbes' political theory[7]. Still in broad terms, the importance attributed to certain offences seems to be interlocked with assumptions about the vulnerability of the expected victim, as is the case with most sex crimes, particularly those involving children. General principles that guide criminal legal thought can also be reshaped with vulnerability in mind: identifying spaces in the social fabric where vulnerability (to crime) thrives is a frequent mechanism to argue for the necessity of legal reform, more severe punishment and the like. Even some core criminal-legal concepts seem to aim at vulnerability, as is the case when premeditation or an abuse of power are considered as aggravating circumstances[8].

That being said, more explicit and systematic protection of vulnerable victims seems to have flown largely under the radar in substantive criminal law until recent times. This is related to the pace at which victims have moved from a mostly testimonial status in an offender-focused criminal procedure[9]

---

7 Thomas Hobbes, *Leviatán* (Madrid: Editora Nacional, 1980), 222.

8 Isidoro Blanco Cordero, 'La Menor Edad Como Fundamento de La Agravación de La Pena: Estudio Crítico de Los Tipos Agravados Por Razón de La Menor Edad y La Especial Vulnerabilidad', in *La Protección de Las Víctimas Especialmente Vulnerables. Aspectos Penales, Procesales y Político-Criminales*, ed. Clara Moya Guillem and Dyango Bonsignore Fouquet (Valencia: Tirant lo Blanch, 2023), 127; Clara Moya Guillem and Juan Carlos Sandoval, 'La Regulación de Los Ataques Contra Víctimas Vulnerables En Los Delitos Contra La Vida. Otro Caso de Irracionalidad Legislativa', in *Manifestaciones de Desigualdad En El Sistema de Justicia Penal. Volumen I*, (Ed.) Antonio Doval Pais and Elena Gutiérrez Pérez (Madrid: Aranzadi, 2023), 263–307; Natalia Sánchez-Moraleda Vilches, 'Mayores Vulnerables y Derecho Penal: Una Aproximación a La Circunstancia Agravante de Especial Vulnerabilidad Por Razón de La (Avanzada) Edad', in *La Protección de Las Víctimas Especialmente Vulnerables. Aspectos Penales, Procesales y Político-Criminales*, (Ed.) Clara Moya Guillem and Dyango Bonsignore Fouquet (Valencia: Tirant lo Blanch, 2023), 165.

9 Cornelius Prittwitz, 'The Resurrection of the Victim in Penal Theory', *Buffalo Criminal Law Review* 3, no. 1 (1 April 1999): 109–29, <https://doi.org/10.1525/nclr.1999.3.1.109>; Carmen Tomás-Valiente Lanuza, 'El Interés de La Víctima En La Pena Del Delito. Algunas Reflexiones', in *El Papel de La Víctima En El Derecho Penal*, ed. Laura Pozuelo Pérez and Daniel Rodríguez Horcajo (Madrid: Boletín Oficial del Estado, 2021), 40–42.

to a more centre-stage position. Although not without issues in a context where victims have been easily instrumentalised by political interests and penal populism, the legal protection of victims has been increasingly consolidated[10]. Within the European context, this has been further reinforced by the enactment of a unitary legal framework regarding victim rights, notably energised by Directive 2012/29/EU of the European Parliament and of the Council of 25 October 2012 establishing minimum standards on the rights, support and protection of victims of crime, and replacing Council Framework Decision 2001/220/JHA,[11] special dispositions regarding victims of terrorism,[12] and the adoption of a victim-centric approach to modern issues such as human trafficking[13].

To this overview, we can also add the EU Strategy on victims' rights for 2020–2025, as it contains not only an assessment of the successes and limitations of the existing legal framework regarding victims of crime, but also the main focus points for the European policy on the matter. It is interesting to note that the EU Strategy pays special attention to some victims considered particularly vulnerable, such as victims of gender-based violence, children,

---

10 Javier Cigüela Sola, 'Populismo Penal y Justicia Paralela: Un Análisis Político-Cultural', *Revista Electrónica de Ciencia Penal y Criminología* 22, no. 12 (2020): 18; José Luis Díez Ripollés, 'El Nuevo Modelo Penal de La Seguridad Ciudadana', *Revista Electrónica de Ciencia Penal y Criminología* 06, no. 03 (2004): 9–10; John Pratt, *Penal Populism* (Abingdon: Routledge, 2007); Daniel Varona Gómez, 'Medios de Comunicación y Punitivismo', *InDret: Revista Para El Análisis Del Derecho*, no. 1 (2011): n. 55.

11 José Manuel Chozas Alonso, 'El Nuevo Estatuto de La Víctima de Los Delitos En El Proceso Penal', in *Los Sujetos Protagonistas Del Proceso Penal*, ed. José Manuel Chozas Alonso (Dykinson, 2015), 193–261; Josep Maria Tamarit Sumalla, 'Los Derechos de Las Víctimas', in *El Estatuto de Las Víctimas de Delitos. Comentarios a La Ley 4/2015*, ed. Josep Maria Tamarit Sumalla (Valencia: Tirant lo Blanch, 2015), 7–60.

12 Luis Roca Agapito, 'Análisis Del Nuevo Régimen Jurídico-Económico de Las Víctimas Del Terrorismo', *Diario La Ley*, no. 7776 (2012): 1–15.

13 Norberto J. De la Mata Barranco, Ana Isabel Pérez Machío, and Leire Berasaluce Gerrkagoitia, 'La Regulación Del Delito de Trata de Seres Humanos y La Protección de Las Víctimas Atendiendo a Las Personas Menores de Edad No Acompañadas y El Anteproyecto de La Ley de Trata', in *Personas Vulnerables y Tutela Penal*, ed. Norberto J. De la Mata Barranco et al. (Aranzadi, 2023), 337–71; Carolina Villacampa Estiarte, 'Acerca Del Anteproyecto de Ley Orgánica Integral Contra La Trata y La Explotación de Seres Humanos', *Diario LA LEY*, no. 10267 (2023): 1. For the sake of reference, the European repertoire of instruments with paramount relevance in regulating the protection of victims, apart from the 2012 Directive, include Council Directive 2004/80/EC of 29 April 2004 relating to compensation to victims of crime; Directive

victims with disabilities, elderly victims, victims of hate crime and terrorism and victims of human trafficking. Some of those categories might even overlap, as human trafficking or elderly victimisation often have a gender bias.

From a legal standpoint, however, most of these advances have been related to the protection and empowerment of the victim within the criminal procedure (such as ensuring access to justice and minimising secondary victimisation), as well as indemnification, psychosocial assistance and recovery[14]. Rather cogently, the directive focuses on protecting the victims through practical measures and a series of rights to ensure that due treatment will be provided by the institutions. Sufficient examples of this can be found in its various chapters, which often organise around key moments or situations where the victim must be properly treated and protected, both from the offender as well as from secondary victimisation (e.g. the right to an adequate information during the criminal procedure, victim support measures, ensuring the optimal participation of the victim, victim protection adapted to the specific needs of each individual, as well as some considerations regarding the criminal justice professionals and their behaviour towards the victims). This is coherent with some of the (rare) explicit references to vulnerability

2011/99/EU of the European Parliament and of the Council of 13 December 2011 on the European protection order and Regulation (EU) No 606/2013 of the European Parliament and of the Council of 12 June 2013 on mutual recognition of protection measures in civil matters; Directive 2011/36/EU of the European Parliament and of the Council of 5 April 2011 on preventing and combating trafficking in human beings and protecting its victims, and replacing Council Framework Decision 2002/629/JHA; Directive 2011/93/EU of the European Parliament and of the Council of 13 December 2011 on combating the sexual abuse and sexual exploitation of children and child pornography, and replacing Council Framework Decision 2004/68/JHA; Directive (EU) 2017/541 of the European Parliament and of the Council of 15 March 2017 on combating terrorism and replacing Council Framework Decision 2002/475/JHA and amending Council Decision 2005/671/JHA; and, of course, the Council of Europe Convention on preventing and combating violence against women and domestic violence (or the Istanbul Convention).

[14] Paz Mercedes De la Cuesta Aguado, 'Sobre La Asistencia a Víctimas de Delitos Más Allá Del Estatuto de La Víctima', *Estudios Penales y Criminológicos*, no. 39 (2019): 403–54; Carmen Durán Silva, 'La Especial Vulnerabilidad de La Víctima En El Derecho Penal Procesal Español', in *La Protección de Las Víctimas Especialmente Vulnerables. Aspectos Penales, Procesales y Político-Criminales*, ed. Clara Moya Guillem and Dyango Bonsignore Fouquet (Tirant lo Blanch, 2023), 250.

contained in the directive, presented as a heightened risk of secondary or repeat victimisation, as well as intimidation or retaliation. The directive also underlines the particular importance of some victims, such as minors or victims of human trafficking,[15] terrorism, or sexual violence, among others, in order to establish specific measures of protection related to their particular needs. What is characteristically absent from this instrument is any reference to punishment.

This is not the place to make an exhaustive retrieval of international instruments that might be more or less tied to the topic at hand, as they tend to be fragmented and thematic in nature (although references will be included when relevant). Rather, the aim here is to focus on national examples of vulnerability protection in criminal law to discuss the main theoretical and criminal policy implications. This is important as it draws from the observation that this is an area with significant irregularities across European penal codes, with some countries like Spain, France, and Belgium containing multiple explicit references to vulnerability, while others have only a couple of mentions, or none at all. In this sense, the penal systems with more comprehensive approaches are of particular interest for the European discussion.

---

[15] Human trafficking, in particular, has provided some of the most interesting developments regarding vulnerability and victim protection. In this context, as it is clear that this is an area where vulnerability is deep and pervasive, special care has been paid to emphasise effective protection. Here, Directive 2011/36/UE of the European Parliament and of the Council of 5 April 2011 on preventing and combating trafficking in human beings and protecting its victims and replacing Council Framework Decision 2002/629/JHA has brought significant advances, particularly in designing a model of victim protection that is notionally emancipated from the objectives of criminal prosecution (see Article 11). Although this directive contains some references to criminal punishment, and particularly a reference to aggravating the offence when it has been committed against particularly vulnerable victims, a clear majority of its content remains aimed at institutional protection and assistance. Globally, this consolidates a victim-centred approach, building upon the Council of Europe Convention on Action against Trafficking in Human Beings, or Warsaw Convention. Carolina Villacampa Estiarte, "La Nueva Directiva Europea Relativa a La Prevención y La Lucha Contra La Trata de Seres Humanos y a La Protección de Las Víctimas ¿Cambio de Rumbo de La Política de La Unión En Materia de Trata de Seres Humanos?", *Revista Electrónica de Ciencia Penal y Criminología* 13–14 (2011): 1–52; Villacampa Estiarte, "Acerca Del Anteproyecto de Ley Orgánica Integral Contra La Trata y La Explotación de Seres Humanos".

Suffice to say that substantive criminal law has remained largely on the margins of this 'rediscovery of the victim,' and the vulnerable in particular, even in countries that now have extensive regulation on the matter.[16] Taking Spain as an example, the 1995 Spanish Criminal Code (still in force, even if widely changed from its original form) originally contained a single example where the vulnerability of the victim was taken into consideration. Specifically, sexual offences were aggravated when the victim was deemed to be 'particularly vulnerable considering their age, illness or situation.'[17] An almost identical starting point has been described for France.[18] From then on, several changes to the Spanish Code expanded the protection afforded to vulnerable victims, with increased breadth from 2015 onwards, due to the multiplication of offences aggravated when committed on vulnerable victims and the widening of the notion of vulnerable victim itself. However, this has come at the price of internal consistency, as this growth has been rather irregular and unsystematic in nature[19]. It remains to be seen whether recent penal reforms on hate crime and gender violence have promoted a group-based victim protection, perhaps bringing about a shift towards a collectivist approach within criminal policy[20].

This tension between group-based and individual-focused notions of victimhood and vulnerability has been an important feature of the evolution of substantive criminal law on these matters, as even particularly vulnerable victims have usually been characterised around collective categories such

16 Olivier Échappé, "Les Personnes Vulnérables En Droit Français", *L'Anée Canonique* 63 (2023): 16, <https://doi.org/10.3917/cano.063.0007>.

17 Clara Moya Guillem, "La Especial Vulnerabilidad Como Circunstancia Agravante. Resultados de Una Investigación Sobre La Jurisprudencia Penal Española", *Revista de Derecho Penal y Criminología* 3ª Época, no. 24 (2020): 15; Moya Guillem and Sandoval, "La Regulación de Los Ataques Contra Víctimas Vulnerables En Los Delitos Contra La Vida. Otro Caso de Irracionalidad Legislativa", 284.

18 Échappé, "Les Personnes Vulnérables En Droit Français", 17.

19 Sergio Pérez González and Norberto J. De la Mata Barranco, "Las Circunstancias Diferenciales y de Vulnerabilidad Del Sujeto Pasivo En El Código Penal", in *Personas Vulnerables y Tutela Penal*, ed. Norberto J. De la Mata Barranco et al. (Aranzadi, 2023), 19–72.

20 José Luis Díez Ripollés, "Alegato Contra Un Derecho Penal Sexual Identitario", *Revista Electrónica de Ciencia Penal y Criminología* 21, no. 10 (2019): 29; José Luis Díez Ripollés, "Los Colectivos Identitarios y La Tutela Penal", *Revista Electrónica de Ciencia Penal y Criminología* 26–01 (2024): 1–46.

as age or disability. This had the symbolic effect of placing the focus on categories the individual victim had to be fitted into, leaving other sources of vulnerability without comparable protection. This has notably been the framework followed by the ECtHR in its case law[21]. As this chapter will show in more detail, the usual issues of over and under-inclusion apply, albeit sometimes mitigated through the incorporation of open clauses referred to 'other circumstances' or similar. When such a technique is used, vulnerability is potentially emancipated from traditional group categories, opening the door to a wider variety of cases and situations.

A similar regulatory procedure is visible in other countries. Again, the French Criminal Code contains references to the vulnerability of the victim as an aggravating circumstance to certain offences, such as sex crimes, torture, assault and fraud, but also as a central aspect of independent offences such as human trafficking (Article 225-4-1), labour exploitation (Article 225-14) and the somewhat peculiar abuse of ignorance or weakness (Article 223-15-2).[22] In many of those cases, the particular vulnerability of the victim is tied to endogenous characteristics such as age, sickness or disability (whether physical or mental) or even pregnancy, but there are also other circumstances of vulnerability that are related to exogenous factors, such as dependency and precarity[23]. Similarly, Belgium offers even more examples of vulnerability clauses,[24] such as in offences against religious freedom (Article 142), hostage taking (Article 347bis 2), sex crimes (Article 376), prostitution (Article 380), some forms of bodily harm (Article 405 bis), torture, inhumane and degrading treatment (Articles 417 *ter, quarter, and quinquies*), and many others, amounting to 44 explicit references to vulnerability. Interestingly, most of the time the vulnerability of the victim receives equal treatment as when the victim is a minor, and is tied to particular causes of vulnerability abused

---

21 Alexandra Timmer, "A Quiet Revolution: Vulnerability in the European Court of Human Rights", in *Vulnerability. Reflections on a New Ethical Foundation for Law and Politics*, (Ed.) Martha Albertson Fineman and Anna Grear (Routledge, 2013), 147–70.

22 Also regulated in Belgium, punishing the abuse of the needs and weaknesses (of passion or of ignorance) of minors or individuals in a situation of vulnerability – Article 493 of the Belgian Criminal Code.

23 Échappé, "Les Personnes Vulnérables En Droit Français", 18–19.

24 Regarding Belgium, the comments in this piece are referred to the still in force version of the Code, and not to the recently approved reform, which is yet in *vacatio*.

by the offender: age, pregnancy, illness, and physical or mental disability. Usually, these vulnerability clauses work as aggravating circumstances to several particular offences, while in some cases they allow criminal punishment (such as in theft committed by close family members, who are excluded from criminal punishment unless committed against a vulnerable victim, Article 462).

Other countries include some references to vulnerable victims in particular contexts, such as the German Criminal Code when punishing sexual abuse of prisoners, the sick or vulnerable institutionalised individuals (section 174a). The Swiss Code, too, contains a limited set of references to vulnerable victims, which are used mostly to regulate measures such as an interdiction of communication, geographic exclusion zones, or even a prohibition on participating in activities, professional or not, if it could imply contact with 'minors or other particularly vulnerable persons'[25] (Article 67), a response that can be intensified in some offences, such as sex crimes, human trafficking, or prostitution, where the victim is particularly vulnerable or in a situation that renders her defenceless.

In broader terms, it is true that, in cases such as when the victim is a minor, there is ample room to argue that vulnerability is not always explicitly mentioned, but works as the rationale behind increased punishment in many countries. That being said, it seems that, when directly mentioned, the most frequent response to vulnerability is not to be found in substantive criminal law but in procedural law. In this context, the French, Belgian and Spanish examples provide some of the best illustrations of wide ranging and somewhat systematic use of vulnerability clauses to determine criminal punishment. It is for this reason that this paper will analyse the Spanish regulation, as it provides a wide number of examples that should be able to fuel comparative reflection.

Using this example, the aim is not only to examine the several ways by which vulnerable victims have been introduced explicitly within the Criminal

---

[25] Interestingly, the Swiss case provides a definition of particularly vulnerable victims, conceived as those in need of assistance of others for their everyday activities, or for self-determination due to their age, illness, or physical/mental disability (Article 67a). This is roughly in line with some of the most usual categories of vulnerability, although it seems point at situations of dependency, which may be a stricter standard than necessarily implied by the notion of vulnerability.

Code, but also to complement the analysis with a parallel reinforcement of the protection of vulnerable groups. The contrast of collective vs individualistic approaches, as we shall see, has analytic importance in distinguishing the protection of 'particularly vulnerable victims' from the protection of vulnerable groups, with the former aiming usually at defencelessness and the latter being directed mostly at discrimination and/or hate crime (albeit not exclusively). Accordingly, this chapter will maintain that thematic distinction when describing, in the following section, the state of present-day protection of the vulnerable in the Spanish Criminal Code, starting with the collective approach.

3. Different approaches, different vulnerabilities

3.1. Vulnerable groups, discrimination and hate crime

The protection of vulnerable groups is not necessarily a new issue. Indeed, as a country traditionally exposed to migration, Spain has had some tradition of facing issues of discrimination through criminal policy, albeit in a somewhat ambiguous manner, sometimes protecting, sometimes excluding[26]. However, the issue has regained traction in recent times through the more systematic tackling of hate speech and hate crime. Such growth in interest is illustrated, for instance, by the Spanish national policy specifically targeted at tackling hate crimes, which was put in motion by the Spanish administration in 2019 and renewed in 2022.

As far as substantive criminal law is concerned, protection against specific forms of discrimination can be found in several offences throughout the Criminal Code: threats against certain protected groups (Article 170.1), torture motivated by discrimination (Article 174.1), or work-related

[26] Isidoro Blanco Cordero and Antonio Doval Pais, 'La Extranjería Como Factor de Discriminación de Los Condenados a Penas de Prisión', in *Crimen Organizado y Extranjería En España y Marruecos*, ed. Luis R Ruiz Rodríguez, Crimen Organizado y Extranjería En España y Marruecos (Valencia: Tirant lo Blanch, 2013), 52; Dyango Bonsignore, 'The Dangerous Individual in a Time of Migration: Periculum, Dominium and Dangerousness', in *From Fear to Hate: Legal-Linguistic Perspectives on Migration*, ed. Victoria Guillén-Nieto, Antonio Doval Pais, and Dieter Stein (De Gruyter, 2023), 36–42, <https://doi.org/10.1515/9783110789157-002>; José Ángel Brandariz García and Cristina Fernández Bessa, '"Perfiles" de Deportabilidad: El Sesgo Del Sistema de Control Migratorio Desde La Perspectiva de La Nacionalidad', *Estudios Penales y*

discrimination (Article 314) among others. There are even examples of group-based protection not based on discrimination (such as most forms of protection of minors). That being said, in this section we will focus on the widely discussed mechanisms of protection against discrimination: the aggravating circumstance from Article 22.4 and the regulation of hate speech crimes in Article 510. We will thus turn to both of them.

a) Hate crimes and biased motives

Starting with the aggravating circumstance, Article 22.4 of the Criminal Code increases the punishment of any crime committed with a specific forbidden motive, such as racism, antisemitism or any other type of discrimination based upon ideology, religion, beliefs, ethnicity, race, nation, gender, sex, age, health, disability, social exclusion, etc. As such, it fits the standard definition of hate crimes, understood as a base offence motivated by discriminatory bias,[27] which is directly in line with Council Framework Decision 2008/913/JHA of 28 November 2008 on combating certain forms and expressions of racism and xenophobia by means of criminal law (see particularly Articles 1 to 4). It bears mentioning that, according to the Spanish regulation, the existence of a motive that qualifies the base offence is enough (issues of proof notwithstanding) to meet the applicability criteria of the aggravating circumstance. To this effect, Article 22.4 explicitly indicates that the victim does not need to actually belong to the protected group, nor have the characteristic on which the discriminatory offence was based (gender, ethnicity…). To put it more simply, whether the offender's motives were based or not in an accurate assessment of the characteristics of the victim is irrelevant (Fuentes Osorio, 2017, p. 6). This was confirmed by the Spanish Public Prosecutor's Office in a 2019 report.

Criminológicos XXXVII (2017): 310–14; Antonio Doval Pais, 'Revisión Del Papel de La Agravante de Discriminación (Art. 22.4ª CP) En La Protección de La Igualdad y La No Discriminación', in *Manifestaciones de Desigualdad En El Sistema de Justicia Penal. Volumen I*, ed. Antonio Doval Pais and Elena Gutiérrez Pérez (Cizur Menor, Navarra: Aranzadi, 2023), 222–23.

27 Jon Mirena Landa Gorostiza, "Delitos de Odio y Estándares Internacionales: Una Visión Crítica a Contra Corriente", *Revista Electrónica de Ciencia Penal y Criminología* 22 (2020): 16; OSCE/ODIHR, *Hate Crime Laws: A Practical Guide* (Varsovia: Office for Democratic Institutions and Human Rights, 2022), 15.

Although this is a rather broad approach to the criminalisation of hate, some doubts remain about the theoretical applicability of the aggravating circumstance to all offences. This is a possibility allowed by the regulatory technique adopted by the Spanish legislator and, as such, every single offence contained in the Criminal Code could be 'turned into' a hate crime, should the specified motives be present. Still, intuition suggests that, although many everyday crimes could be motivated by discrimination,[28] in practice violent incidents seem to be the main stage where biased motivation will be brought up by the courts.

From the perspective of the legal protection of the vulnerable, some features can be outlined. First, it seems obvious that not every sense of vulnerability is important here. On the contrary, it is vulnerability as exposure to discrimination that is at stake[29]. This is important, as it should not be confused with other metrics of vulnerability, such as general exposure to crime (risk), nor individual capabilities to, for instance, repel aggression[30]. Second, a collective notion of vulnerability prevails here, as the individual characteristics of the victim are virtually irrelevant from an applicability standpoint. As already stated, it could even be a victim 'by association' (for example, someone defending the cause of a discriminated collective to which they do not belong) or a victim 'by mistake'.[31]

The fact that none of this changes the legal playing field points to the idea that the particular victim serves as a guarantee that at least a crime was committed. But from that point on, it is the symbolic meaning of that

[28] One could imagine the case of a fraudster that would only target women, driven by the assumption that they are "worse with numbers", "superficial and materialistic" or any other misogynistic stereotyping of the sort. Even more exaggerated examples could be imagined, but surely there would be no reason to doubt the applicability of the aggravating circumstance at face value.

[29] Jon Mirena Landa Gorostiza, 'El Delito de Incitación al Odio (Artículo 510 Cp): Quo Vadis', *Azafea: Revista de Filosofía* 23 (2021): 73, <https://doi.org/10.14201/azafea2021235781>.

[30] Clara Moya Guillem, 'La Protección Penal de Las Víctimas Vulnerables. Pautas Interpretativas y Propuestas de Mejora', in *La Protección de Las Víctimas Especialmente Vulnerables. Aspectos Penales, Procesales y Político-Criminales*, ed. Clara Moya Guillem and Dyango Bonsignore Fouquet (Valencia: Tirant lo Blanch, 2023), 303; Naxhelli Ruiz Rivera, 'La Definición y Medición de La Vulnerabilidad Social. Un Enfoque Normativo', *Investigaciones Geográficas*, no. 77 (2012): 64.

[31] Doval Pais, 'Revisión Del Papel de La Agravante de Discriminación (Art. 22.4ª CP) En La Protección de La Igualdad y La No Discriminación', 234.

crime and its actual target (the discriminated group) that have the central role. So, in a sense, while the base offence has a particular victim, its 'hate' dimension is a communicative act that intends to harm the social status of the targeted group. It is a representation of discrimination and, as such, it is countered through criminalisation, even when no direct harm (i.e. to persons or property) was produced to the targeted group or its members (Bonsignore Fouquet, 2023, p. 53).

There is a final aspect of this mechanism that is shared with hate speech regulation (or should be, as this has raised some issues we will examine shortly). Being the case that vulnerability should be understood here as exposure to discrimination, arguably not every form of discrimination is relevant. On the contrary, while there are many possible grounds for bias (for example, bias against the rich, against communists or against supporters of a certain soccer team), only a selection of such motives is granted reinforced protection. Although there is ample room for discussion over the historical reasons and different pathways followed by nation states in tackling hate crime,[32] it seems that the over-arching rationale for protection lies in combating socially entrenched patterns of discrimination against minority groups[33]. Such minorities should not be understood merely in terms of quantity, but more so as 'qualitative minority'. In other words, a group should be considered vulnerable in this sense when, irrespective of its actual numbers, its social existence is characterised by subalternity, disadvantage or disparagement, as pointed out by the Office of the High Commissioner for Human Rights of the United Nations[34]. In this sense, non-minority groups in quantitative terms, such as women or the poor, could be included under the umbrella of vulnerability. In most cases, this cannot be separated from a history of actual discrimination that is

---

32 Landa Gorostiza, 'Delitos de Odio y Estándares Internacionales: Una Visión Crítica a Contra Corriente'; Enrique Peñaranda Ramos, 'Delitos de Odio y Derecho Penal de La Culpabilidad', in *Reflexiones Académicas Sobre Delitos de Odio*, ed. Juan Alberto Díaz López (Madrid: Observatorio Español del Racismo y la Xenofobia, 2022), 5.

33 Jon Mirena Landa Gorostiza, *Los Delitos de Odio. Artículos 510 y 22.4º CP 1995* (Valencia: Tirant lo Blanch, 2018), 102; Patricia Tapia Ballesteros, 'El Discurso de Odio Del Art. 510.1.a) Del Código Penal Español: La Ideología Como Un Caballo de Troya Entre Las Circunstancias Sospechosas de Discriminación', *Política Criminal* 16, no. 31 (2021): 303.

34 OHCHR, *Minority Rights: International Standards and Guidance for Implementation*, 2010, 3–4, <https://www.refworld.org/reference/themreport/ohchr/2010/en/79004>.

sufficiently pervasive in present-day societies as to warrant increased protection. However, as we will examine next, the lack of a specific reference to this type of socially entrenched vulnerability has allowed for surprising efforts to extend protection to groups that could hardly be described as disadvantaged in a discriminatory sense[35].

b) Hate speech, discourse intoxication and struggles over vulnerability

As mentioned, another avenue for the protection of vulnerable groups against discrimination in Spanish criminal law comes through the criminalisation of hate speech. To this end, Article 510 of the Criminal Code devises a fairly complex, albeit technically unsatisfying[36] system to tackle hateful discourse directed at largely the same groups targeted by hate crime.[37] In this case, it concerns a strictly communicative act aimed at maintaining a group in a preexisting (and usually historically grounded) situation of social inferiority and discrimination. Metaphorically, it appears as a form of intoxication of the public discourse by spreading hatred against discriminated minorities. This is by no means new behaviour, but it is no surprise that it has become especially worrying with the proliferation of contemporary means of mass

---

35 Jorge Correcher Mira, 'Discurso Del Odio y Minorías: Redefiniendo La Libertad de Expresión', *Teoría y Derecho*, no. 28 (2020): 175, <https://doi.org/doi.org/10.36151/td.2020.016>; Landa Gorostiza, 'El Delito de Incitación al Odio (Artículo 510 Cp): Quo Vadis', 76; Tapia Ballesteros, 'El Discurso de Odio Del Art. 510.1.a) Del Código Penal Español: La Ideología Como Un Caballo de Troya Entre Las Circunstancias Sospechosas de Discriminación', 285–86.

36 Sergio Cámara Arroyo, 'El Concepto de Delitos de Odio y Su Comisión a Través Del Discurso. Especial Referencia al Conflicto Con La Libertad de Expresión', *Anuario de Derecho Penal y Ciencias Penales* 70, no. 1 (2017): 203; Juan Luis Fuentes Osorio, 'El Odio Como Delito', *Revista Electrónica de Ciencia Penal y Criminología*, no. 19 (2017): 27.

37 This is a necessary simplification, as Article 510 would be quite unwieldy otherwise, at least within the thematic confines of this piece. Suffice to say that the complete regulation mentions discriminatory motives, several ways of promoting or contributing to hate and discrimination, as well as aggravating clauses when some form of mass media is used or when the behaviour is sufficient to alter the peace or seriously frighten the members of the protected groups. Significantly, Article 510 includes both the individual victim and the collective under its protection, but here it is necessary for the individual victim to actually belong to that group. Landa Gorostiza, 'El Delito de Incitación al Odio (Artículo 510 Cp): Quo Vadis', 59–61.

communication, political polarisation, disinformation, and rampant inequality[38]. Implicitly, behind this viewpoint seems to lie the assumption that contemporary public spheres are subject to threats that exceed the possibilities of redress traditionally conceded to free speech within democratic systems. However, it is unclear whether hate speech has become too sophisticated and thus needs active institutional intervention, or whether fear, hate, and bias simply grow strong where social solidarity lacks solid ground in law and economics[39].

Be that as it may, the criminalisation of hate speech is deeply problematic, even in comparison to hate crime, as the frontier with free speech seems hard to establish with precision. This is certainly the case in Spain, where the law lacks sufficient clarity to allow for proper predictions over what will or will not be considered hate speech by the courts. Adding to this, some grounds for hate speech seem particularly prone to appropriation and deviation from the aim of protecting vulnerable groups. The inclusion of 'ideology' as a cause for discrimination, for instance, not only exemplifies that Spanish legislation has exceeded international obligations in its regulation, but also introduces a degree of uncertainty over who could claim to deserve protection against

---

[38] Correcher Mira, 'Discurso Del Odio y Minorías: Redefiniendo La Libertad de Expresión', 168; Tapia Ballesteros, 'El Discurso de Odio Del Art. 510.1.a) Del Código Penal Español: La Ideología Como Un Caballo de Troya Entre Las Circunstancias Sospechosas de Discriminación', 285.

[39] Jacob R. Gunderson, 'When Does Income Inequality Cause Polarization?', *British Journal of Political Science* 52, no. 3 (14 July 2022): 1315–32, <https://doi.org/10.1017/S0007123421000053>; Torben Iversen and David Soskice, 'Information, Inequality, and Mass Polarization: Ideology in Advanced Democracies', *Comparative Political Studies* 48, no. 13 (1 November 2015): 1781–1813, <https://doi.org/10.1177/0010414015592643>; Sascha Riaz, 'Does Inequality Foster Xenophobia? Evidence from the German Refugee Crisis', *Journal of Ethnic and Migration Studies*, 2023, <https://doi.org/10.1080/1369183X.2023.2259108>; Hernan Winkler, 'The Effect of Income Inequality on Political Polarization: Evidence from European Regions, 2002–2014', *Economics and Politics* 31, no. 2 (1 July 2019): 137–62, <https://doi.org/10.1111/ecpo.12129>.

hate speech.[40] This malleability, in part due to the lack of express links with vulnerability in the legal text, has been described by some authors as a potential risk whereby hate speech offences could be redirected against the same minorities they should be protecting[41]. The risk is accentuated by popularity, so to speak, as ideology is one of the most frequent reasons behind hate incidents, besting even racism in 2020[42].

Even when aptly aimed, there is still a significant risk of the overinclusion and, consequently, overcriminalisation of forms of communication that, while generally considered distasteful, should still remain within the confines of lawful discourse (which should be the overwhelming majority, under liberal politics). Spanish case law has already provided some high-profile examples of the punishment or judicialisation of music and satire,[43] which is hardly reassuring. Similarly, there is reason to fear that the crime-prevention aims of criminal law could be severely undermined if this type of case grew in

---

40 Case in point, the already agitated political debate between the left-wing government in force and the right-wing opposition has reached new heights with the possible judicialisation of some unsavoury declarations of the far-right leadership directed at political adversaries as a form of hate speech. This is not the only case, however, and recent history has provided examples of hate speech accusations across the political spectrum (in fact, the same far-right political party 'Vox' has a pretty open stance when it pushes legal action towards the alleged use of hate speech against them, as can be seen in their webpage: <https://www.voxespana.es/noticias/vox-querella-ser-delito-sentimientos-religiosos-pedir-dinamite-valle-caidos-20220704>). Whatever the empirical situation may be, this clearly exemplifies the lack of clarity of the regulation, as well as the unhealthy levels of verbal aggression in the political realm, which together have provided ample ground for "lawfare" tactics (interestingly enough, in this context of political tension, the term "lawfare" itself has reached significant popularity in Spanish media outlets). Ana María Pascual, 'La Fiscalía Del Supremo Estudiará La Denuncia Del PSOE Contra Abascal Por Delito de Odio', *Público*, 13 December 2023, <https://www.publico.es/politica/fiscalia-supremo-estudiara-denuncia-psoe-abascal-delito-odio.html>.

41 Correcher Mira, 'Discurso Del Odio y Minorías: Redefiniendo La Libertad de Expresión'; Fuentes Osorio, 'El Odio Como Delito'.

42 Landa Gorostiza, 'El Delito de Incitación al Odio (Artículo 510 Cp): Quo Vadis', no. 30.

43 Patricia Tapia Ballesteros, 'La Especial Vulnerabilidad de La Víctima Por Razón de La Discapacidad o Enfermedad', in *La Protección de Las Víctimas Especialmente Vulnerables. Aspectos Penales, Procesales y Político-Criminales*, ed. Clara Moya Guillem and Dyango Bonsignore Fouquet (Valencia: Tirant lo Blanch, 2023), 286–87.

number, as institutional legitimacy seems at odds with cyclical scandal. From the perspective of a criminal policy aimed at protecting vulnerable groups, if nothing else, this is highly undesirable, as it provides fertile ground for public reaction against the judiciary and, ultimately, against the vulnerable groups themselves, reconstructed by some as unfairly prioritised. This poses the risk of turning anti-discrimination legislation on its head when, in an ill-calibrated effort to protect vulnerable groups, it ends up fuelling public opposition against those groups. In this sense, clearer and better regulation, from a technical standpoint, seems to be of paramount importance also from a policy standpoint.

3.2. The vulnerable victim

As suggested earlier, Spanish substantive criminal law does not have a unitary approach towards the protection of vulnerable victims. Here, we have opted for a two-pronged description, with the first aspect being the protection of vulnerable groups against discrimination through hate crimes and hate speech legislation. The second aspect, which we will now turn to, concerns the protection provided to individual victims in a position of vulnerability. This has been executed mainly through the proliferation of aggravating circumstances that, while not fully homogenous, convey a similar purpose and approach.

Some examples of this have been provided above for several countries and, as shown, there is notable similarity between them, especially in cases such as Spain, France, and Belgium, where regulation has been more prolific. In the case of Spain, this regulatory technique was already present at the inception of the current Criminal Code and, with time, aggravating circumstances related to 'particularly vulnerable victims' grew in number and disseminated. However, the protection of the vulnerable victim was not (is not) universally applicable to every criminal offence. Rather, it has become an archipelago of sorts: it can be found associated with many offences as a specific aggravation, but it leaves lots of empty space in between too, with many crimes left outside of the realm of vulnerability protection. This description seems applicable to the French and Belgian examples as well.

The historical evolution of such aggravating circumstances is interesting from a conceptual perspective too, as the prevailing wording up until recently was based on a selection of protected characteristics (such as age, illness, or disability) that served to identify the vulnerable victim. However, these lists functioned as *numerus clausus*, implicitly associating vulnerability to particular groups (the young, the elderly…) while excluding the rest. These groups were usually different from those protected by anti-discrimination regulations, as the rationale seemed different too: it is a vulnerability akin to defencelessness that seems at play here, which is different from the vulnerability of discriminated groups and, to some extent, strictly specific to the type of crime and the circumstances of its unravelling[44].

This notion of vulnerability (which comes from an interpretation *de lege lata*, not a legal definition of any kind)[45] has remained largely consistent, though the approach has significantly changed and, in its present form, most of these aggravating circumstances include some form of open clause. As illustrated earlier by Article 180.1, the sentence for the corresponding sexual offence will be aggravated when committed against someone in a situation of particular vulnerability due to their 'age, illness, disability or any other circumstance'. In this case, this could imply a very significant increase, depending on the type of sexual offence directed at the victim: even in a non-violent form, a sex crime punished with one to four years of imprisonment grows to a range of two to eight years, effectively duplicating the upper and lower limits and thus the potential time served in prison. The severity of the aggravation according to the law is nevertheless offence-specific most of the time, which produces an inconsistent picture overall. For instance, when aggravating the act of stalking (Article 172 *ter* 1), the particular vulnerability

---

44 Dyango Bonsignore Fouquet, 'Bases Teóricas y Aspectos Político-Criminales Acerca de La Vulnerabilidad', in *La Protección de Las Víctimas Especialmente Vulnerables. Aspectos Penales, Procesales y Político-Criminales*, ed. Clara Moya Guillem and Dyango Bonsignore Fouquet (Valencia: Tirant lo Blanch, 2023), 55; Moya Guillem, 'La Protección Penal de Las Víctimas Vulnerables. Pautas Interpretativas y Propuestas de Mejora', 310; Clara Moya Guillem and Carmen Durán Silva, 'La Inconsistente Presunción de Fragilidad de Las Víctimas Menores En El Derecho Penal (Sustantivo y Procesal). A Propósito de La Ley Orgánica 8/2021', *InDret* 2022, no. 1 (2022): 418–19, <https://doi.org/10.31009/InDret.2022.i1.10>.

45 There is also support from the case law. Most clearly, the Supreme Court has defined the type of vulnerability here analysed as a concept that should be understood from the perspective of the "subjective fragility" of the victim (reference: STS 677/2022, 4 July 2022). For an in-depth analysis see Moya Guillem, 'La Protección Penal de Las Víctimas Vulnerables. Pautas Interpretativas y Propuestas de Mejora', 306–8.

of the victim, although defined in the same way as above, only determines a rise in the lower limit of the imposable sentence. We thus end up going from a possible range of three months to two years of imprisonment, to six months to two years when the victim is particularly vulnerable. Paying attention to comparable cases confirms that, while the wording of the law has become increasingly homogeneous, the associated punishment remains largely inconsistent and without any discernible pattern or justification for the differences.

Going back to conceptual considerations, the introduction of open clauses when defining the vulnerable victim is of great significance, as it has several relevant consequences, both theoretical and practical. The reference to 'any other circumstance' has the effect of a) rendering redundant the remaining criteria for vulnerability, such as age or illness, as those become nothing but examples of circumstances of vulnerability, necessarily *inter alia*. As such, they can be understood as an emphatic reminder to the court, but not much else. Related to this, b) tying vulnerability to an indeterminate reference can be expected to imply a more fine-grained and individualised approach to vulnerability. As 'classes' are rendered less determinant in favour of 'circumstances', the courts will have to make an effort to examine such circumstances in detail and justify their contribution to the vulnerability of the victim. This is different from the tendency to over-rely on vulnerability labels[46] to produce semi-automatic decisions based on cursory or formalistic assessment of vulnerability, as happens on occasion,[47] although it is unclear whether the courts will embrace these possibilities. Implicit in this discussion is also c) the fact that open clauses also help dispel, or at least mitigate, the fears of collectivism or identitarianism raised by some authors[48] against perceived shifts in criminal law from the abstract-individualistic model of the citizen to the differential protection of collectives (based on their lobbying capabilities or any other implicit or explicit cause). Paying attention to circumstances of vulnerability leads more easily into the examination of how they interact in the specific situation of the individual (and away from

46 Luna, 'Elucidating the Concept of Vulnerability : Layers Not Labels'.
47 Moya Guillem, 'La Especial Vulnerabilidad Como Circunstancia Agravante. Resultados de Una Investigación Sobre La Jurisprudencia Penal Española', 23.2
48 Díez Ripollés, 'Alegato Contra Un Derecho Penal Sexual Identitario'; Díez Ripollés, 'Los Colectivos Identitarios y La Tutela Penal'.

generalisation), in a similar fashion to intersectional analysis[49]. Lastly, d) this opens the door to more nuanced constructions of vulnerability, allowing for higher diversity and sensibility with the factors that, taken together, end up making someone particularly vulnerable to the victimisation of crime. Evidence of this is still scarce, although it suggests that open clauses have allowed courts to consider peculiar situations that are not specifically mentioned by the law, such as inebriation, pregnancy or living in isolation, as manifestations of vulnerability[50].

4. Concluding remarks about vulnerability and criminal policy

As we have seen, the protection of vulnerable individuals and groups has expanded notably in recent times. Although this can be considered broadly positive, certain issues can still be raised to elicit further reflection.

For instance, some technical difficulties arise in the Spanish regulation regarding the appropriate fitting of the 'particularly vulnerable victim' aggravation with other instruments that convey a power asymmetry between offender and victim. Such is the case with the aggravating circumstance of 'premeditation' (a somewhat loose translation for *alevosía*), as well as others such as abuses of power, trust or authority. This might be a relevant factor to explain the why some criminal codes do not contain vulnerability clauses, as they could appear as redundant when the power asymmetry is already accounted for by various instruments. Should that be the case, it remains unclear whether 'regulationist' countries such as Spain are overcriminalising, or whether it is the 'abstentionist' side that is failing to protect vulnerable victims.

---

49 Crenshaw, 'Demarginalizing the Intersection of Race and Sex: A Black Feminist Critique of Antidiscrimination Doctrine, Feminist Theory and Antiracist Politics'; Crenshaw, 'Mapping the Margins: Intersectionality, Identity Politics, and Violence against Women of Color'; Christian Henrik Alexander Kuran *et al.*, 'Vulnerability and Vulnerable Groups from an Intersectionality Perspective', *International Journal of Disaster Risk Reduction* 50 (1 November 2020), <https://doi.org/10.1016/j.ijdrr.2020.101826>.

50 Moya Guillem, 'La Especial Vulnerabilidad Como Circunstancia Agravante. Resultados de Una Investigación Sobre La Jurisprudencia Penal Española', 30.

To make things more complicated, the Spanish Criminal Code also makes occasional use of the wording 'abusing a situation of vulnerability', although the prevailing criterion seems to be that aggravations based on abuse are different to those based on the 'particular vulnerability' of the victim. This is a relevant regulatory debate for the European legislators, as there are examples of both technical approaches elsewhere. For instance, the French Criminal Code aggravates rape when committed on a particularly vulnerable victim, while requiring an abuse of vulnerability in the aforementioned 'abuse of ignorance or weakness', or as one of the manifestations of human trafficking. The Belgian case also provides examples of both: aggravating hostage-taking when committed on minors or vulnerable individuals, while requiring an abuse of such vulnerability in cases of forced prostitution or mendicity. This is not to say that this distinction has no merit or rationale, but simply to underline visible trends and their underlying risks if regulated without sufficient care.

More broadly, the lack of conceptual clarity and legal determination is an overarching tendency that has been criticised time and time again in the Spanish criminal justice system. Turning to vulnerable groups, special care should have been taken to avoid jurisdictional uncertainty and, above all, the risks of deviation and co-opting that are particularly present in anti-discrimination offences such as hate speech. Similarly, some grounds for discrimination, such as 'ideology', although completely sound at face value, might be a bit too malleable and indeterminate to fit the standards of criminal law.

Furthermore, vulnerability protection should not become a playground for struggles for labels, nor foster spurious competition over which stakeholder can appear as the greater victim. This is an increasingly important criminal policy precaution, as recent decades have shown that the (necessary) recognition of harm and victimisation has been swiftly understood as having significant political value. This is no ill in itself, but experience shows that the needs of victims can all-too-quickly be reduced to symbolic measures that bring high returns for the occasional victim's advocate, but not nearly as much for the actual victims themselves[51]. Vulnerability is rooted in needs

---

51 Tom Daems, '¿Tienen Las Sociedades Las Víctimas Que Se Merecen? Un Estudio Sociológico Sobre La Victimación', *InDret* 2 (2020): 363, <https://doi.org/10.31009/InDret.2020.i2.10>; Díez Ripollés, 'El Nuevo Modelo Penal de La Seguridad Ciudadana', 10–11.

and rights and, as such, it demands a response in terms of needs and rights, not Manichean discourse and ritual punitiveness.

This, in turn, is related to another important policy lesson that can be derived from criminological thought. There seems to be significant evidence pointing to the fact that offenders and victims are usually in proximity, with victimisation positively correlated with offending[52]. Should this be the case, particularly in 'ordinary' criminal activity, then one could start to see that much crime and victimisation could have a common denominator, precisely, in vulnerability. This is hardly a novel idea within the sociology of crime and criminal justice, and yet, contemporary discussion over vulnerable victims, particularly in the legal field, has tended to overlook this basic consideration, turning, perhaps unwittingly, to the classical opposition between malicious offender and innocent victim.

This is not to say that no crime involves exploitative relationships among individuals, but rather that offenders and victims do not exist in a vacuum. Wide ranging sources of vulnerability are both capable of pressuring some individuals into crime and exposing them to victimhood, even to a degree that would almost make them interchangeable[53]. We should, at this point, remember the interconnection between criminal 'risk' and criminogenic 'needs' in the influential framework provided by the work of Andrews and Bonta.[54]

It is for this very reason that one should be cautious of trying to 'solve' vulnerability (only) through criminal law, as it is usually ill-equipped to provide integrative and long-lasting solutions. This is not to say that we should dismiss this entirely, far from it, but rather that we should actively oppose the frequent kind of 'penal fetishism' that assumes victims are adequately attended through the severe punishment of offenders. This assumption has

---

52 Mark T. Berg and Christopher J. Schreck, 'The Meaning of the Victim-Offender Overlap for Criminological Theory and Crime Prevention Policy', *Annual Review of Criminology* 5 (2022): 277–97; Stephen Farrall and Adam Calverley, *Understanding Desistance from Crime. Theoretical Directions in Resettlement and Rehabilitation* (Nueva York: Open University Press, 2006), 170.

53 Paul Rock, 'Theoretical Perspectives on Victimisation', in *Handbook of Victims and Victimology*, ed. Sandra Walklate (Abingdon, Oxon: Routledge, 2018), 44.

54 Donald Arthur Andrews and James Bonta, *The Psychology of Criminal Conduct* (New Providence: LexisNexis, 2010).

been challenged by victimological research[55] and found to be only to the benefit of those *outside* the conflict.[56]

I would be tempted to argue, as a final remark, that most stories lying behind the types of crime and victimisation that feed the prisons are more akin to tragedy than to epic narrative. This is actually well-attuned to a kind of sensibility and reflection that places vulnerability unapologetically at the forefront. This type of perspective seems most necessary and promising, for as long as criminal justice systems maintain their current form and demographics, they will remain a subsystem intimately related to the management of the most vulnerable segments of society. For such a system to be rational and humane, attending to the needs of all those involved in a criminal event can be expected to produce better results than sterile punishment and exclusion.

Bibliography

OHCHR. (2010). *Minority Rights: International Standards and Guidance for Implementation*. United Nations.

Andrews, D. A., & Bonta, J. (2010). *The Psychology of Criminal Conduct* (5th ed.). LexisNexis.

Berg, M. T., & Schreck, C. J. (2022). The Meaning of the Victim-Offender Overlap for Criminological Theory and Crime Prevention Policy. *Annual Review of Criminology*, *5*, 277–297.

Blanco Cordero, I. (2023). La menor edad como fundamento de la agravación de la pena: estudio crítico de los tipos agravados por razón de la menor edad y la especial vulnerabilidad. In C. Moya Guillem (Dir.) & D. Bonsignore Fouquet (Coord.), *La protección de las víctimas especialmente vulnerables. Aspectos penales, procesales y político-criminales* (pp. 121–160). Tirant lo Blanch.

Blanco Cordero, I., & Doval Pais, A. (2013). La extranjería como factor de discriminación de los condenados a penas de prisión. In L. R. Ruiz Rodríguez (Dir.), *Crimen organizado y extranjería en España y Marruecos* (pp. 51–84). Tirant lo Blanch.

---

[55] Leah E Daigle, *Victimology: The Essentials.* (SAGE Publications, 2018), 87; Meredith Rossner, 'Restorative Justice and Victims of Crime', in *Handbook of Victims and Victimology*, ed. Sandra Walklate (Routledge, 2018), 230.

[56] Cigüela Sola, 'Populismo Penal y Justicia Paralela: Un Análisis Político-Cultural', 21.

Bonsignore, D. (2023). The dangerous individual in a time of migration: Periculum, dominium and dangerousness. In V. Guillén-Nieto, A. Doval Pais, & D. Stein (Eds.), *From Fear to Hate: Legal-Linguistic Perspectives on Migration* (pp. 23–47). De Gruyter. <https://doi.org/10.1515/9783110789157-002>.

Bonsignore Fouquet, D. (2023). Bases teóricas y aspectos político-criminales acerca de la vulnerabilidad. In C. Moya Guillem (Dir.) & D. Bonsignore Fouquet (Coord.), *La protección de las víctimas especialmente vulnerables. Aspectos penales, procesales y político-criminales* (pp. 19–64). Tirant lo Blanch.

Brandariz García, J. Á., & Fernández Bessa, C. (2017). 'Perfiles' de deportabilidad: El sesgo del sistema de control migratorio desde la perspectiva de la nacionalidad. *Estudios Penales y Criminológicos*, *XXXVII*, 307–347.

Butler, J. (2006). *Vida precaria: El poder del duelo y la violencia*. Paidós.

Cámara Arroyo, S. (2017). El concepto de delitos de odio y su comisión a través del discurso. Especial referencia al conflicto con la libertad de expresión. *Anuario de Derecho Penal y Ciencias Penales*, *70*(1), 139–225. <https://dialnet.unirioja.es/servlet/articulo?codigo=6930585>.

Chozas Alonso, J. M. (2015). El nuevo estatuto de la víctima de los delitos en el proceso penal. In J. M. Chozas Alonso (Dir.), *Los sujetos protagonistas del proceso penal* (pp. 193–261). Dykinson.

Cigüela Sola, J. (2020). Populismo penal y justicia paralela: un análisis político-cultural. *Revista Electrónica de Ciencia Penal y Criminología*, *22*(12), 1–40. <http://criminet.ugr.es/recpc>.

Correcher Mira, J. (2020). Discurso del odio y minorías: redefiniendo la libertad de expresión. *Teoría y Derecho*, *28*, 166–191. <https://doi.org/doi.org/10.36151/td.2020.016>.

Crenshaw, K. (1989). Demarginalizing the Intersection of Race and Sex: A Black Feminist Critique of Antidiscrimination Doctrine, Feminist Theory and Antiracist Politics. *The University of Chicago Legal Forum*, *140*, 139–167.

Crenshaw, K. (1991). Mapping the Margins: Intersectionality, Identity Politics, and Violence against Women of Color. *Source: Stanford Law Review*, *43*(6), 1241–1299.

Daems, T. (2020). ¿Tienen las sociedades las víctimas que se merecen? Un estudio sociológico sobre la victimación. *InDret*, *2*, 350–372. <https://doi.org/10.31009/InDret.2020.i2.10>.

Daigle, L. E. (2018). *Victimology: The essentials.* SAGE Publications.

De la Cuesta Aguado, P. M. (2019). Sobre la asistencia a víctimas de delitos más allá del Estatuto de la Víctima. *Estudios Penales y Criminológicos, 39*, 403–454.

De la Mata Barranco, N. J., Pérez Machío, A. I., & Berasaluce Gerrkagoitia, L. (2023). La regulación del delito de trata de seres humanos y la protección de las víctimas atendiendo a las personas menores de edad no acompañadas y el anteproyecto de la ley de trata. In N. J. de la Mata Barranco, A. I. Pérez Machío (Dirs.), L. Berasaluze Gerrikagoitia, & H. Colomo Iraola (Coords.), *Personas vulnerables y tutela penal* (pp. 337–371). Aranzadi.

Díez Ripollés, J. L. (2004). El nuevo modelo penal de la seguridad ciudadana. *Revista Electrónica de Ciencia Penal y Criminología, 06*(03), 1–34.

Díez Ripollés, J. L. (2019). Alegato contra un derecho penal sexual identitario. *Revista Electrónica de Ciencia Penal y Criminología, 21*(10), 1–29.

Díez Ripollés, J. L. (2024). Los colectivos identitarios y la tutela penal. *Revista Electrónica de Ciencia Penal y Criminología, 26–01*, 1–46.

Doval Pais, A. (2023). Revisión del papel de la agravante de discriminación (Article 22.4ª CP) en la protección de la igualdad y la no discriminación. In A. Doval Pais & E. Gutiérrez Pérez (Dirs.), *Manifestaciones de desigualdad en el sistema de justicia penal. Volumen I* (pp. 219–262). Aranzadi.

Durán Silva, C. (2023). La especial vulnerabilidad de la víctima en el Derecho Penal Procesal español. In C. Moya Guillem (Dir.) & D. Bonsignore Fouquet (Coord.), *La protección de las víctimas especialmente vulnerables. Aspectos penales, procesales y político-criminales* (pp. 245–281). Tirant lo Blanch.

Échappé, O. (2023). Les personnes vulnérables en droit français. *L'Anée Canonique, 63*, 7–21. <https://doi.org/10.3917/cano.063.0007>.

Farrall, S., & Calverley, A. (2006). *Understanding desistance from crime. Theoretical directions in resettlement and rehabilitation*. Open University Press.

Fineman, M. A. (2008). The vulnerable subject: Anchoring equality in the human condition. *Yale Journal of Law and Feminism, 20*(1), 1–23.

Fineman, M. A. (2013). Equality, autonomy, and the vulnerable subject in Law and politics. In M. A. Fineman & A. Grear (Eds.), *Vulnerability. Reflections on a New Ethical Foundation for Law and Politics* (pp. 13–28). Routledge.

Fuentes Osorio, J. L. (2017). El odio como delito. *Revista Electrónica de Ciencia Penal y Criminología, 19*, 1–52.

Gunderson, J. R. (2022). When Does Income Inequality Cause Polarization? *British Journal of Political Science*, *52*(3), 1315–1332. <https://doi.org/10.1017/S0007123421000053>.

Hobbes, T. (1980). *Leviatán* (2nd ed.). Editora Nacional.

Iversen, T., & Soskice, D. (2015). Information, Inequality, and Mass Polarization: Ideology in Advanced Democracies. *Comparative Political Studies*, 48(13), 1781–1813. <https://doi.org/10.1177/0010414015592643>.

Kuran, C. H. A., Morsut, C., Kruke, B. I., Krüger, M., Segnestam, L., Orru, K., Nævestad, T. O., Airola, M., Keränen, J., Gabel, F., Hansson, S., & Torpan, S. (2020). Vulnerability and vulnerable groups from an intersectionality perspective. *International Journal of Disaster Risk Reduction*, *50*. <https://doi.org/10.1016/j.ijdrr.2020.101826>.

Landa Gorostiza, J. M. (2018). *Los delitos de odio. Artículos 510 y 22.4º CP 1995*. Tirant lo Blanch.

Landa Gorostiza, J. M. (2020). Delitos de odio y estándares internacionales: una visión crítica a contra corriente. *Revista Electrónica de Ciencia Penal y Criminología*, 22, 1–34.

Landa Gorostiza, J. M. (2021). El delito de incitación al odio (artículo 510 CP): Quo Vadis. *Azafea: Revista de Filosofía*, 23, 57–81. <https://doi.org/10.14201/azafea2021235781>.

Luna, F. (2009). Elucidating the Concept of Vulnerability : Layers Not Labels. *International Journal of Feminist Approaches to Bioethics*, 2(1), 121–139.

Moya Guillem, C. (2020). La especial vulnerabilidad como circunstancia agravante. Resultados de una investigación sobre la jurisprudencia penal española. *Revista de Derecho Penal y Criminología, 3ª Época*(24), 13–58.

Moya Guillem, C. (2023). La protección penal de las víctimas vulnerables. Pautas interpretativas y propuestas de mejora. In C. Moya Guillem (Dir.) & D. Bonsignore Fouquet (Coord.), *La protección de las víctimas especialmente vulnerables. Aspectos penales, procesales y político-criminales* (pp. 283–318). Tirant lo Blanch.

Moya Guillem, C., & Durán Silva, C. (2022). La inconsistente presunción de fragilidad de las víctimas menores en el Derecho penal (sustantivo y procesal). A propósito de la Ley Orgánica 8/2021. *InDret*, *2022*(1), 414–451. <https://doi.org/10.31009/InDret.2022.i1.10>.

Moya Guillem, C., & Sandoval, J. C. (2023). La regulación de los ataques contra víctimas vulnerables en los delitos contra la vida. Otro caso de irracionalidad legislativa. In A. Doval Pais & E. Gutiérrez Pérez (Dirs.), *Manifestaciones de desigualdad en el sistema de justicia penal. Volumen I* (pp. 263–307). Aranzadi.

Nussbaum, M. C. (2006). *El ocultamiento de lo humano. Repugnancia, vergüenza y ley*. Katz.

OSCE/ODIHR. (2022). *Hate Crime Laws: A Practical Guide*. Office for Democratic Institutions and Human Rights.

Pascual, A. M. (13 December 2023). La Fiscalía del Supremo estudiará la denuncia del PSOE contra Abascal por delito de odio. *Público*. <https://www.publico.es/politica/fiscalia-supremo-estudiara-denuncia-psoe-abascal-delito-odio.html>.

Peñaranda Ramos, E. (2022). Delitos de odio y Derecho penal de la culpabilidad. In J. A. Díaz López (Dir.), *Reflexiones académicas sobre delitos de odio* (pp. 7–21). Observatorio Español del Racismo y la Xenofobia.

Pérez González, S., & de la Mata Barranco, N. J. (2023). Las circunstancias diferenciales y de vulnerabilidad del sujeto pasivo en el Código Penal. In N. J. de la Mata Barranco, A. I. Pérez Machío (Dirs.), L. Berasaluze Gerrikagoitia, & H. Colomo Iraola (Coords.), *Personas vulnerables y tutela penal* (pp. 19–72). Aranzadi.

Pratt, J. (2007). *Penal Populism*. Routledge.

Prittwitz, C. (1999). The Resurrection of the Victim in Penal Theory. *Buffalo Criminal Law Review*, *3*(1), 109–129. <https://doi.org/10.1525/nclr.1999.3.1.109>.

Riaz, S. (2023). Does inequality foster xenophobia? Evidence from the German refugee crisis. *Journal of Ethnic and Migration Studies*. <https://doi.org/10.1080/1369183X.2023.2259108>.

Roca Agapito, L. (2012). Análisis del nuevo régimen jurídico-económico de las víctimas del terrorismo. *Diario La Ley*, *7776*, 1–15.

Rock, P. (2018). Theoretical perspectives on victimisation. In S. Walklate (Ed.), *Handbook of Victims and Victimology* (2nd ed., pp. 30–58). Routledge.

Rogers, W., MacKenzie, C., & Dodds, S. (2012). Why bioethics needs a concept of vulnerability. *International Journal of Feminist Approaches to Bioethics*, *5*(2), 11–38. <https://doi.org/10.1353/ijf.2012.0024>.

Rossner, M. (2018). Restorative justice and victims of crime. In S. Walklate (Ed.), *Handbook of Victims and Victimology* (pp. 229–246). Routledge.

Ruiz Rivera, N. (2012). La definición y medición de la vulnerabilidad social. Un enfoque normativo. *Investigaciones Geográficas*, *77*, 63–74.

Sánchez-Moraleda Vilches, N. (2023). Mayores vulnerables y Derecho penal: una aproximación a la circunstancia agravante de especial vulnerabilidad por razón de la (avanzada) edad. In C. Moya Guillem (Dir.) & D. Bonsignore Fouquet (Coord.), *La protección de las víctimas especialmente vulnerables. Aspectos penales, procesales y político-criminales* (pp. 161–204). Tirant lo Blanch.

Tamarit Sumalla, J. M. (2015). Los derechos de las víctimas. In J. M. Tamarit Sumalla (Dir.), *El Estatuto de las Víctimas de Delitos. Comentarios a la Ley 4/2015* (pp. 7–60). Tirant lo Blanch.

Tapia Ballesteros, P. (2021). El discurso de odio del Article 510.1.a) del Código Penal español: la ideología como un Caballo de Troya entre las circunstancias sospechosas de discriminación. *Política Criminal*, 16(31), 284–320.

Tapia Ballesteros, P. (2023). La especial vulnerabilidad de la víctima por razón de la discapacidad o enfermedad. In C. Moya Guillem (Dir.) & D. Bonsignore Fouquet (Coord.), *La protección de las víctimas especialmente vulnerables. Aspectos penales, procesales y político-criminales* (pp. 205–220). Tirant lo Blanch.

Timmer, A. (2013). A quiet revolution: Vulnerability in the European Court of Human Rights. In M. A. Fineman & A. Grear (Eds.), *Vulnerability. Reflections on a New Ethical Foundation for Law and Politics* (pp. 147–170). Routledge.

Tomás-Valiente Lanuza, C. (2021). El interés de la víctima en la pena del delito. Algunas reflexiones. In L. Pozuelo Pérez & D. Rodríguez Horcajo (Dirs.), *El papel de la víctima en el Derecho Penal* (pp. 31–72). Boletín Oficial del Estado.

Turner, B. S. (2006). Vulnerability and human rights. In *Vulnerability and Human Rights*. Pennsylvania State University Press.

Varona Gómez, D. (2011). Medios de comunicación y punitivismo. *InDret: Revista Para El Análisis Del Derecho*, *1*, 1–34.

Villacampa Estiarte, C. (2011). La nueva Directiva europea relativa a la prevención y la lucha contra la trata de seres humanos y a la protección de las víctimas ¿Cambio de rumbo de la política de la Unión en materia de trata de seres humanos? *Revista Electrónica de Ciencia Penal y Criminología*, *13–14*, 1–52.

Villacampa Estiarte, C. (2023). Acerca del Anteproyecto de Ley Orgánica Integral contra la Trata y la Explotación de Seres Humanos. *Diario LA LEY*, *10267*, 1–14.

Winkler, H. (2019). The effect of income inequality on political polarization: Evidence from European regions, 2002–2014. *Economics and Politics*, *31*(2), 137–162. <https://doi.org/10.1111/ecpo.12129>.

Rights of Vulnerable Groups in EU Environmental Law

Ewa Radecka, Gabriel Radecki ***

Abstract: The link between the state of the environment and human health is undeniable. Environmental pollution is responsible for around 7 million premature deaths worldwide. In Poland alone, 46,000 people die annually due to the poor quality of one of the environmental components – air. In general, children and pregnant women, the elderly, certain occupational groups, people with disabilities, and people with chronic medical conditions are more vulnerable to health stressors such as extreme heat, floods, poor air quality and other environmental-related events. It is necessary to determine whether the above mentioned individuals or groups have the tools to protect their fundamental human right to a 'clean, healthy environment in an appropriate state of balance' (Resolution 48/13 of the UN Human Rights Council of 8 October 2021 on the human right to a clean, healthy and sustainable environment).

The chapter will focus on issues related to the rights of public participation as an instrument for protecting the vulnerable, particularly with the participation of environmental organisations as representatives of these people's interests in administrative and court proceedings. It is not uncommon that vulnerable people cannot effectively assert their rights in environmental matters and require support from environmental organisations. Importantly, sometimes even these organisations do not have sufficient instruments to protect human rights (an example is the inability to challenge forest management plans – see the judgment of the Court of Justice of the EU of 2 March 2023, case C-432/21; the issue of the legal standing of an environmental protection organisation in a vehicle approval case – see: judgment of the Court of Justice of the EU of 8 November 2022, case C-873/19; as the last reference to the amendment to the Czech Nature and Landscape Protection Act). Hence, it is necessary to identify the reasons for this state of affairs.

Keywords: environmental, environmental organisations, public participation

* Ph.D., Associate Professor, Faculty of Law and Administration of the University of Silesia, Poland. ORCID: 0000-0003-4669-3327.

** Ph.D., Associate Professor, Faculty of Law and Administration of the University of Silesia, Poland. ORCID: 0000-0003-1311-5635.

1. Introduction

The environment is a common and indivisible good and its protection is an important part of public life. The Treaty on EU[1] explicitly states that the Union 'shall work for the sustainable development of Europe based on balanced economic growth (…) and a high level of protection and improvement of the quality of the environment'. The environment can be subject to legal obligations (e.g. prescribed or prohibited behaviour of specific addressees towards the environment). It is possible to speak of the 'empowerment' of the environment as a good protected by law, making it possible to protect the common interest directly and not only by protecting individual interests. However, this direct protection is not irrelevant to those individual interests; it even fulfils these interests, as it contributes to improving the living conditions of individuals who, after all, function in the environment, concentrating all their activities, especially living and working in it. This also, or even primarily, applies to those individuals who are classed as vulnerable. These are often not in a position to protect their individual interests themselves, including those relating to the environment, i.e. in practice their daily environment, which determines their health, comfort and thus their ability to overcome constraints affecting their weaker societal position. Thus, environmental protection becomes an instrument or a factor that is indispensable for equalising opportunities, thereby acquiring a social value. This is the case irrespective of the fact that the law treats humans and their environment as separate subjects of regulation. For example, one can cite Article 3(49) of the Polish Environmental Protection Law of 27 April 2001, in which pollution is defined as an emission that may harm human health or the environment.

The state of the environment and human health are inextricably linked. Air pollution alone is considered one of the biggest environmental threats to human health, resulting in an estimated 7 million premature deaths every

---

1 Consolidated version, Journal of Laws Device EU C 202 of 7 June 2016. <https://eur-lex.europa.eu/resource.html?uri=cellar:9e8d52e1-2c70-11e6-b497-01aa75ed71a1.0018.01/DOC_2&format=PDF> (accessed on 20 December 2023).

year.[2] In Poland, a country with some of the most polluted air in the EU, 46,000 people die prematurely each year due to poor air quality.[3] Pressures on the environment influence such things as biodiversity loss, ocean acidification, land degradation and water scarcity. Environmental impacts pose especially urgent threats to vulnerable populations.[4] These hazards can include natural hazards such as flooding, earthquakes, events related to climate change such as droughts, wildfires and rises in sea level, as well as air and water pollution. Understanding population vulnerability is critical to ensuring that the needs of vulnerable population groups are considered in the law-making process. This enables hazards to be prevented where possible, or at least their impact minimised.[5]

The chapter attempts to answer the question of whether environmental protection law solutions regarding public participation can constitute an instrument for protecting the vulnerable. These solutions are intended to provide society, of which the vulnerable are a part, with an opportunity to express their position on environmental issues, including – to the extent limited to ecological organisations – in proceedings where representatives of society participate as parties with a full spectrum of procedural rights, including in particular, those involving appealing against decisions. The answer to this question requires first considering the specific nature of sensitive entities in the context of the environment and its protection based on environmental protection law, including values and legislative assumptions

---

2 Promoting environmental justice Securing our right to a clean, healthy and sustainable environment through UNDP programming, New York 2022, <https://www.undp.org/sites/g/files/zskgke326/files/2022-06/Environmental%20justice-Guidance%20Note.pdf> (accessed on 20 December 2023).

3 Poland is one of the countries where PM2.5 dust is recorded as having the greatest impact on premature deaths <https://www.eea.europa.eu/en/topics/in-depth/air-pollution?activeAccordion=4268d9b2-6e3b-409b-8b2a-b624c120090d> (accessed on 30 November 2023).

4 <https://gheli.harvard.edu/vulnerability-and-environment> (accessed on 30 November 2023).

5 <https://www.ehinz.ac.nz/indicators/population-vulnerability/what-are-vulnerable-populations/> (accessed on 30 November 2023). Lisa Rygel, David O'Sullivan, Brent Yarnal, "A Method for Constructing a Social Vulnerability Index: An Application to Hurricane Storm Surges in a Developed Country", *Mitigation and Adaptation Strategies for Global Change* 11 (2006): 36–61, <https://doi.org/10.1007/s11027-006-0265-6>.

presented in the preambles of individual legal acts. Then, it is necessary to show selected examples of legal regulations regulating social participation, especially the rights of ecological organisations, along with important matters where social initiative played (or could have played) a key role. This, in turn, will allow appropriate conclusions to be drawn, particularly assessing the effectiveness of the regulations presented.

2. The concept of vulnerable people from an environmental law perspective

For the purposes of this chapter, it is necessary to establish the concept of a 'vulnerable person' in general and in the specific environmental context. Starting from a broad view, as given by Mariano Longo and Vincenzo Lorubbio:[6] following Fineman's work, vulnerability has been thematised in the wide field of social sciences, which has made a relevant semantic turn possible. The Western conception of the paradigmatic legal subject as an abstract, self-sufficient, rational individual, able to control themselves and the environment, has given way to a new model – a concrete, contextualised individual, needing mutuality and support, and connected with the social and natural environment.[7]

Turning to the meaning of a 'vulnerable person' on environmental grounds, several acts can be drawn upon. Worthy of note is the Preamble to the Paris Agreement,[8] which sets out that states should 'respect, promote and consider their respective obligations on human rights, the right to health, the rights of indigenous peoples, local communities, migrants, children, persons with disabilities and people in vulnerable situations and the right to development (…)'. Reference should also be made to the resolution adopted

---

6 Mariano Longo, Vinzenzo Lorubbio, "Ecosystem Vulnerability. New Semantics for International Law", *International Journal for the Semiotics of Law* 36 (2023): 1611–1628.

7 Longo, Lorubbio, Ecosystem…

8 Paris Agreement to the United Nations Framework Convention on Climate Change, done at New York on 9 May 1992, adopted in Paris on 12 December 2015 (Journal of Laws 2017, item 36).

by the Parliamentary Assembly of the Council of Europe[9] in 2021. The groups mentioned in the resolution include women, children, the elderly, sick persons, minorities and the poor. In addition to these, 'vulnerable groups' the European Parliament resolution of 19 May 2021 on the effects of climate change on human rights and the role of environmental defenders on this matter[10] also included people with disabilities and indigenous people.

Furthermore, in order to clarify the vulnerability of these people is in the context of environmental protection, it is helpful to refer to the European Environment Agency's report 'Unequal exposure and unequal impacts: social vulnerability to air pollution, noise and extreme temperatures in Europe' (2019).[11] In the scope under consideration, two of the conclusions formulated in this report in particular should be noted:

- people who are already disadvantaged in socioeconomic terms or, because of their age, are also disproportionately affected by environmental risks,
- there are large regional differences in Europe in terms of where the most disadvantaged regions are located and where pollution is concentrated. Some regions are relatively richer and less polluted, while others are poorer or more disadvantaged, more polluted and more exposed to extreme temperatures.[12]

Further discussion will aim to determine whether vulnerable people have the tools to protect their fundamental human right to a 'clean, healthy environment in a proper state of equilibrium' (UN Human Rights Council

9 Anchoring the right to a healthy environment: need for enhanced action by the Council of Europe. Resolution no. 2396, 29 September 2021. <https://pace.coe.int/en/files/29499/html> (accessed on 30 November 2023).

10 <https://www.europarl.europa.eu/doceo/document/TA-9-2021-0245_EN.html> (accessed on 30 November 2023).

11 <https://www.eea.europa.eu/highlights/protect-vulnerable-citizens> (accessed on 20 December 2023).

12 <https://www.eea.europa.eu/articles/how-do-environmental-hazards-affect> (accessed on 20 December 2023).

Resolution 48/13 of October 8 2021 on the human right to a clean, healthy, and sustainable environment[13]).[14]

3. International standards for public participation, including environmental organisations, in environmental protection. Selected legal bases

The essential legal act regulating this issue is the Convention on access to information, public participation in decision-making and access to justice in environmental matters adopted in Aarhus, on 25 June 1998[15] (hereinafter referred to as Aarhus Convention). According to the preamble of the Aarhus Convention, the powers of members of an interested community are intended to contribute, among other things, to raising awareness of environmental issues, increasing responsibility and openness in decision-making, strengthening public support for environmental decisions, and improving the quality and implementation of decisions.

It is designed to help protect the right of every person of present and future generations to live in an environment suited to their health and well-being. To this end, the convention provides for action in three areas:

a) ensuring public access to environmental information held by the public authorities;
b) fostering public participation in decision-making that affects the environment;
c) extending the conditions of access to justice in environmental matters.

It is worth mentioning that ensuring this public participation in environmental protection in accordance with the three pillars of the Aarhus Convention

---

13 <https://undocs.org/Home/Mobile?FinalSymbol=A%2FHRC%2FRES%2F48%2F13&Language=E&DeviceType=Desktop&LangRequested=False> (accessed on 20 December 2023).

14 See more: Vivien Köböl-Benda, "The current status of the right to the environment in the global international law", *Opolskie Studia Administracyjno-prawne*, vol. 20, 1 (2022): 117–143.

15 Convention adopted in Aarhus on 25 June 1998 on access to information, public participation in decision-making and access to justice in environmental matters, <https://eur-lex.europa.eu/legal-content/PL/TXT/?uri=CELEX%3A02005A0517%2801%29-20061218> (accessed on 30 November 2023).

is an extremely difficult task due to the process of globalisation, which at the beginning of the 21st century led to an increase in environmental degradation at an unprecedented rate and scale.[16]

The Aarhus Convention is a continuation of Principle 1 of the Stockholm Declaration,[17] which states that 'man has the fundamental right to (…) adequate conditions of life in an environment of a quality which makes it possible to live in dignity and well-being. At the same time, he has a solemn responsibility to protect and improve the environment for present and future generations'. It also refers to Principle 10 of the Rio Declaration[18] on Environment and Development, which emphasises that 'environmental issues are best addressed, at the appropriate level, with the participation of all citizens'.

According to Article 2 of the Aarhus Convention, the public is one or more natural or legal persons and, in accordance with national legislation or practice, their associations, organisations or groups. The Aarhus Convention also introduces a definition of the public concerned, which is the part of the public that is or may be affected by or has an interest in environmental decision-making; for the purposes of this definition, NGOs working for the protection of the environment and meeting the requirements under national law are deemed to have an interest. One mechanism for achieving the previously invoked objectives of the Aarhus Convention are the provisions on access to complaints codified in Article 9. Pursuant to Article 9, access to justice covers three categories of acts or omissions by public authorities or private individuals. The most relevant, from the perspective of this text, is expressed in Article 9(3) of the Aarhus Convention, providing access to judicial or other review procedures to challenge the acts and omissions of private individuals and public authorities in violation of environmental law. According to Article 2 of the Directive of the European Parliament and of

16 Magdalena Micińska, *Udział społeczeństwa w ochronie środowiska. Instrumenty administracyjno-prawne*, (Wydawnictwo Adam Marszałek, 2011), 17.

17 Declaration of the United Nations Conference on the Human Environment, 16 June 1972, <http://undocs.org/en/A/CONF.48/14/Rev.1> (accessed on 20 December 2023).

18 Rio Declaration on Environment and Development, 14 June 1992, <http://libr.sejm.gov.pl/tek01/txt/inne/1992.html> (accessed on 20 December 2023).

the Council of 26 May 2003,[19] Member States must ensure that the public is given early and effective opportunities to participate in the preparation and modification or review of the plans or programmes required to be drawn up under the provisions listed in Annex I. To that end, Member States must ensure that e.g. (a) the public is entitled to express comments and opinions when all options are open before decisions on the plans and programmes are made; (b) in making those decisions, due account will be taken of the results of the public participation.

In turn, the Directive of the European Parliament and of the Council of 13 December 2011[20] formulates the general conditions and requirements for the manner in which public participation in environmental decision-making is to take place. According to Article 11 of this directive, members of the public concerned have access to a review procedure before a court of law or another independent and impartial body established by law to challenge the substantive or procedural legality of decisions, acts or omissions subject to the public participation provisions of this directive. However, the detailed arrangements for consulting the public concerned are left to the legislative competence of the Member States, and the scope for regulatory discretion is quite wide.

4. The implementation of the principles of public participation in the national legal orders

The degree to which public participation is ensured, and thus also the resulting possibilities of protecting the rights of the vulnerable, can only be considered on the basis of individual national legal orders providing for specific legal solutions in the area under consideration. This is the only way to move

19 Directive 2003/35/EC of the European Parliament and of the Council of 26 May 2003 providing for public participation in respect of the drawing up of certain plans and programmes relating to the environment and amending with regard to public participation and access to justice Council Directives 85/337/EEC, <https://eur-lex.europa.eu/legal-content/PL/TXT/?uri=CELEX%3A02003L0035-20161231> (accessed on 20 December 2023).

20 Directive 2011/92/EU of the European Parliament and of the Council of 13 December 2011 on the assessment of the effects of certain public and private projects on the environment, <https://eur-lex.europa.eu/legal-content/PL/TXT/?uri=CELEX%3A02011L0092-20140515> (accessed on 20 December 2023).

from abstract general observations to a more specific level and to trace which rights are available and who is entitled to them in individual cases. This, in turn, makes it possible to answer the question of the effectiveness of the legal instruments and what objectives they can achieve, especially whether they adequately serve to protect the values recognised by the legal system, such as the environment and the safeguarding of the interests or rights of vulnerable entities. At the same time, of course, one must not lose sight of the impact on each national legal order of international rules, especially those that are applied directly or require implementation.

In this context, it is important to note that the impact can be twofold for the EU Member States that have ratified the Aarhus Convention. Indeed, the Aarhus Convention was incorporated into the European legal order by Council Decision No. 2005/370/EC of 17 February 2005, which opens up space to take it into account when interpreting EU legislation.[21] European law, which has to be adjusted to the Aarhus Convention as a result of its ratification by the EU, is subject to implementation, the direction and framework of which are determined not only by the legislation itself, but also by the case law of the European Court of Justice and the position of the other EU institutions.[22]

An example illustrating this observation is the Polish Act on the Provision of Information on the Environment and its Protection, Public Participation in Environmental Protection and Environmental Impact Assessment of 3 October 2008.[23] This act was adopted as a result of the infringement procedure initiated by a letter from the European Commission to the Polish Minister of Foreign Affairs, pointing out the overly restrictive requirements of the law in force at the time with regard to public participation; more specifically, it concerned the possibility for environmental organisations to

---

21 Janusz Niczyporuk, "Organizacja ekologiczna w ogólnym postępowaniu administracyjnym", in: *Ocena modelu prawnego organizacji ochrony środowiska w Polsce i na Słowacji*, ed. Stanisław Pieprzny, Jerzy Stelmasiak, Elżbiera Ura (RS Druk, 2021), 374.

22 Journal of Laws 2023, item. 1094. See also Bartosz Draniewicz, "Uprawnienia organizacji ekologicznych w postępowaniach wymagających udziału społeczeństwa", *Monitor Prawniczy* 1 (2011): 13.

23 Bartosz Draniewicz, "Udział organizacji ekologicznych w postępowaniu niewymagającym udziału społeczeństwa. Glosa do wyroku WSA w Krakowie z 22 lipca 2010 r. (II SA/Kr 272/10)", *Prawo i Środowisko* 3 (2010): 116.

participate in administrative proceedings.[24] Within the framework of public participation, which in its essential form consists of the possibility of submitting comments and proposals, it also grants procedural rights, although only to environmental organisations, i.e. in light of the definition in Article 3(1)(10) of the act in question, to social organisations whose statutory objective is the protection of the environment.[25] These rights were regulated in Article 44 of the act, setting out that environmental organisations whose statutory objectives declare their willingness to participate in certain proceedings requiring public participation, can participate in them as a party if they have been carrying out statutory activities in the field of environmental protection or nature protection for at least twelve months prior to the date of initiating such proceedings. Such an organisation has the right to appeal against a decision issued in proceedings requiring public participation and is entitled to complain to the administrative court, even if it did not participate at an earlier stage of the proceedings.

The cited provision may therefore serve to protect the interests of the vulnerable to a relatively narrow extent. It limits the procedural rights of environmental organisations exclusively to administrative proceedings, before a public administration body, and to proceedings before an administrative court reviewing the legality of an act issued by that body. As a result, what was completely disregarded was the issue of civil proceedings, in which many individual rights or interests may be asserted, including those related to the environment and its protection, e.g. the right to ecological safety or to an adequate state of the environment, considered by part of legal scholarship and case law as subjective rights subject to protection provided for by civil

---

24 Draniewicz, Uprawnienia..., 13–14. These restrictions consisted of the obligation to maintain the domicile, i.e. making the ability of an ecological organisation to exercise its rights dependent on the place where the organisation is based and stipulating the deadline within which the organisation could join the proceedings and making it conditional on submitting comments and motions.

25 Paweł Daniel, "Udział organizacji ekologicznej w postępowaniu w przedmiocie wydania decyzji o pozwoleniu na budowę", *Przegląd Ochrony Środowiska* 4 (2012): 20–21.

law.[26] In this framework, vulnerable people can only benefit from the general solutions available to all civil and non-environmental litigants.

Furthermore, it should be noted that environmental organisations may not participate in all administrative proceedings, but only those in which an administrative decision requiring – according to a specific statutory provision – public participation may be issued.[27] In doing so, they have not been granted the possibility to file appeals triggering extraordinary forms of review of final decisions, i.e. outside the ordinary instance review procedure, such as an application to annul or to resume administrative proceedings.[28] In this context, however, what requires attention is the increasingly widespread position of the literature and case law, referring to standards arising from EU law and the Aarhus Convention, emphasising the need to ensure broad access to the courts, one of the pillars of that convention.[29] It is argued, in particular, that the protection of the interest raised by environmental organisations must not be weaker than the protection of the interest of individuals and their position weaker than that of the parties to proceedings, which in turn implies the right to participate in all proceedings in which a decision requiring public participation may be reviewed, including the extraordinary administrative procedure.

This position may, however, have negative consequences for parties who may be vulnerable, since the interest represented by an environmental organisation may not necessarily be in line with their legal interest, as pursued in given administrative proceedings or subsequently before an administrative court. The granting of procedural powers to environmental organisations is intended to enable the authority to become comprehensively acquainted with the case and to take an objective decision, rather than one corresponding to

---

26 Kinga Flaga-Gieruszyńska, "Udział organizacji pozarządowych w postępowaniach w sprawach cywilnych z zakresu ochrony środowiska", in: *Administracja a środowisko. Prace dedykowane prof. zw. dr hab. Markowi Górskiemu z okazji 45-lecia pracy naukowej*, (Ed.) Anna Barczak, Piotr Korzeniowski (Wydawnictwo Naukowe Uniwersytetu Szczecińskiego, 2018): 393–409.

27 See: Draniewicz, Udział…, 118.

28 See more: Daniel, Udział…, 25.

29 See more: Joanna Wegner-Kowalska, "Glosa do wyroku Naczelnego Sądu Administracyjnego z dnia 7 kwietnia 2016 r., II OSK 1627/14", *Orzecznictwo Sądów Polskich* 9 (2017): 117–124.

the subjective expectations of a party.[30] The participation of environmental organisations in proceedings is not always beneficial to the parties to the proceedings, and never indifferent to them, especially when their interests are in conflict.[31] Significant here is the lack of mechanisms for verifying whether the objectives an environmental organisation intends to pursue in proceedings requiring public participation are indeed compatible with the needs of the environment or the public interest, and thus whether the organisation is not abusing its procedural rights,[32] for example by wanting to block an important investment by taking actions leading only to protraction of the proceedings.[33] Concerns have even been expressed in the literature that an environmental organisation may use these powers to pursue its own interest, which for the purposes of the proceedings will be elevated to the status of a social interest, without it actually being one.[34] The legislator must therefore find a golden mean, allowing on the one hand the full fulfilment of the statutory objectives of environmental organisations, while on the other hand preventing the abuse of their procedural powers and all the time respecting the legitimate interests of the parties.[35] The comments so far justify the thesis that this task is very difficult and that the Polish legislator has not completed it. The complexity of this task and the inadequacy of legal instruments that can be used to perform it are confirmed by specific case law examples cited later in the study.

---

30 Paweł Milewski, "Status prawny organizacji ekologicznych w ujęciu porównawczym", *Kwartalnik Prawa Publicznego* 3–4 (2008): 191.

31 Krzysztof Gruszecki, "Udział organizacji ekologicznych w postępowaniu administracyjnym w sprawach ochrony środowiska", *Państwo i Prawo* 2 (2002): 93–94.

32 Anna Barczak, "Udział organizacji ekologicznych w ochronie środowiska a granice realizacji przez nie prawa do udziału w postępowaniu wymagającym udziału społeczeństwa", *Studia Prawnicze KUL* 3 (2020): 29–44. <https://doi.org/10.31743/sp.5450>.

33 Wojciech Federczyk, "Organizacja ekologiczna jako uczestnik postępowania administracyjnego w zakresie ochrony środowiska", *Kwartalnik Prawa Publicznego* 3–4 (2008): 72–73 and 80–81.

34 Tomasz Jezierski, "Glosa do wyroku Naczelnego Sądu Administracyjnego z 19.01.2018 r., II OSK 833/16", *Przegląd Prawa Publicznego* 1 (2019): 108.

35 Milewski, Status…, 192 and 206.

5. Public participation – selected examples

It is not uncommon for vulnerable people to be unable to effectively enforce their rights due to certain limitations, e.g. of a financial nature or related to living conditions, and therefore to seek the assistance of environmental organisations in representing their rights, hoping for a favourable outcome. There is no doubt that, as far as environmental organisations are concerned, the protection of human rights of what is known as the third generation,[36] among which is the right to a clean and ecologically sustainable environment, is of particular importance.[37] The field of action of these organisations will therefore not only be educational activities, but specific actions taken against those responsible for violating the environment or supporting individuals,[38] including vulnerable people, who undertake such activities themselves but, due to the circumstances, need organisational assistance or financial help from an organisation. This action through environmental organisations ensures a higher level of professionalism (organisations bring together a variety of professionals and use a wide range of experts) and, at later stages, protects the courts from overload and paralysis.[39] Adjudicatory practice confirms that, thanks to the participation of environmental organisations, blatant violations of the law are relatively often uncovered in the course

---

36 Wegner-Kowalska, Glosa…, 117–124.

37 Flaga-Gieruszyńska, Udział…, 408.

38 In particular, there are many studies on the importance of organisations in connection with climate change. According to the Climate Litigation in Europe A Summary Report for the European Union Forum of Judges for the Environment, almost 50% of European climate cases have been filed by individuals or civil society organisations, or by both acting together (Joana Setzer, Harj Narulla, Catherine Higham, Emily Bradeen, Climate litigation in Europe A summary report for the European Union Forum of Judges for the Environment, December 2022, <https://www.lse.ac.uk/granthaminstitute/wp-content/uploads/2022/12/Climate-litigation-in-Europe_A-summary-report-for-the-EU-Forum-of-Judges-for-the-Environment.pdf> (accessed on 20 December 2023). See also about supporting organisations to protect the rights of children and young people in the context of climate change: Nina Koistinen, "Looking forward: An analysis of global climate litigation invoking intergenerational equity and the interests of future generations", October 2023, <https://erepo.uef.fi/bitstream/handle/123456789/31032/urn_nbn_fi_uef-20231515.pdf?sequence=1&isAllowed=y> (accessed on 20 December 2023).

39 Barbara Iwańska, "*Koncepcja skargi zbiorowej* w *prawie ochrony środowiska*" (Wolters Kluwer, 2013): 329–330.

of inspections.[40] Research has shown the effectiveness of environmental movements in changing the policies and behaviours of corporations and governments, as well as promoting local pro-environmental behaviour.[41] Unfortunately, it is not uncommon for these organisations to be unable to effectively claim protection in environmental cases. There have been several such situations in the last few years, which should be regarded as worrying to say the least.

As an example, it is worth mentioning the judgment of the Court of Justice of the EU (European Commission vs the Republic of Poland)[42] of 2 March 2023 in case C-432/21. This judgment stated that there was a failure to adopt all the legislative provisions necessary to ensure that nature conservation organisations could apply to the courts for an effective examination of the substantive and formal legality of forest management plans[43] within the meaning of the Polish Forestry Act. This ruling must be considered in conjunction with the second CJEU judgment of 17 April 2018 in case C-441/17. One of conclusions of the judgment states that Poland had failed to fulfil its obligations as a Member State by adopting an annex to the forest management plan of the Białowieża Forest District without ensuring that the annex would not adversely affect the integrity of a site of Community

---

40 Marcin Pchałek, Michał Behnke, "Postępowanie w sprawie oceny oddziaływania na środowisko w prawie polskim i europejskim, (C.H. Beck, 2009): 223.

41 Edward J. Carberry, Pratyush Bharati, David L. Levy, Abhijit Chaudhury, "Social movements as catalysts for corporate social innovation: environmental activism and the adoption of green information systems", *Business & Society* 58(2017): 1083–1127; Vivek Shandas, W. Barry Messer, Fostering green communities through civic engagement: Community-based environmental stewardship in the Portland area, *Journal of the American Planning Association*, 74(2008): 408–418; Wibowo H. Prasetiyo, Kamarul R. Kamarudin, Jagad A. Dewantara, "Surabaya green and clean: Protecting urban environment through civic engagement community", *Journal of Human Behavior in the Social Environment*, 29 (2019): 997–1014.

42 <https://eur-lex.europa.eu/search.html?scope=EURLEX&text=w+sprawie+C-432%2F21&lang=en&type=quick&qid=1703015682328> (accessed on 20 December 2023).

43 It is a basic forest management document developed for a specific facility, containing a description and assessment of the condition of the forest as well as objectives, tasks and methods of forest management (Article 6(1)(6) of the Polish Forestry Act of 28 September 1991, Journal of Laws 2023.1356, as amended). See more Article 18(1) and (2) of the Polish Forestry Act.

importance and the Białowieża Forest Special Protection Area. It was impossible to challenge both the forest management plan and the annex under Polish law, and therefore neither individuals nor environmental organisations had the legal possibility to counteract the massive[44] and uncontrolled felling of the Białowieża Forest.[45] The importance of this felling to the ecosystem is undeniable.[46] Certainly, the effects of this measure will also be experienced by individuals in the long term.[47]

Another example of when it was difficult for environmental organisations to seek protection in environmental cases are the cases related to what came to be known as the dieselgate scandal. These concerned the approval of Volkswagen Group vehicles in Germany (licensing). The environmental association Deutsche Umwelthilfe filed a complaint against the Volkswagen Group, claiming that the software used in Volkswagen Group vehicles was an unlawful 'performance-limiting device'. This complaint was dismissed by a German court, which denied the association's *locus standi*. The case was finally resolved in the judgment of the Court of Justice of the EU of 8 November 2022 in Case C 873/19 (Deutsche Umwelthilfe eV v Bundesrepublik Deutschland, with the participation of: Volkswagen AG).[48] According to the Advocate General's opinion, a recognised environmental association that

---

44 Furthermore, according to the Commission, which relies on data from the State Forests, the cuts in the Białowieża Forest, carried out since the beginning of 2017, amount to a total of more than 35,000 m^3 of timber, including more than 29,000 m^3 of spruce, i.e. about 29,000 trees.

45 The Białowieża Forest is a forest complex with an area on the Polish-Belarusian border. According to the EU Commission, the Białowieża Forest, Natura 2000 site is one of the best preserved natural forests in Europe, characterised by large amounts of dead wood and historic stands of trees, especially stands which are 100 years old.

46 Grzegorz Mikusiński, Jakub W. Bubnicki, Marcin Churski, Dorota Czeszczewik, Wiesław Walankiewicz, Dries P.J. Kuijper, "Is the impact of loggings in the last primeval lowland forest in Europe underestimated? The conservation issues of Białowieża Forest", *Biological Conservation*, 227 (2018): 266–274.

47 The importance of forests, especially in the context of emphasised climate change, is undeniable. Forests play a significant role in both mitigating climate change and adapting to the negative consequences of this process. Ewa Radecka, "Legal consequences of the Judgment of the Court of the Justice of the European Union in case C-432/21", *Acta Univeristatic Carolinae. Iuridica* 1(2024): 147–158.

48 <https://eur-lex.europa.eu/legal-content/PL/TXT/?uri=CELEX:62019CJ0873> (accessed on 20 December 2023).

is entitled to bring proceedings under national law should be able to challenge before a national court an administrative decision granting European Community (EC) vehicle type-approval. This case was particularly important from the perspective of one of the environmental components, which is clean air. The installation of tampering software in Volkswagen Group vehicles led to significant emissions into the air. This, in turn, certainly did not have a positive impact on the health of the general public,[49] including those vulnerable groups who are particularly exposed to poor air quality, such as pregnant women, children or the elderly.[50]

Another topic worth mentioning is the amendment of the Czech Act č. 114/1992 Sb. on the protection of nature and landscape.[51] According to the original wording of § 70 of this act, civic associations (environmental associations, non-governmental organisations) engaged in nature and landscape protection as part of their activities could participate in administrative proceedings in which nature and landscape protection interests could be affected. Participation was not only possible in proceedings conducted on the basis of the Nature and Landscape Protection Act, but also in other acts under which investment project permits were sought. Unfortunately, as a result of several amendments between 2015 and 2023, the scope of this right was gradually reduced from the originally broad concept of community participation in proceedings conducted under the Nature and Landscape Protection Act and under other laws of the environmental law system. At first, these restrictions were introduced in such a way that civic associations, whose main mission according to their statutes was the protection of nature and landscape, could participate in all administrative proceedings in which the interests of nature and landscape protection protected according to this act might be affected, with the exception of proceedings relating to environmental impact assessment according to § 3(g) of Act č. 100/2001 Sb.[52] Subsequently, the Nature

---

[49] Higher concentrations of nitrogen dioxide (one of the main sources of emissions is road transport) may cause problems with the respiratory and circulatory systems. <https://healpolska.pl/aktualnosci/czym-jest-dwutlenek-azotu-i-jak-jego-wdychanie-wplywa-na-zdrowie-infografika/>, accessed on 20 December 2023.

[50] < https://www.epa.gov/air-research/research-health-effects-air-pollution > (accessed on 20 December 2023).

[51] Zákon č. 114/1992 Sb., o ochraně přírody a krajiny.

[52] Zákon ć. 100/2001 Sb., o posuzování vlivů na životní prostředi

and Landscape Protection Act was amended by Act č. 225/2017 Sb.,[53] which led to limiting the participation of these organisations to administrative proceedings conducted only based on the Nature and Landscape Protection Act. The latest amendment, made by Act č. 149/2023 Sb.,[54] with effect from 1 January 2024, at first sight extends the right of environmental associations to participate in administrative proceedings, but this extension is in relation to 2017 and not the original broad catalogue of rights. In addition, there are views in the literature that this amendment will not change much in practice,[55] ergo the role of organisations in these procedures will still be limited.

6. Conclusions

The observations made so far lead to the conclusion that legal solutions regarding social participation do not adequately protect the needs of sensitive groups. They serve to protect the public or general interest in environmental protection, rather than considering individual interests, even justified ones and those related to the environment. In particular, ecological organisations themselves define the general interest that they will represent in the proceedings and may do so in a manner contrary to individual interests, including when it comes to the interest of a party to the proceedings in which they participate, including a party that is a sensitive entity. Consequently, the interest of the vulnerable may be protected only indirectly and provided that this interest is consistent with the general interest raised by the ecological organisation in the proceedings. However, practice proves that this convergence occurs very often since, for example, in about half of climate protection cases, the participation of a social organisation comes down to supporting an individual asserting their rights in the proceedings and actively advocating on their side, presenting broader and more professional arguments, sometimes

---

53 Zákon č. 225/2017 Sb., kterým se mění zákon č. 183/2006 Sb., o územním plánování a stavebním řádu (stavební zákon), ve znění pozdějších předpisů, a další související zákony, Parlamentu České republiky.

54 Zákon č. 149/2023 Sb., kterým se mění některé zákony v souvislosti s přijetím zákona o jednotném environmentálním stanovisku.

55 For more, see: Vojtech Stejskal, "Účast spolků zabývajících se ochranou přírody v navazujících řízenich ve světle judikatury Ústavního soudu ČR", *Prawne Problemy Górnictwa i Ochrony Środowiska* 1(2024): 1–12.

going beyond the individual's individual needs or conditions.[56] Therefore, social initiative or activity precedes the legal provisions on social participation based on which it is manifested. These provisions do not provide for any mechanisms to protect individual interests, particularly the interests of the vulnerable, in cases where an ecological organisation acts contrary to these interests. This issue cannot be verified by the authority conducting the proceedings and the parties are not entitled to any procedural rights, as they cannot oppose either the inclusion of an ecological organisation in their proceedings or any procedural steps taken by the organisations that are unfavourable to them.

Bibliography

Barczak Anna, "Udział organizacji ekologicznych w ochronie środowiska a granice realizacji przez nie prawa do udziału w postępowaniu wymagającym udziału społeczeństwa", *Studia Prawnicze KUL* 3 (2020): 29–44. <https://doi.org/10.31743/sp.5450>.

Carberry Edward J., Bharati Pratyush, Levy David L., Chaudhury Abhijit, "Social movements as catalysts for corporate social innovation: environmental activism and the adoption of green information systems", *Business & Society* 58(2017): 1083–1127.

Daniel Paweł, "Udział organizacji ekologicznej w postępowaniu w przedmiocie wydania decyzji o pozwoleniu na budowę", *Przegląd Ochrony Środowiska* 4 (2012): 9–29.

Draniewicz Bartosz, "Udział organizacji ekologicznych w postępowaniu niewymagającym udziału społeczeństwa. Glosa do wyroku WSA w Krakowie z 22 lipca 2010 r. (II SA/Kr 272/10)", *Prawo i Środowisko* 3 (2010): 110–119.

Draniewicz Bartosz, "Uprawnienia organizacji ekologicznych w postępowaniach wymagających udziału społeczeństwa", *Monitor Prawniczy* 1 (2011): 12–18.

Federczyk Wojciech, "Organizacja ekologiczna jako uczestnik postępowania administracyjnego w zakresie ochrony środowiska", *Kwartalnik Prawa Publicznego* 3–4 (2008): 71–81.

---

[56] See footnote no. 39.

Flaga-Gieruszyńska Kinga, “Udział organizacji pozarządowych w postępowaniach w sprawach cywilnych z zakresu ochrony środowiska”, in: *Administracja a środowisko. Prace dedykowane prof. zw. dr hab. Markowi Górskiemu z okazji 45-lecia pracy naukowej*, (Ed.) Anna Barczak, Piotr Korzeniowski (Wydawnictwo Naukowe Uniwersytetu Szczecińskiego, 2018): 393–409.

Gruszecki Krzysztof, “Udział organizacji ekologicznych w postępowaniu administracyjnym w sprawach ochrony środowiska”, *Państwo i Prawo* 2 (2002): 89–97.

Iwańska Barbara, “*Koncepcja skargi zbiorowej* w *prawie ochrony środowiska*” (Wolters Kluwer, 2013).

Jezierski Tomasz, “Glosa do wyroku Naczelnego Sądu Administracyjnego z 19.01.2018 r., II OSK 833/16”, *Przegląd Prawa Publicznego* 1 (2019): 108–114.

Koistinen Nina, “Looking forward: An analysis of global climate litigation invoking intergenerational equity and the interests of future generations”, October 2023, <https://erepo.uef.fi/bitstream/handle/123456789/31032/urn_nbn_fi_uef-20231515.pdf?sequence=1&isAllowed=y> (accessed on 20 December 2023).

Köböl-Benda Vivien, “The current status of the right to the environment in the global international law”, *Opolskie Studia Administracyjno-prawne*, vol. 20, 1 (2022): 117–143.

Longo Mariano, Lorubbio Vinzenzo, “Ecosystem Vulnerability. New Semantics for International Law”, *International Journal for the Semiotics of Law* 36 (2023): 1611–1628.

Micińska Magdalena, *Udział społeczeństwa w ochronie środowiska. Instrumenty administracyjno-prawne* (Wydawnictwo Adam Marszałek, 2011).

Milewski Paweł, “Status prawny organizacji ekologicznych w ujęciu porównawczym”, *Kwartalnik Prawa Publicznego* 3–4 (2008): 191–207.

Mikusiński Grzegorz, Bubnicki Jakub W., Churski Marcin, Czeszczewik Dorota, Walankiewicz Wiesław, Kuijper Dries P.J., “Is the impact of loggings in the last primeval lowland forest in Europe underestimated? The conservation issues of Białowieża Forest”, *Biological Conservation*, 227 (2018): 266–274.

Niczyporuk Janusz, “Organizacja ekologiczna w ogólnym postępowaniu administracyjnym”, in: *Ocena modelu prawnego organizacji ochrony środowiska w Polsce i na Słowacji*, (Ed.) Stanisław Pieprzny, Jerzy Stelmasiak, Elżbiera Ura (RS Druk, 2021).

Pchałek Marcin, Behnke Michał, "Postępowanie w sprawie oceny oddziaływania na środowisko w prawie polskim i europejskim" (C.H. Beck, 2009).

Prasetiyo Wibowo H., Kamarudin Kamarul R., Dewantara Jagad A., "Surabaya green and clean: Protecting urban environment through civic engagement community", *Journal of Human Behavior in the Social Environment*, 29 (2019): 997–1014.

Radecka Ewa, "Legal consequences of the Judgment of the Court of the Justice of the European Union in case C-432/21", *Acta Univeristatic Carolinae. Iuridica* 1(2024): 147–158.

Rygel Lisa, O'Sullivan David, Yarnal Brent, "A Method for Constructing a Social Vulnerability Index: An Application to Hurricane Storm Surges in a Developed Country", *Mitigation and Adaptation Strategies for Global Change* 11 (2006): 36–61, <https://doi.org/10.1007/s11027-006-0265-6>.

Shandas Vivek, Messer W. Barry, Fostering green communities through civic engagement: Community-based environmental stewardship in the Portland area, *Journal of the American Planning Association*, 74(2008): 408–418.

Setzer Joana, Narulla Harj, Higham Catherine, Bradeen Emily, Climate litigation in Europe A summary report for the European Union Forum of Judges for the Environment, December 2022, <https://www.lse.ac.uk/granthaminstitute/wp-content/uploads/2022/12/Climate-litigation-in-Europe_A-summary-report-for-the-EU-Forum-of-Judges-for-the-Environment.pdf> (accessed on 20 December 2023).

Stejskal Vojtech, "Účast spolků zabývajících se ochranou přírody v navazujících řízenich ve světle judikatury Ústavního soudu ČR", *Prawne Problemy Górnictwa i Ochrony Środowiska* 1(2024): 1–12.

Wegner-Kowalska Joanna, "Glosa do wyroku Naczelnego Sądu Administracyjnego z dnia 7 kwietnia 2016 r., II OSK 1627/14", *Orzecznictwo Sądów Polskich* 9 (2017): 117–124.

The Protection of Minority Shareholders: A Comparative Approach to a 'Trapped' Shareholder

*Piotr Pinior**

Abstract: Shareholders are not, in principle, a vulnerable group, as they are investors who decide to take up shares and participate in the company in light of contractual freedom. In the practice of a company's operations, particularly in private limited companies, due to potential conflicts of interest, circumstances may arise in which shareholders can be considered vulnerable. This concept refers particularly to minority shareholders, whose position towards the dominant shareholder (or controlling shareholders) may be at stake due to the majority rule. The paper aims to identify examples of the abuse of the rights of minority shareholders in corporate relations and find the optimal method to protect them in the event of conflicts of interest.

Keywords: minority shareholder, conflict of interest, abuse of rights, buyout of shares

1. Introduction

The term 'vulnerable' addresses a number of various groups, primarily individuals; however, it may also refer to other groups in corporate relations, particularly minority shareholders, as their position towards the dominant shareholder (or controlling shareholders) may be at stake due to the majority rule. The majority rule (capital primacy) in companies means that the capital commitment of shareholders, and thus the number of shares held, refers directly

* Full Professor at the Faculty of Law and Administration of the University of Silesia in Katowice, Poland. ORCID: 0000-0003-2084-0325.

to participation in the company's decision-making process.[1] Consequently, shareholders enjoy their rights in relation to the corporation by virtue of their ownership position. However, the more negligible capital involvement of minority shareholders may not lead to the exclusion of protection of their interests. As a result, the concept of the protection of minority shareholders is commonly adopted in the commercial law doctrine to ensure that minority shareholders are treated fairly and have their rights upheld within a company.

It should be emphasised that shareholders are not, in principle, a vulnerable group, as they are investors who decide to take up shares and participate in the company in light of contractual freedom. However, in the practice of a company's operations, particularly in private limited companies, due to potential conflicts of interest, circumstances may arise in which shareholders can be considered a vulnerable group, though this only really applies to minority shareholders. Less visible are conflicts of interest in listed companies, where a large number of shareholders may be solely investors, not engaged directly in the company's operations.

It is quite a different situation when dealing with groups of companies (holdings) where a dominant shareholder is a legal entity and the interest of the group of companies determines the specific legal relationship between shareholders and the interest of every subsidiary company. In the case of group companies, domestic legal orders introduce particular mechanisms to protect minority shareholders, but the issue of groups of companies will not be presented in this chapter due to the distinct legal character of the relationships in the group.

The paper aims to identify examples of the abuse of rights in corporate relations and demonstrate the existing legal mechanisms and safeguards

---

[1] See among others, Wojciech Jan Katner, "Prawa mniejszości w spółkach kapitałowych (I)", *Przegląd Prawa Handlowego*, 2 (2002): 3; Andrzej Kidyba, "Ochrona praw mniejszości w spółce z ograniczoną odpowiedzialnością" in *Księga pamiątkowa dla uczczenia pracy naukowej Prof. K. Kruczalaka*, Gdańskie Studia Prawnicze Vol. V (1999), 190; Józef Okolski, Jerzy Modrzejewski, Łukasz Gasiński, "Zasada równego traktowania akcjonariuszy na gruncie KSH", *Przegląd Prawa Handlowego*, 10 (2002): 22; Andrzej Szumański in *System Prawa Prywatnego. Prawo papierów Wartościowych, Vol. 19.* (Ed.) Andrzej Szumański, C.H. Beck, Warszawa, (2006): 222; Wojciech Popiołek, "Akcja – prawo podmiotowe", C.H. Beck, Warszawa, (2010): 129; Katarzyna Kopaczyńska – Pieczniak, "Spółka z ograniczoną odpowiedzialnością", (Ed.) Andrzej Kidyba, Wolters Kluwer, Warszawa, (2007): 332.

designed to prevent minority shareholders from abuse by majority (controlling) shareholders, particularly in limited liability companies. A limited liability company is the most common legal form of a company used in corporate practice, and for that reason, cases of abuse of rights by majority shareholders in this legal form occur often. Consequently, the paper aims to find the optimal method to protect minority shareholders in the event of conflicts among shareholders and to formulate proposals *de lege ferenda* on amendments to the law.

2. The vulnerability of minority shareholders

The source of a violation of the rights of minority shareholders is most frequently a conflict of interests between the majority (controlling) shareholders and the minority shareholder, particularly in a situation where the majority shareholders also act as members of the management board in a limited liability company. This conflict may come about due to the fact that the company's authorities are able to take advantage of being the majority shareholders to deprive the minority shareholder of significant contractual or statutory rights, making their participation in the company pointless. If that happens, then regaining these rights in another way is extremely difficult, as a result of abuse of rights by the majority shareholder.[2] At the same time, the withdrawal from the company or the sale of shares in the company may not be possible, which leaves minority shareholders 'trapped' in the company without the prospect of participating in profits or recovering a return on their investment.

A conflict between shareholders and the company's authorities is not, by itself, sufficient grounds to assume an abuse of rights. An abuse of rights by controlling shareholders occurs where a conflict results in a detriment to the minority shareholders, or the conflict results in the deprivation of shareholder rights. The most spectacular examples of violating shareholder rights are the denial of a dividend – where the controlling shareholders refuse the distribution of dividends in order to weaken the minority shareholders'

2 Supreme Court Judgment of 12 January 2018, II CSK 207/17, Lex No 25558235; Supreme Court Judgment of 16 April 2019, II CSK 66/18, OSNC-ZD 2020, No 3, p.41.

position, and related-party transactions – understood as unfair transactions between the company and its controlling shareholders.

In particular, as the shareholders' resolution on the distribution of profits requires an absolute majority of votes, it means that the right to obtain the payment of profits depends totally on the dominant shareholder. The Polish judicature underlines, e.g. in the Supreme Court judgments of 16 April 2004 and of 29 October 2008,[3] that the significant degree of discretionary power of the majority shareholder, who is able to adopt a resolution to refrain from paying dividends, does not mean unrestricted freedom, because a resolution regarding the distribution of profit cannot violate the principle of equal rights of shareholders or otherwise harm shareholders, especially minority ones. The right to a dividend is one of the fundamental property rights arising from shares, so its permanent exclusion limits the ownership right in terms of the possibility of achieving financial benefits, resulting in the shares losing their essence and being, as it were, devoid of economic value.

Consequently, in its ruling of 10 July 2009,[4] the Supreme Court stated that if a shareholders' resolution on the distribution of profit in a limited liability company, adopted in a dynamically operating company, allocates almost the entire profit to reserve capital, then it may be considered as aimed at harming the shareholder. The Supreme Court presented the same line in its judgments of 3 December 2021 and 16 March 2022,[5] whereby the constant, long-term allocation of profit to reserve capital and refraining from paying dividends may harm a minority shareholder because holding shares in a company is usually motivated by the expectation of a dividend, especially by a minority shareholder deprived of other benefits related to the sound financial result of the company. Therefore, excluding a shareholder from profit participation, unless related to a particular situation occurring in the company in connection with the implementation of intended and purposeful projects requiring the strengthening of its financial status, should be considered harming the shareholder.

---

3 Supreme Court Judgment of 16 April 2004, I CK 537/03, OSNC 2004, No 12, p. 204; Supreme Court Judgment of 29 October 2008, IV CSK 242/08, Lex No 590266.

4 Supreme Court Judgment of 10 July 2009, II CSK 91/09, Glosa, 2010, No 3, p. 14.

5 Supreme Court Judgment of 3 December 2021, V CSK 117/21, Lex No 3271098; Supreme Court Judgment of 16 March 2022, II CSKP 191/22, Lex No 3417258.

Another problem that frequently occurs as a form of abuse of corporate rights is the transfer of a company's assets to one of the shareholders or company's organs, leading to the depletion of the assets or the exclusion of the payment of potential dividends. In a typical abuse of rights, the controlling shareholders provide services to the company and the payment exceeds the average market price. Such a transfer of assets requires cooperation between the company's boards and the controlling shareholders. Another frequent situation is the case where the shareholders also sit on the management board and receive remuneration under a management contract or an employment contract. In both cases, the transfer of assets to the controlling shareholders deprives the minority shareholders of receiving dividends, or significantly reduces the amount of profit distributed among shareholders.

In other words, an economically unjustified, long-term hoarding of profit in the company, caused by decisions of the majority shareholder(s), which results in depriving the minority shareholder of the possibility of receiving a dividend, especially if, at the same time, the company transfers profit to the controlling shareholders as a result of non-corporate transactions concluded between them and the company, constitutes an abuse of majority rule. A large number of Supreme Court rulings, not mentioning the adjudications of lower instances courts, prove that a denial of dividend payments frequently occurs as a form of abuse of rights by majority shareholders.

These examples demonstrate that a robust protection of minority shareholders is essential for a healthy corporate environment. The problem mostly affects the shareholders in limited liability companies, because the sale of shares held by a minority shareholder may be difficult due to the lack of potential purchasers, while the redemption of shares is hindered by the need to adopt a shareholders' resolution with an absolute majority of votes, or the need for authorisation from the company's boards. The abuse of rights and deprivation of protection of a shareholder who must remain in the company due to the inability to sell or redeem shares while being deprived of any benefits from the shares held due to the transfer of assets from the company by other shareholders or members of the board means that his status in the company is similar to that of an injured party. It is even possible to identify a minority shareholder, taking into account the circumstances indicated above, with a vulnerable person due to the lack of mechanisms allowing for the protection of the rights of such a person.

3. The 'typical' instruments of minority shareholder protection

In the Polish literature, the concept of protecting the rights of minority shareholders is presented in two senses.[6] In a broad sense (*sensu largo*), the protection of minority shareholders' rights consists of all corporate mechanisms of a protective nature for shareholders, including individual rights such as the ability to appeal against resolutions. In a narrow sense (*sensu stricto*), however, minority rights are exercised while representing a specific number of shares or a specific part of the share capital, as the protection mechanisms refer only to those connected with representing part of the share capital or shares (or sometimes a specified threshold of votes).

The protection of minority shareholders should ensure fairness and prevent exploitation and is recognised on European and domestic regulatory levels. The introduction of these instruments is intended to prevent the total supremacy of majority shareholders towards a minority shareholder, also through the actions of the company's bodies, in particular the managing body, undertaken 'in agreement' with the majority shareholder.[7] Nevertheless, the safeguards differ significantly among different types of companies. Moreover, the effectiveness of the instruments discussed is not always satisfactory for the injured shareholder in conflict with majority shareholders, particularly in the circumstances described in the previous part of this chapter.

---

6 Katner, "Prawa mniejszości w spółkach kapitałowych (I)": 3; Kidyba, "Ochrona praw mniejszości w spółce z ograniczoną odpowiedzialnością": 191; Okolski, Modrzejewski, Gasiński, "Zasada równego traktowania akcjonariuszy na gruncie KSH": 22; Kopaczyńska – Pieczniak, "Spółka z ograniczoną odpowiedzialnością": 332; Dominika Wajda, "Ochrona akcjonariuszy mniejszościowych w kodeksie spółek handlowych", C.H. Beck, Warszawa, (2007): 47; Paweł Błaszczyk, "Ochrona wspólników mniejszościowych spółki zależnej należącej do grupy spółek", *Państwo i Prawo*, 10 (2010): 22; Szumański in *System Prawa Prywatnego. Prawo papierów Wartościowych, Vol. 19*: 221; Popiołek, "Akcja – prawo podmiotowe": 128; Olga Lipińska – Długosz, "Ochrona spółki akcyjnej i jej akcjonariuszy przed niewłaściwym wykonywaniem prawa", C.H. Beck, Warszawa, (2006): 15; Krzysztof Oplustil, "Instrumenty nadzoru korporacyjnego (corporate governance) w spółce akcyjnej", C.H. Beck, Warszawa, (2010): 558; Piotr Pinior, "Nadzór wspólników w spółce z ograniczoną odpowiedzialnością", C.H. Beck, Warszawa, (2013): 371; Jakub Jan Zięty, "Uprawnienia akcjonariuszy polskich spółek publicznych, w świetle dyrektywy 2007/36/WE", C.H. Beck, Warszawa, (2015): 27.

7 Pinior, "Nadzór wspólników w spółce z ograniczoną odpowiedzialnością": 373,

In many legal systems, companies are required to treat shareholders equally. One aspect of equal treatment is introduced by Directive 2007/36.[8] Under Art. 4 of this directive, the company must ensure equal treatment for all shareholders in the same position regarding participation and the exercise of voting rights at the general meeting. Based on this rule, particular measures to protect minority shareholders have been established, guaranteeing the minimum protection on the exercise of their rights connected with the shareholders' meeting. The instruments for protecting minority shareholders under European law include the right to request shareholders' meetings and to place items on the agenda, as well as the right to draft resolutions for items included on the agenda. These instruments are regulated at the European level by Directive 2007/36 (SRD I) on the exercise of shareholders' rights in listed companies, which aims to encourage the shareholders in a listed company to participate actively at the company's meetings. Directive 2017/828[9] (SRD II) identifies, among other things, the issue of related-party transactions in listed companies. It explains that transactions with related parties may cause prejudice to companies and their shareholders, as they may give the related party an opportunity to appropriate value belonging to the company. Therefore, appropriate safeguards for protecting the interests of both companies and shareholders are essential. Even though these instruments strengthen the position of minority shareholders, they do not guarantee a 'safe environment' in relation to the controlling shareholders. It should also be underlined that the aim of these directives does not refer strictly to the protection of minority shareholders, but to enable the exercise of shareholders' rights and to encourage them to engage more in the company's operations[10]

The national legislators have tended to mostly introduce provisions on minority protection in listed companies and in non-listed joint stock

---

8 Directive (EU) 2007/36 of the European Parliament and of the Council of 11 July 2007 on the exercise of certain rights of shareholders in listed companies (O.J.EU.L.2007.184.11).

9 Directive (EU) 2017/828 of the European Parliament and of the Council of 17 May 2017, amending Directive 2007/36/EC on the encouragement of long-term shareholder engagement (O.J.EU.L.2017.132.1).

10 Pierre-Henri Conac, "The shareholders' duty not to abuse rights" in *Shareholders' duties*, ed. Hanne S. Birkmose, Kluwer Law International, (2017): 364; Zięty, "Uprawnienia akcjonariuszy polskich spółek publicznych, w świetle dyrektywy 2007/36/WE": 27.

companies.[11] The protection of minority shareholders, as provided in Directive SRD I, usually appears in domestic legislation in limited liability companies as well.

However, minority shareholders in listed companies are in a different position to their counterparts in private companies because they can usually sell their shares without obstacles. In addition, they may be able to take advantage of the right to demand that the company purchase their shares (sell-out). Directive 2004/25[12] on takeover bids introduces an obligation whereby if, following a takeover bid, an offeror has acquired a certain percentage of a company's capital with voting rights, the holders of the remaining shares should be able to require that the offeror also buy their securities (Article 16 of Directive 2004/25[13]). A similar institution, but not connected with takeover bids, also appears in non-listed companies (see Article 418[1] of the Polish Commercial Companies Code[14]). The right of minority shareholders

---

11 The Continental system differs from the Anglo-Saxon one, which needs explaining. In the Anglo-Saxon system, there are two main types of companies, depending on how the shares are disposed of, namely public limited companies (listed companies), with shares admitted to be traded on the regulated market, and private limited companies (non-listed companies). The continental system recognises primarily two types of company – joint stock companies (e.g. Aktiengesellschaft, sociedad anónima, società per azioni, société anonyme) and limited liability companies (e.g. Gesellschaft mit beschränkter Haftung, sociedad de responsabilidad limitada, aocietà a responsabilita limitata; société à responsabilité limitée). Among joint stock companies, there are companies whose shares are admitted to be traded on the regulated market (listed companies) and joint stock companies not admitted to the regulated market (non-listed companies). On the contrary, the shares in limited liability companies may never be admitted to a regulated market, as the shares have a different legal nature and are not securities.

12 Directive (EU) 2004/25 of the European Parliament and of the Council of 21 April 2004 on takeover bids (O.J.EU.L.2004.142.12).

13 Under Article 15 sec. 2, Member States have to introduce that right where the offeror holds securities representing not less than 90% of the capital carrying voting rights and 90% of the voting rights in the offeree company. Member States may set a higher threshold, but not higher than 95% of the capital carrying voting rights and 95% of the voting rights.

14 The Commercial Companies Code of 15 September 2000, the Official Journal of Laws of the Republic of Poland, 2024.18, as amended, hereinafter abbreviated as CCC.

to sell their shares on demand is also incorporated in the European Model Company Act (Sec. 11.35).[15]

Another right intended to protect a shareholder's interest (minority protection *sensu largo*), commonly found in national legal systems in all types of companies, is the right to appeal against shareholder resolutions. The right to file a statement of claim against a resolution is independent of the number of shares held by a shareholder and may be exercised by a shareholder holding at least one share.[16] Under Polish law, any resolution of the shareholders that conflicts with the provisions of the articles of association or good practice and is detrimental to the company's interest or aimed at harming a shareholder may be appealed against by filing a statement of claim against the company for repealing the resolution. A shareholder also has the right to file a statement of claim against the company to declare a shareholders' resolution adopted in breach of the law invalid. However, it requires an outlay of financial resources due to the need to make a payment for filing a lawsuit. A shareholders' resolution on denying a dividend may be challenged due to the conflict with good practice and being harmful to the minority shareholder, but it does not prevent the re-adoption of a resolution unfavourable to the shareholder or further abuse by the majority shareholder. This right is also ineffective while transferring assets from the company to the controlling shareholders based on other contractual relations, where the transfer does not require a shareholders' resolution.

These rights, unfortunately, do not improve the position of minority shareholders, particularly in limited liability companies, where the majority

[15] Nordic & European Company Law, LSN Research Paper Series, No 16–26, European Model Company Act 2017, by Paul Krüger Andersen & Jan Bertil Andersson, (Sec. 11.35 If a shareholder holds more than nine-tenths of the shares in a company and a corresponding share of the votes, each minority shareholder of the company may demand redemption by that shareholder).

[16] The legitimacy to file a statement of claim under Polish law appertains to a shareholder who voted against the resolution and, upon the adoption thereof, requested that their objection be recorded in the minutes; a shareholder who was prevented from participating in the shareholders' meeting without a sound reason; a shareholder who was absent from the shareholders' meeting, only in the event of defects in convening a meeting or adopting a resolution on a matter not included in the agenda; and in the case of a written vote in a private limited company, a shareholder who was omitted in voting or who did not consent to a written vote.

shareholders hold the majority of votes and can deprive the minority shareholders of their corporate rights. In the event of a conflict of interest, where the typical examples of the abuse of the dominant position appear, the disposal of shares seems the most desirable solution.

4. Remedy for a 'trapped' shareholder

Unlike partnerships, the provisions on companies do not involve the company's withdrawal mechanism. However, some national orders allow shareholders to exit the company in a manner other than the regular disposal or redemption of shares. The mechanisms may be connected either with the court's decision on shareholders' exclusion, or with the fulfilment of conditions (premises) provided by law.

One of the most recent amendments to the Polish Commercial Companies Code[17] introduced a new type of company – simple joint stock company – which created a new legal mechanism for protecting minority shareholders from majority abuse. The right to demand the disposal of shares aims to protect the rights of minority shareholders in the event of a permanent conflict with other shareholders or actions of shareholders or members of bodies resulting in harming a minority shareholder. The right to demand the disposal of shares may be defined as '*ius dissidentium*'.[18] However, the shareholders exercise this right only in the cases provided by law on particular premises.

Under Article 300^{50} § 1 CCC, at the demand of a shareholder, a court may rule on their exclusion from the company, provided that there is a material reason justified by relations between the shareholders of the company and the departing shareholder, resulting in a glaring detriment to the departing shareholder. The act also provides protection on the manner of a shareholder buyout and the price of shares, because the shares held by a departing shareholder will be subject to buyout at a price corresponding to the fair value determined by a court as of the day of serving the complaint. The court will also determine the time limit within which the buyout price will be paid to

---

17 Act on the Amendment of the Commercial Companies Code, of 9 February 2022, Journal of Laws, 2022, item 807. The amendment of the code entered into force on 13 October 2022.

18 Arkadiusz Radwan, "*Ius dissidentium*. Granice konsensusu korporacyjnego i władzy większości w spółkach kapitałowych", C.H. Beck, Warszawa, (2016): 288.

the departing shareholder and interest accrues from the day of serving the complaint. The shares held by the departing shareholder will be bought out by the company on the account of other shareholders, pro rata to the number of shares they hold. Additionally, the company and the shareholders will be jointly and severally liable for the payment of the buyout price (Article 300^{50} § 3–4 CCC). As indicated in the justification of the amendment, this mechanism aims to protect minority shareholders in the case of a conflict of interest, in particular, due to the long-lasting, economically unjustified hoarding of the company's profits, which results from the controlling shareholders' decision, especially if the profit is transferred to the controlling shareholders in the form of transactions not resulting from the corporate relationship.[19]

Consequently, the Polish literature indicates that in the vast majority of cases, in trade practice, the reason referred to in Article 300^{50} § 1 CCC will usually be an extended conflict between shareholders, or between shareholders and the company's management board.[20] This mechanism aims to protect the shareholder from being the 'corporate prisoner' who cannot leave the company despite infringing his or her interest.[21]

A similar mechanism is provided in the European Model Company Act in Section 11.37. If any shareholder has, intentionally or by gross negligence, caused a loss to the company, individual shareholders, the company's creditors, or other third parties, and there is a risk of continued abuse, in that case, the court may order that shareholder to redeem the shares belonging to the shareholder who suffers a loss or to sell his shares to the other shareholders.

---

19 Justification to the governmental amendment draft – Parliamentary Draft, 2019, No 3236, p. 58.

20 Grzegorz Kozieł, "Prosta spółka akcyjna. Komentarz", C.H. Beck, Warszawa, (2020): Art. 300 (50), Legalis; Piotr Pinior, "Ochrona praw akcjonariuszy mniejszościowych a prawo ustąpienia akcjonariusza", in *Non omne quod licet honestum est. Studia z prawa cywilnego i handlowego w 50-lecie pracy naukowej Profesora Wojciecha Jana Katnera*, ed. Szymon Byczko, Aleksander Kappes, Bartosz Kucharski, Urszula Promińska, Wolters Kluwer, Łódź – Warszawa, (2022): 670; Marcin Mazgaj in *Kodeks spółek handlowych. Komentarz.* ed. Zbigniew Jara, C. H. Beck, Warszawa, (2023): Art. 300 (50), Legalis; Robert Głowacki, "Powództwo o ustąpienie akcjonariusza", *Przegląd Prawa Handlowego*, 1 (2022): 38.

21 Mateusz Żaba in *Kodeks spółek handlowych. Komentarz*, ed. Piotr Pinior, Janusz Andrzej Strzępka, C.H. Beck, Warszawa, (2024): 727.

The redemption or sale is made at a reasonable price, fixed with respect to the company's financial position and circumstances of the case.[22]

In the British Companies Act,[23] the protection of minority shareholders is guaranteed by proceedings against unfair prejudice. Under Article 994 (1) CA, a shareholder may petition the court for an order on the grounds that the company's affairs are being or have been conducted in a manner that is unfairly prejudicial to the interests of members generally, or of some of its members (including at least the petitioner), or that an actual or proposed act or omission of the company (including an act or omission on its behalf) is or would be prejudicial. Among other things, a court's order may, under Article 996 (2) CA, require the company to refrain from doing or continuing the act being complained about, or may provide for the purchase of the shares of any shareholders, either by other shareholders or by the company itself. The unfair prejudice remedy enables a minority shareholder to exit the company under the court's decision in the case of suffering harm from other shareholders or the company's authorities. It is underlined in the literature that the most common order of the court is to provide for the purchase of the shares.[24]

Different legal mechanisms may be found in other national orders. A prime example of this is in the Spanish Companies Act,[25] which allows shareholders in limited liability companies or joint-stock companies to demand their release from the company in the case of insufficient dividend payment. Under Article 348 bis of the SCA, unless otherwise provided in the company's bylaws, after the fifth financial year from the registration of the company, a shareholder who has recorded in the minutes a protest against the insufficiency of the recognised dividends will have the right to separation (withdrawal) if the shareholders' meeting does not agree to the distribution as a dividend of at least 25% of the legally distributable profits

22 As explained in the comment, Section 37 is inspired by Nordic law (Danish Companies Act §§ 362 and 363, Finnish Companies Act Chapter 23, Section 2 and Swedish Companies Act Chapter 29, 3 § and following).

23 Companies Act 2006, <www.legislation.gov.uk/ukpga/2006/46/>, hereinafter abbreviated as CA.

24 Carsten Gerner-Beuerle, Michael Schillig, "Comparative Company Law", Oxford, (2020): 611.

25 Real Decreto Legislativo 1 / 2010, de 2 de julio, por el que se aprueba el texto refundido de la Ley de Sociedades de Capital, BOE-A-2010-10544, Art. 227–229, hereinafter abbreviated as SCA (Spanish Companies Act).

obtained during the previous year, on the condition that the company has been profitable profits in each of the three previous years. However, even if the above circumstance occurs, the right of separation will not arise if the total dividends distributed during the last five years are equivalent to at least 25% of the legally distributable profits recorded in that period. In the event that there is a lack of agreement between the company and the shareholder on the fair value of the shares, or on the person or persons who must value them and the procedure to follow for their valuation, the shares will be valued by an independent expert, appointed by the commercial registrar at the request of the company or any of the shareholders who own the shares being valued (Article 353 SCA). The mechanisms mentioned above, as well as typical minority protection rights, demonstrate that the national legislator has identified the problems of vulnerable shareholders. However, the withdrawal mechanisms are not widely provided by law and if they exist at all, they are limited to specific circumstances.

As for the second aspect of typical abuse, national legislators also provide protection mechanisms. For example, Article 300[21] CCC introduces an obligation concerning Polish simple joint-stock companies whereby the value of any benefits provided by the company to shareholders other than rights arising from shares, as well as to companies or cooperatives related to them or remaining in a relationship of dominance or dependence towards them, may not exceed the fair value of the mutual benefit received by the company. A shareholder who received a payment made contrary to that provision is obliged to return it (Article 300[22] § 1 CCC). According to the justification for the amendment, this provision aims to prevent minority shareholders from a 'hidden payout' in the form of a transfer of the company's assets beyond *causa societatis*, i.e. in the form of sale, lease, or mandate contract, as the addressee of the 'hidden payout' is almost always the controlling shareholder in practice. These transfers are detrimental to minority shareholders as they reduce the potential investment capital or participation in the company's profits.[26] This solution protects the company because the board members responsible for excessive payments will be liable for the damage incurred by the company. However, it may still not be satisfactory in some cases, for

[26] Justification to the governmental amendment draft – Parliamentary Draft 2019, No. 3236.

example, where the board member is also a shareholder and has a labour or mandate contract with the company. In the legal doctrine, the view appears that such a mechanism is aimed at protecting the integrity of a company's assets, primarily in the interest of creditors and minority shareholders.[27] However, it requires cooperation with the company's boards.

In the case of an abuse of rights due to related party transactions, the unfair prejudice remedy provided in the UK Companies Act may also be used by disadvantaged shareholders.

Considering the forms of shareholder protection mentioned above, the proposal to create optimal protection in limited liability companies means a choice between a court decision on shareholders' withdrawal and the introduction of shareholders' withdrawal premises by law. Both possibilities have their advantages and disadvantages. In the first case, the disadvantage is the initial fee for filing a claim against the company and its shareholders. In the second, the disadvantage is that introducing all the potential premises of a conflict of interest by law is impossible. Additionally, even in the case of a voluntary withdrawal, there might be a problem with a satisfactory payoff for the leaving shareholder, which may finally result in a court dispute.

5. Conclusions

Protecting minority shareholders is crucial in order to maintain a balance of power and prevent abuse by majority shareholders. It contributes to transparent and accountable corporate practices. The need to introduce additional protective mechanisms for shareholders occurs when their interests are violated, and there are no instruments to protect their rights. The violation of the interests of a minority shareholder appears when a shareholder is deprived of the right to a dividend for a long time, while at the same time, the company's assets are transferred to the majority shareholders, and there is no possibility of selling or redeeming the shareholder's shares. Such circumstances allow

---

[27] Kozieł, "Prosta spółka akcyjna. Komentarz": Art. 300 (21), Legalis; Andrzej Kidyba, Małgorzata Dumkiewicz, "Komentarz aktualizowany do kodeksu spółek handlowych". Wolters Kluwer, Warszawa, Lex/el. (2023): Art. 300 (21); Wojciech Wyrzykowski in *Kodeks spółek handlowych. Komentarz*, ed. Piotr Pinior, Janusz Andrzej Strzępka, C.H. Beck, Warszawa, (2024): 694.

the identification of the shareholder as a vulnerable person due to the lack of legal protection.

The mechanisms indicated in the fourth part of this chapter enabling a shareholder to exit the company based on a court decision help guarantee proper protection of minority shareholders in conflict situations and constitute a remedy for 'trapped' shareholders. These instruments should also guarantee appropriate remuneration (fair value) for the purchased shares.

The mechanism of a shareholder's right to exit the company is undoubtedly a desirable institution, the introduction of which should also be considered in all types of companies, in particular in limited liability companies, where the problem of shareholders' vulnerability may occur.

Bibliography

Paul Krüger Andersen, Jan Bertil Andersson, Nordic & European Company Law, LSN Research Paper Series, No 16-26, European Model Company Act (2017).

Paweł Błaszczyk, "Ochrona wspólników mniejszościowych spółki zależnej należącej do grupy spółek", *Państwo i Prawo*, 10 (2010).

Pierre-Henri Conac, "The shareholders' duty not to abuse rights" in *Shareholders' duties*, ed. Hanne S. Birkmose, Kluwer Law International (2017).

Carsten Gerner-Beuerle, Michael Schillig, "Comparative Company Law", Oxford (2020).

Robert Głowacki, "Powództwo o ustąpienie akcjonariusza", *Przegląd Prawa Handlowego*, 1 (2022).

Wojciech Jan Katner, "Prawa mniejszości w spółkach kapitałowych (I)", *Przegląd Prawa Handlowego*, 2 (2002).

Andrzej Kidyba, "Ochrona praw mniejszości w spółce z ograniczoną odpowiedzialnością" in *Księga pamiątkowa dla uczczenia pracy naukowej Prof. K. Kruczalaka*, Gdańskie Studia Prawnicze, Vol. V (1999).

Andrzej Kidyba, Małgorzata Dumkiewicz, "Komentarz aktualizowany do kodeksu spółek handlowych". Wolters Kluwer, Warszawa, Lex/el. (2023).

Katarzyna Kopaczyńska – Pieczniak, "Spółka z ograniczoną odpowiedzialnością", ed. Andrzej Kidyba, Wolters Kluwer, Warszawa (2007).

Grzegorz Kozieł, "Prosta spółka akcyjna. Komentarz", C.H. Beck, Warszawa (2020).

Olga Lipińska – Długosz, "Ochrona spółki akcyjnej i jej akcjonariuszy przed niewłaściwym wykonywaniem prawa", C.H. Beck, Warszawa (2006).

Marcin Mazgaj in *Kodeks spółek handlowych. Komentarz.* ed. Zbigniew Jara, C. H. Beck, Warszawa (2023).

Józef Okolski, Jerzy Modrzejewski, Łukasz Gasiński, "Zasada równego traktowania akcjonariuszy na gruncie KSH", *Przegląd Prawa Handlowego*, 10 (2002).

Krzysztof Oplustil, "Instrumenty nadzoru korporacyjnego (corporate governance) w spółce akcyjnej", C.H. Beck, Warszawa (2010).

Piotr Pinior, "Ochrona praw akcjonariuszy mniejszościowych a prawo ustąpienia akcjonariusza", in *Non omne quod licet honestum est. Studia z prawa cywilnego i handlowego w 50-lecie pracy naukowej Profesora Wojciecha Jana Katnera*, ed. Szymon Byczko, Aleksander Kappes, Bartosz Kucharski, Urszula Promińska, Wolters Kluwer, Łódź – Warszawa (2022).

Piotr Pinior, "Nadzór wspólników w spółce z ograniczoną odpowiedzialnością", C.H. Beck, Warszawa (2013).

Wojciech Popiołek, "Akcja – prawo podmiotowe", C.H. Beck, Warszawa (2010).

Arkadiusz Radwan, "*Ius dissidentium*. Granice konsensusu korporacyjnego i władzy większości w spółkach kapitałowych", C.H. Beck, Warszawa (2016).

Andrzej Szumański in *System Prawa Prywatnego. Prawo papierów Wartościowych, Vol. 19*. ed. Andrzej Szumański, C.H. Beck, Warszawa (2006).

Dominika Wajda, "Ochrona akcjonariuszy mniejszościowych w kodeksie spółek handlowych", C.H. Beck, Warszawa (2007).

Wojciech Wyrzykowski in *Kodeks spółek handlowych. Komentarz*, ed. Piotr Pinior, Janusz Andrzej Strzępka, C.H. Beck, Warszawa (2024).

Jakub Jan Zięty, "Uprawnienia akcjonariuszy polskich spółek publicznych, w świetle dyrektywy 2007/36/WE", C.H. Beck, Warszawa (2015).

Judicial Review of Local Anti-LGBT Resolutions in Light of the Principles of Polish and European Law

*Dawid Gregorczyk**

Abstract: The issue of the rights of the lesbian, gay, bisexual, and transgender (LGBT)[1] community has been used for political purposes in Poland since 2019. Local government bodies have adopted resolutions introducing so-called LGBT-free zones, expressing their opposition to an ideology that they claimed seeks to 'sexualise children' and destroy traditional values such as family. However, these resolutions violated the principle of non-discrimination expressed in the Polish constitution and European law, being homophobic and excluding sexual minorities, making them a particularly vulnerable group. Despite the actions of European institutions in this matter, challenging anti-LGBT resolutions in Polish courts has proven to be a complicated matter. Therefore, the institutional vulnerability of LGBT community and LGBT persons can be viewed in two key areas. First, their relationship with local government bodies, which represent the entire community but often claim to be free from 'LGBT ideology'. Second, their interaction with the judiciary, where courts are expected to protect human rights against discriminatory actions by public administration. This work specifically examines whether LGBT individuals and LGBT organisations have effective means to challenge such discrimination under current laws and judicial practices.

Keywords: judicial review of administrative action, jurisdiction of administrative courts, local government bodies, polish LGBT-free zones, rights of LGBT persons

1. Introduction

The concept of vulnerability and vulnerable groups is used to describe specific groups that are experiencing hardship in society because of their disabilities and lack of social support. Sociological approaches to vulnerability can be based on the general theory of risk, or health risks, or by examining the

* PhD, Assistant Professor at the Faculty of Law and Administration of the University of Silesia in Katowice, Poland. ORCID: 0000-0001-7740-2540.

1 For the purposes of this paper, the term LGBT will be used to cover the whole spectrum of LGBT+ individuals: lesbian, gay, bisexual, transgender, and more, like queer or questioning, intersex, asexual.

effects of individualisation on human vulnerability.[2] The topic of vulnerability and the protection of marginalised groups is a recurring issue in the field of protecting fundamental rights. In recent years, the EU has recognised and addressed the situation and needs of vulnerable groups in various general documents. One of the criteria used to identify vulnerability is minority status, which includes individuals who identify as LGBT.[3] There is no doubt in psychological science that LGBT people are at high risk of suicidal behaviour due to perceived stigma and psychopathology.[4] Protective factors, such as community connectedness[5] and the work of school-based health centres that support mental health indicators among sexual minority youths,[6] may reduce that risk. Irresponsible discriminatory actions have the opposite effect, especially if they are undertaken in the name of the local community. A study conducted in 2023 concluded that the adoption of anti-LGBT resolutions in local government units in Poland was detrimental to the population's mental health by establishing a direct link between anti-LGBT resolutions, suicide attempts and deaths from suicide. This rise in suicide attempts was concentrated among men and was associated with 11 additional suicides per

---

2 Barbara A. Misztal, "The Challenges of Vulnerability: In Search of Strategies for a Less Vulnerable Social Life", *Palgrave Macmillan London*, 2011, 2–4; <https://doi.org/10.1057/9780230316690>.

3 Agnė Limantė & Artūras Tereškinas, "Definition of Vulnerable Groups", in (Eds.) A. Limantė & D. Pūraitė-Andrikienė, *Legal Protection of Vulnerable Groups in Lithuania, Latvia, Estonia and Poland. European Union and its neighbours in a globalized world*, 2022 (vol. 8), Springer, 12–13; <https://doi.org/10.1007/978-3-031-06998-7_1>.

4 Stephen T. Russell, Jessica N. Fish, "Mental Health in Lesbian, Gay, Bisexual, and Transgender (LGBT) Youth", *Annual Review of Clinical Psychology*, 2016 12:1, 465–487; <https://doi.org/10.1146/annurev-clinpsy-021815-093153>.

5 Andrea Kaniuka, Kelley C. Pugh, Megan Jordan, Byron Brooks, Julia Dodd, Abbey K. Mann, Stacey L. Williams & Jameson K. Hirsch, "Stigma and suicide risk among the LGBTQ population: Are anxiety and depression to blame and can connectedness to the LGBTQ community help?", *Journal of Gay & Lesbian Mental Health*, 2019, 23(2), 205–220. DOI: 10.1080/19359705.2018.1560385.

6 Lei Zhang, Laura J. Finan, Melina Bersamin, Deborah A. Fisher, "Sexual Orientation-Based Depression and Suicidality Health Disparities: The Protective Role of School-Based Health Centers", *Journal of Research on Adolescence*, 2020 January, 134–142; <https://doi.org/10.1111/jora.12454>.

100k individuals aged 30–49.[7] Moreover, it was noted that, regardless of the intentions, the actions of the local governments have a significant impact on the development of socially accepted norms of behaviour; such resolutions may cause a chilling effect in subordinate units and increase the incidence of hate crimes.[8]

From a legal point of view, anti-LGBT resolutions seem to violate the principle of non-discrimination expressed in Article 32 of the Polish constitution[9] and in European law, especially in Article 14 of the ECHR,[10] Article 10 of the TFEU,[11] and Article 21(1) of the Charter of Fundamental Rights of the EU.[12] On 18 December 2019, the European Parliament adopted a resolution in which it '[c]alls on Poland to firmly condemn discrimination against LGBT people, including when it originates from local authorities, and to revoke resolutions attacking LGBTI rights, including local provisions against "LGBT ideology", in accordance with its national law as well as its obligations under EU and international law'.[13] On 14 July 2021, the European Commission announced the decision to start infringement procedures against Poland in relation to the process of creating LGBT ideology-free zones.[14] On 16 June 2021, the Congress of Local and Regional Authorities of the Council of Europe passed

7 Chad Meyerhoefer, Xue Bingjin, Anna Poznańska, "Implications of the Decline in LGBT Rights for Population Mental Health: Evidence from Polish LGBT-free zones", Cambridge, MA: National Bureau of Economic Research, September 2023 (No 31702), 18-19; <http://dx.doi.org/10.3386/w31702>.

8 Legal opinion of Marek Szolc for the Polish Anti-Discrimination Law Society, 13–14, <http://ptpa.org.pl/site/assets/files/1845/samorza_dy_ekspertyza_19_07_2019.pdf> (accessed on 11 September 2023).

9 Constitution of the Republic of Poland of April 2, 1997 (Journal of Laws 1997.78.483)

10 The Convention for the Protection of Human Rights and Fundamental Freedoms signed in Rome (Italy) on 4 November 1950 by 12 member states of the Council of Europe.

11 Treaty on the Functioning of the European Union - Consolidated version: Official EN Journal of the EU, C 326, 26.10.2012.

12 Official EN Journal of the EU, C 364/1, 18 December2000.

13 European Parliament resolution of 18 December 2019 on public discrimination and hate speech against LGBTI people, including LGBTI free zones (2019/2933(RSP)) (Official EN Journal of the EU. C 255, 29 June 2021).

14 <https://ec.europa.eu/commission/presscorner/detail/en/ip_21_3668> (accessed on 11 September 2023).

Resolution 471 (2021)23 calling on Polish local and regional authorities to withdraw all declarations and resolutions on so-called LGBT ideology.[15]

Furthermore, the possibility of appealing against anti-LGBT resolutions may be considered in the context of the right to an administrative court, which has its source not only in Article 45(1) of the Polish constitution but also in European law.[16] Particularly important here is Article 6(1) of the ECHR. Although this directly concerns civil and criminal cases, the case law of the ECtHR gives it an autonomous character, also covering certain cases considered by administrative courts.[17] However, appealing against anti-LGBT resolutions to the Polish courts turned out to be a complicated matter. It was unclear whether and how courts could control these resolutions, and who was eligible to appeal against them. This paper is devoted to these legal issues.

2. The origin and the definition of anti-LGBT resolutions

The past two decades have seen a flurry of laws addressing the legal entitlements of LGBT individuals. However, both in the United States and in some EU Member States – Poland and Hungry – there is a growing backlash from conservative political groups against the expansion of LGBT rights.[18] The legal situation of LGBT people in Poland has been difficult and has been deteriorating since the change of the ruling party in 2015. A 2018 report[19] stated a regression in eight areas of the life of LGBT people, highlighted

---

[15] <https://rm.coe.int/CoERMPublicCommonSearchServices/DisplayDCTMContent?documentId=0900001680a287d7> (accessed on 11 September 2023).

[16] Cf. Michał Kowalski, *Prawo do sądu administracyjnego. Standard międzynarodowy i konstytucyjny oraz jego realizacja*, ed. Wolters Kluwer Polska (Warszawa 2019), 38 et seq.

[17] Cf. Judgment ECtHR: 6 November 2007, 61967/00, SERNAWIT v. POLAND; 18 December 2007, 12550/02, OLESINSKI v. POLAND; 9 December 1994, 19005/91, SCHOUTEN AND MELDRUM v. THE NETHERLANDS; 24 February 1994, 12547/86, BENDENOUN v. FRANCE; 3 May 2001, 31827/96, J.B. v. SWITZERLAND. All judgments are available at: <https://hudoc.echr.coe.int>.

[18] Meyerhoefer, Bingjin, Poznańska (2023), 1.

[19] "Three years of bad change for LGBTI people - summary of PiS rule", 2018, by Lambada Warsaw associations and the Campaign for Homophobia, <https://kph.org.pl/wp-content/uploads/2018/11/Raport_podsumowanie_rzadow_pis.pdf> (accessed on 11 September 2023).

in the recommendations of the Committee of Ministers of the Council of Europe.[20] According to a Rainbow Europe ranking by ILGA-Europe, in 2019 Poland took the penultimate place among the EU Member States, receiving just 18 out of 100 points.[21] Another report by the same organisation stated: 'Over the past number of years, LGBTI people have come under increasing attack from ruling politicians, religious leaders and other public figures in Poland. This has come in the form of dangerous and false framing of LGBTI people as a threat to children, and as a threat to Christianity'.[22] The words of Jarosław Kaczyński, leader of the ruling conservative Law and Justice (PiS) party, speaking on 15 April 2018, were considered the first loud political hate speech against LGBT people in Poland: 'No homosexual marriages will occur; we will wait peacefully for the European Union countries to sober up'.[23] The study indicates that this type of action is part of the tendency of other populist governments, especially in Hungary,[24] to wage a 'culture war' and defend society against so-called 'enemies' like the LGBT community.[25]

A step towards improving the situation of LGBT people was the inclusion of LGBT issues in anti-discrimination programmes and sexual education in all schools. The Warsaw LGBT Declaration (LGBT+ Charter) was signed on 18 February 2019, by the mayor of Warsaw – Rafał Trzaskowski – of the opposition political party. His actions were considered by the far-right environment and then the ruling party as an 'ideological offensive' enabling the introduction of sexual education to Warsaw schools according to WHO

---

20 Recommendation CM/Rec (2010) 5 of the Committee of Ministers to member states on measures to combat discrimination based on sexual orientation or gender identity; <https://search.coe.int/cm/Pages/result_details.aspx?ObjectID=09000016805cf40a> (accessed on 11 September 2023).

21 <https://ilga-europe.org/press-release/10th-rainbow-europe-confirmed-stagnation-and-regression-on-lgbti-equality-calls-for-immediate-action/> (accessed on 11 September 2023).

22 Poland Anti-LGBT Timeline, 2022, <https://www.ilga-europe.org/files/uploads/2022/06/Poland-Anti-LGBT-Timeline.pdf> (accessed on 11 September 2023).

23 Ibidem.

24 Adam Bodnar, "Polish Road toward an Illiberal State: Methods and Resistance", Indiana Law Journal No. 96 (2021), 1059.

25 Adam Ploszka, "From human rights to human wrongs: how local government can negatively influence the situation of an individual : the case of Polish LGBT ideology-free zones", *The international journal of human rights*, 2023, Vol. 27, No 2, 361; <https://doi.org/10.1080/13642987.2022.2121708>.

guidelines, which they considered controversial. In the opinion of these bodies, the local authority resolutions express opposition to the ideology that seeks to 'sexualise children' and to 'destroy traditional values, such as the family.'[26] In this way, the matter of LGBT rights became a political issue used in the fight between polarised political parties. On the initiatives of right-wing and Catholic circles, local government bodies adopted opposite declarations, recognising their territories as 'LGBT ideology-free zones' or 'LGBT-free zones.' At one time, a third of Poland was under an LGBT-free zone.[27]

The anti-LGBT resolutions should be understood as various types of resolutions against the 'LGBT ideology' taken by local government bodies (cities and other levels of local government units). There should be no doubt that this is about LGBT people themselves, because there is no single ideology that such people would accept, just as there is no single ideology of heterosexual people.[28] It also does not matter whether they were given the form of a declaration, resolution, or opinion, as an act adopted by a collegial public administration body constitutes a resolution.[29] Hence the name 'anti-LGBT resolutions' seems most appropriate.

The first resolution of this type was adopted on 26 March 2019 by the Świdnik County Council.[30] It stated: Due to the ideological war started by some politicians, the Świdnik County Council adopts the declaration

---

26 <https://ordoiuris.pl/edukacja/presja-ordo-iuris-i-innych-organizacji-prorodzinnych-przynosi-efekty-warszawski-ratusz> (accessed on 11 September 2023).

27 Ploszka (2023), 360.

28 This was stated by the Provincial Administrative Court in Gliwice judgment of 14 July 2020, III SA/Gl 15/20, LEX No 3042555. The court added that, even if it were assumed that the resolution was about "ideology", it should be taken into account that ideology does not occur in nature in a free state, isolated from people. [...] The term "LGBT ideology-free zone" de facto refers to people from this group and directly affects them. Explaining that LGBT are not people, but an ideology, is turning a blind eye to reality when one does not want to see the full consequences of such words.

29 Similarly Dorota Dąbek, "Zakres sądowej kontroli administracji : aktualne tendencje na tle sporu o kognicję w sprawach stref wolnych od LGBT", in eds. Maksymilian Cherka, Piotr Gołaszewski, Jacek, Piecha, Marek Wierzbowski *Kryzys, stagnacja, renesans? Prawo administracyjne przyszłości. Księga jubileuszowa profesora dr hab. Jacka Jagielskiego*, Wolters Kluwer Polska (Warszawa 2021), 922–923; also Supreme Administrative Court judgment of 27 September 2017, I OSK 1066/17, LEX No 2371162.

30 <https://spswidnik.bip.lubelskie.pl/?id=518&action=details&document_id=1591655> (accessed on 11 September 2023).

'Świdnik County free from LGBT ideology'. Radicals seeking a cultural revolution in Poland attacked freedom of speech, the innocence of children, the authority of the family and school, and the freedom of enterprise. That is why we will consistently defend our local government community!

It went on to express disagreement with 'installing political correctness officers in schools (known as lighthouse keepers)' and with 'the entry of scandalists interested in the early sexualisation of Polish children by the WHO standards'. It declared that there is no consent to 'exerting administrative pressure to apply political correctness (sometimes rightly called homopropaganda) in selected professions. We will protect, among others: teachers and entrepreneurs from imposing unprofessional criteria on them, e.g. in educational work, when selecting employees or contractors!'

3. Anti-LBGT resolutions as the subject of a complaint to the Polish courts

According to Article 184 of the Polish constitution: the Supreme Administrative Court and other administrative courts shall exercise, to the extent specified by statute, control over the performance of public administration. Such control shall also extend to judgments on the conformity to the statute of resolutions of organs of local government and normative acts of territorial organs of government administration.

The scope of this control is determined by Article 3(2) of the Act on Proceedings before Administrative Courts (APAC),[31] which lists possible objects of appeal. Therefore, anti-LGBT resolutions can be subject to judicial review only if they can be classified as one of the objects of control indicated in this article, especially as 'acts of local law' (point 5) or as 'other acts of local government bodies and their associations adopted in matters related to public administration' (point 6). The nature of local law, as specified in Articles 87 and 88 of the Polish constitution, does not cover anti-LGBT resolutions, because they were issued without authorisation in a specific act of Parliament and without the intention of containing legally binding orders or prohibitions addressed to residents. The subject of an appeal under

[31] Act on Proceedings before Administrative Courts of 30 August 2002 (Journal of Laws 2023.1634).

Article 3 (2) point 6 APAC was defined broadly. The following features can be deduced from the content of this provision and its relationship with others: 1) legal act (an individual or general, abstract or specific, external or internal act of applying law or normative acts[32]); 'other' (than local law and other types of acts indicated in separate grounds for appeal[33]); undertaken by local government bodies or their associations; in a matter relating to public administration. The courts examining complaints against anti-LGBT resolutions had to determine, primarily, whether the anti-LBGT resolutions met these conditions, in particular the condition for action in a case related to public administration.

In the beginning, provincial (first instance) administrative courts (hereinafter: 'PA Court') found that the resolutions could not be challenged because they were not adopted 'in matters relating to public administration'. It was pointed out that they do not constitute the implementation of a public task assigned by law to a local government body and they do not contain any element of administrative authority,[34] do not constitute the basis for imposing any obligations or granting or confirming rights[35] and do not have a specific addressee (general or individual). This resulted from the position adopted over the years in science and jurisprudence that the subject of an appeal to the court under Article 3 (2) point 6 APAC can only be a legal act, understood as an act with the effect of imposing an obligation, granting a right, or abolishing an existing legal relationship, rather than an actual action.[36] As a result, various types of activities of local government bodies that did not have any legal effects were not subject to the court's jurisdiction. The same

32 Cf. Jan P. Tarno, "Prawo o postępowaniu przed sądami administracyjnymi. Komentarz", ed. LexisNexis Polska (Warszawa 2012), 39.

33 Cf. Małgorzata Jaśkowska, "Sądowoadministracyjna kontrola aktów z zakresu administracji publicznej, niebędących aktami prawa miejscowego, podejmowanych przez organy samorządu terytorialnego i ich związków", in: Marek Szewczyk, Maria Jędrzejczak, *Prawne formy działania stosowane przez organy samorządu terytorialnego. Księga jubileuszowa Profesora Krystiana Ziemskiego*, (Ed.) C.H. Beck (Warszawa 2022), 103.

34 PA Court in Rzeszów resolution of 8 September 2020, II SA/Rz 27/20, LEX No 3070924.

35 PA Court in Kraków resolution of 23 June 23, 2020, III SA/Kr 105/20, LEX No 3020596 and PA Court in Poznań resolution of 16 April 2020, II SA/Po 188/20, LEX No. 3009301.

36 Cf. justification for the resolution of the Supreme Administrative Court of 26 June 2014, I OPS 14/13, ONSAiWSA 2015, No 1, item 2 and Tarno (2012), 39.

conclusion was also derived from the premise of 'matters within the scope of public administration'.[37] The requirement of legal effect was also derived from the fact that the contestable act must infringe the legal interest or right of the complainant.[38] Since the act did not produce any legal effect, it could not have infringed anyone's interest, making its judicial review impossible.

The above theses of the courts were questioned. It should be taken into account that the requirement of a 'violation of a legal interest' and 'the matter remaining within the scope of public administration' do not limit public interest complainants: a supervisory authority, a prosecutor or one of the public ombudsmen.[39] Therefore, the objective requirements of the subject of the complaint cannot be understood through the prism of the requirements of certain categories of complaining entities. In addition, it is hard to disagree with the opinions of the doctrine that Article 3(2) point 6 APAC also includes acts of a general nature not containing orders or prohibitions,[40] especially where such non-authoritative actions may influence the legal situation of their recipients indirectly.[41] This situation occurred in the case of anti-LGBT resolutions, because the local government body made a recommendation on what sex education and education should look like in local government schools. Moreover, even if these resolutions were considered non-normative (having no legal effect), they are undoubtedly adopted in matters of public

---

[37] Cf. PA Court in Kraków resolution of 23 June 2020, III SA/Kr 105/20, LEX No 3020596 and other resolution of PA Court in Rzeszów(8 September 2020, II SA/Rz 27/20, LEX No 3070924); in Gdańsk (24 September 2020, II SA/Gd 702/20, LEX No 3056375); in Białystok (3 December 2020, II SA/Bk 736/20, LEX No 3088948); in Lublin (17 February 2021, III SA/Lu 312/20, LEX No 3125850).

[38] Andrzej Matan, Art. 101, in (Eds.) Bogdan Dolnicki, *Ustawa o samorządzie gminnym. Komentarz*, ed. Wolter Kluwer Polska (Warszawa 2021), 1020; Similarly Dorota Dąbek, Art. 101, in (Eds.) Paweł Chmielnicki, *Ustawa o samorządzie gminnym*, ed. Wolter Kluwer Polska (Warszawa 2022), 1212–1213.

[39] Magdalena Gurdek, "Glosa do wyroku TK z 13.03.2007 r., K 8/07", *Przegląd Prawa Publicznego* 2007, No. 10, 92–94 and Supreme Administrative Court judgment of 13 December 1999, IV SA 872/99, LEX No. 48223.

[40] Krystian M. Ziemski, *Indywidualny akt administracyjny jako forma prawna działania administracji*, (Ed.) Wydawnictwo Naukowe UAM (Poznań 2005), 169.

[41] Jaśkowska (2022), 102.

administration and should be subject to review by an administrative court.[42] This interpretation seems to be consistent with the intention of the legislator, who covered not only the provisions of local law with external legal effect, but also other general acts of local government bodies.

The first ruling on the admissibility of a judicial review of anti-LGBT resolutions came in the judgment of the Provincial Administrative Court in Gliwice on 14 July 2020, III SA/Gl 15/20 (LEX nr 3042555). It was emphasised that the contested anti-LGBT resolution meets all the features of the act stipulated in Article 3(2) point 6 APAC: it is an act adopted by a public administration body in the form of a resolution of its body (the District Council) and concerns matters in the area of public administration (municipal tasks specified in Article 7 Municipal Local Government Act[43]). At the same time, it authoritatively outlines the directions of action and responsibilities for the municipal executive body and other entities, mainly educational ones. The resolution is therefore of a mixed nature: individual, because it refers to the mayor (under Article 18(2) point 2 Municipal Local Government Act), as well as general, as it applies to other municipal entities whose tasks and competencies concern the issues raised in the resolution, and to private entities and businesses that the Municipal Council intended to 'protect'. Therefore, a resolution is not an act that without an addressee and does not address directives to anyone for a specific action, as should be considered in the case of a declaration of worldview, ideology or any other kind. Moreover, it was emphasised that a judicial review of the legality of local government resolutions should provide citizens with a real defence against the illegal actions of public administration bodies. The narrowing of the content of Article 3(2) point 6 APAC was deemed unconstitutional, resulting in the refusal to grant legal recourse to citizens who consider that acts of this type

[42] Supreme Administrative Court resolution of 2 July 2021, III OSK 3353/21, OSP 2022/7-8/69; Iwona Niżnik-Dobosz, "Podstawy i znaczenie prawne rezolucji, deklaracji, apelów i oświadczeń organów stanowiących jednostek samorządu terytorialnego jako formy działania administracji publicznej", in: Szewczyk, Jędrzejczak (2022), 224–225.

[43] Act, on Municipal Local Government of 8 March 1990 (Journal of Laws 2023.40), hereinafter: "Municipal Local Government Act".

violate their constitutional rights. This position was also adopted by some other courts of first instance.[44]

The opinion of the court of the second instance played a crucial role in the final decision, as it questioned the inadmissibility of reviewing anti-LGBT resolutions.[45] The Supreme Administrative Court stated that, according to the Constitution, all activities of local government are subject to the judicial system and the administrative court has the presumption of jurisdiction in this respect, in particular adjudicating on the legal compliance of resolutions of local government bodies. To rebut this presumption, the administrative court must demonstrate that the case brought before this court, as a result of a challenge to the act issued therein, falls within the jurisdiction of another court. Therefore, acts in matters related to public administration are all acts of local government bodies that are not subject to the jurisdiction of other courts, in particular common courts. An administrative court may question the nature of a given act as an act issued in a case in the area of public administration by demonstrating that the act is subject to the administration of justice by a court other than the administrative court, in particular by a common court. Thus, the Supreme Administrative Court distanced itself from its previous position, according to which the acts of Article 3(2) point 6 APAC must 'impose an obligation, establish a right or obligation or create or abolish an existing legal relationship'.[46] The court drew attention to the direction of the evolution of views over the years, regarding the interpretation of the concept of acts taken in matters of public administration, i.e. the direction that guarantees the right to a court to the greatest extent possible, and thus indicates the need for a broad understanding of this concept. This includes preventing manifestations of public administration activity that are aimed at avoiding judicial control.

It should be added that such a broad approach to the jurisdiction of administrative courts corresponds to the broad approach to the right to an

---

[44] Cf. judgment of the PA Court in: Lublin (6 August 2020, III SA/Lu 7/20, LEX No. 3055157); in Warsaw (15 July 2020, VIII SA/Wa 42/20, LEX No. 3047928); in Kielce (11 September 2020, II SA/Ke 382/20, LEX No. 3110483); in Krakow (10 January 2022, III SA/Kr 975/21, LEX No 3291841).

[45] Judgment of 2 July 2021, III OSK 3353/21, LEX No. 3193519.

[46] Cf. the previously cited judgments, especially the resolution of the Supreme Administrative Court of 26 June 2014, I OPS 14/13, ONSAiWSA 2015, No 1, item 2.

administrative court, which, as indicated in the introduction, also has its source in European law. In particular, it should be noted that the soft law clarifying the standards set out in Article 6 of the ECHR – Recommendation No. 20 of 2004 of the Committee of Ministers of the Council of Europe on the judicial review of administrative acts[47] – recognises as 'physical acts of administration taken in the exercise of public authority that may affect the rights or interests of natural or legal persons'.

4. Entities authorised to appeal against an anti-LBGT resolution

Recognising the admissibility of a judicial review of anti-LGBT resolutions opens another problem: who is entitled to appeal? The court cannot conduct a control *ex officio*. At first glance, it may appear that LGBT individuals should have the right to appeal, since they are the ones facing discrimination due to the title resolutions. However, in the Polish model, only citizens who have 'a legal interest in filing a complaint' are granted the *locus standi* to do so, according to Article 50 APAC: having a legal interest means that an entity has a specific legal provision that authorises them to request a public administration body. This legal provision establishes a direct, real and actual relationship between the law and the interest of the entity, rather than an indirect relationship that is justified by future, hypothetical events.[48] Legal interest is therefore understood quite narrowly. Moreover, a complaint to an administrative court does not require demonstrating a violation of an individual's legal interest. It is enough to have an interest in verifying the legality of the resolution, which is not limited only to the allegations in the complaint. However, for district (gmina) and county (powiat) local government resolutions, complainants must demonstrate that their legal interest

47 <https://rm.coe.int/cmrec-2004-20-on-judicial-review-of-administrative-acts/1680a43b5b> (accessed on 11 September 2023).

48 Tarno (2012), 159–162 and the publications indicated therein.

or entitlement has been violated.[49] This requirement has been extended to acts of voivodeship local government bodies.[50]

If an LGBT individual wishes to file a complaint against a discriminatory resolution, they must demonstrate a direct violation of their rights and obligations. Hence, a significant problem arises, because anti-LGBT resolutions do not have a direct legal effect. The statement that a local government body is against LGBT ideology, even though it concerns LGBT people, does not change their legal situation. These resolutions, even those that address the lack of consent to conduct sexual education by WHO guidelines, or the criteria for selecting contractors by businesses, cannot have any impact on the relevant issues because local government bodies do not have the authority to influence them. For these reasons, recognising the legal interest of LGBT people in challenging resolutions that discriminate against them, especially the violation of their interests or rights, turned out to be very complicated and the courts did not recognise the complaints as admissible.[51]

Another entity whose legitimacy to file a complaint should be considered is a social organisation. It would seem obvious that an organisation fighting for the rights of LGBT people would be able to initiate a judicial review. In practice, however, it turned out not to be the case. Article 50(1) APAC provides that a social organisation, within the scope of its statutory activities, may submit a complaint to the administrative court in matters relating to the legal interests of others if it participated in administrative proceedings. First, this still leaves doubts as to whether the modification of the right to file a complaint in special provisions has excluded the possibility of a complaint being filed by social organisations that have no other legal basis than Article 50 APAC.[52] Second, this legal provision requires the participation of a social organisation in administrative proceedings, and anti-LGBT resolutions were

---

[49] Art. 101(1) Municipal Self-Government Act and Art. 87 of the Act on County Local Government of 5 June 1998 (Journal of Laws of 2022.1526).

[50] Supreme Administrative Court resolution of 22 September 2021, III OSK 4685/21, LEX No. 3226436.

[51] Supreme Administrative Court resolution of 22 September 2021, III OSK 4685/21, LEX No. 3226436; PA Court in Rzeszów resolution of 22 November 2019, II SA/Rz 1118/19, LEX No. 3038444; PA Court in Bialystok resolution of 10 October 2019, II SA/Bk 651/19, LEX No. 2726133.

[52] Tarno (2012), 163–164.

not issued in such proceedings. Polish law limits administrative proceedings mainly to individual decisions. Therefore, the question is whether, in such a situation, this requirement does not apply at all, which would make it possible to grant the social organisation legitimacy, or whether this requirement applies but will never be met, which excludes the possibility of social organisations appealing against any resolutions. Unfortunately, science and jurisprudence have opted for the last solution,[53] which makes it impossible for social organisations to challenge anti-LGBT resolutions.

Relevant public entities may also submit a complaint to the administrative court. This applies in particular to the appropriate voivode, the prosecutor, the Ombudsman and the Ombudsman for Children. These entities operate in the public interest, so the requirement to prove the existence and infringement of an individual legal interest does not apply to them. It would therefore seem that a wide list of public entities authorised to initiate a judicial review would guarantee its implementation in cases requiring the intervention of an administrative court. However, the example of anti-LGBT resolutions raised justified doubts in this respect. When the issue turned political, the agencies under the ruling political party declined to contest the resolutions in the administrative court.[54] This is because, the supervisory body is legally obliged to share the political position of the government,[55] the prosecutor's office is subordinate to the Minister of Justice[56] and the Ombudsman for Children opposed support for LGBT people.[57] Luckily, the political circumstances of the

---

53 Taudeusz Woś, in: Hanna Knysiak-Sudyka, Marta Romańska, Tadeusz Woś, *Prawo o postępowaniu przed sądami administracyjnymi. Komentarz,* ed. Wolters Kluwer Polska (Warszawa 2016), 426; also Supreme Administrative Court judgment of 31 January 2018, II OSK 1558/17, LEX No. 2466812.

54 Cf. Ploszka (2023), 365–366.

55 According to Art. 24 of the Act on Voivodes and Government Administration in Voivodeships of 23 January 2009 (Journal of Laws 2023.190): In his speeches, the voivode represents a position in accordance with the arrangements adopted by the Council of Ministers.

56 According to Art. 1 (2) of the Act on the Public Prosecutor's Office of 28 January 2016 (Journal of Laws 2023.1360).

57 Cf. report by the Helsinki Foundation for Human Rights "Children's rights in the shadow of the rule of law crisis. Functioning of the office of the Ombudsman for Children in 2015-2022", 44–48, <https://hfhr.pl/upload/2022/12/raport-prawa-dziecka-w-cieniu-kryzysu-praworzadnosci_1.pdf> (accessed on 11 September 2023).

Ombudsman were different and Adam Bodnar, who served as Ombudsman, showed civil courage in the face of government criticism. He did not hesitate to exercise the right of complaint, which turned out to be the only effective way to initiate a judicial review of anti-LGBT resolutions.

5. Material patterns of control over anti-LGBT resolutions

The effective initiation of proceedings before an administrative court does not yet guarantee effective control. Therefore, it is necessary to consider whether the formula of judicial control only over the legality of the administration's actions was sufficient to verify anti-LGBT resolutions. To determine the legality of a public administration body's resolution, it is necessary to examine its compliance with both the substantive law (related to the content of the resolution) and the formal law (which includes the requirements for the adoption and the introduction of the resolution into legal circulation). A substantive legal assessment involves Article 7 of the Polish constitution, according to which public authorities act on the basis and within the limits of the law. As a result, the legality of all acts, including resolutions issued by local government bodies, must be scrutinised to determine whether there was a valid legal basis for issuing them, and whether their use violated any other legal provisions, in particular the principles of Polish and European law.

A problem arises because the restrictive requirements of having a clear legal basis in the form of a specific competence provision do not apply to resolutions that do not have a universally binding force, like anti-LGBT resolutions. Therefore, such resolutions can only be issued on the basis of general regulations specifying the tasks of given local government bodies.[58] Moreover, the lack of a legal basis that would set the boundaries and direction of the legal content of the resolution makes it difficult to build an effective control pattern. Entities defending anti-LGBT resolutions claimed that these are legally meaningless, subjective assessments and the views of people acting as a local government body, which should be assessed in light of the freedom of expression, rather than in terms of the legality of the actions of public

[58] Cf. Supreme Administrative Court judgments of 25 May 2017, I OSK 297/17, LEX No. 2442347 and of 18 April 2018, I OSK 552/18, LEX No. 2494132.

administration bodies. In one of judgment by a court of first instance, which was ultimately overturned, the court approved this narrative, stating that: (…) a resolution of the district council containing a declaration of an ideological and philosophical nature, consistent with the views of the majority of councillors, cannot be the subject of control in judicial and administrative proceedings, as long as it does not concern the presentation of an ideology that is prohibited by law and does not interfere with its content in the public law sphere (…).[59]

However, the courts that confirmed the admissibility of appealing against anti-LGBT resolutions had no problem creating control patterns from general principles of Polish and European law and they found the complaints justified. Some argued that the resolutions were mixed in nature not only agreed with an unspecified 'LGBT ideology' but also opposed the presence of certain people called 'lighthouse keepers' in schools.[60] Anti-LGBT resolutions refused to agree to specific content being introduced into the school curriculum and announced interference when specific criteria of action and selection were imposed on teachers and employees or contractors. The courts found that anti-LGBT resolutions were authoritative in this regard and required a precise legal basis. This matter did not fall within the scope of the tasks of the council of local government bodies. Therefore, the resolutions were illegal as they were adopted without the required detailed legal basis and outside the statutory tasks of the issuing body.[61]

Despite the above, the courts examined the legality of the further content of the resolutions. First of all, it was found that there had been a violation of the principle of equality and the prohibition on discrimination under Article 32 of the Polish constitution, Article 14 of the ECHR, and Article 21(1) of the Charter of Fundamental Rights of the EU. It was found that 'LGBT ideology' did actually concern LGBT people and was therefore discriminatory. It is worth noting that the court did not agree with the prosecutor's position that

---

59 PA Court in Krakow resolution of 23 June 2020, III SA/Kr 105/20, LEX No. 3020596.

60 The "Lighthouse keeper" programme aimed to ensure that every school has at least one person (teacher, school counsellor or psychologist) prepared to prevent and respond to violence against LGBT+ students and to cooperate with teaching staff (providing knowledge, intervening in crises) – <https://mnw.org.pl/program_samorzadowy_dla_lgbt> (accessed on 11 September 2023).

61 PA Court in Gliwice judgment of 14 July 2020, III SA/Gl 15/20, LEX No. 3042555.

examining the social effects of the contested resolutions goes beyond an examination of legal compliance, because in the court's opinion this issue cannot be limited to examining the letter of the law itself. The resolution must be assessed in terms of its compliance with basic constitutional principles, such as the prohibition on discrimination, the right to private life, and freedom of expression. This assessment must take into account the real effects of the resolution on the life of the municipal community, it is not only about the assessment of the legal text, but also about its effects, because these effects may or may not express a violation of the rights and freedoms of citizens.[62]

Moreover, in the court's opinion, the wording of the contested resolution violates the dignity of LGBT people. It raises serious accusations against them without any justification, using slogans and attributing unworthy intentions and actions, which is a violation of the principle of inherent human dignity according to Article 30 of the Polish constitution. In turn, interference in the sphere of citizens' private life, which undoubtedly includes their sexual life, sexual orientation, and gender identity, violates their right to privacy protection under Article 47 of the Polish constitution and Article 8(1) ECHR. In addition, according to the court, the anti-LGBT resolutions violated freedom of expression under Article 54(1) of the Polish constitution and Article 10(1) ECHR, because in each of the three points of the resolution, the Municipal Council specified what it does not agree to in public debate and community life. Participating in a public debate as an exercise of this right is one thing, but administratively influencing its content and deciding what will be allowed and what will not be is another thing. In addition, the resolution included content according to which the District Council will not allow the transfer of specific knowledge to students, which is a violation of the constitutional freedom to learn and teach, breaching Article 70(1) and Article 73 of the Polish constitution. The court also referred to the judgment of the Constitutional Tribunal,[63] which explained that the right to access scientific knowledge and to receive this knowledge does not interfere with the parental right to raise children according to their own beliefs. A violation of this right may be interference in the transmitted scientific knowledge seen from the perspective of

---

62 Ibidem.

63 Constitutional Tribunal judgment of 12 April 2011, SK 62/08, OTK-A 2011, No 3, item 22, 4.7.

parents with a different worldview and value system than the one referred to in the resolution.[64] The Supreme Administrative Court fully shared the above position,[65] adding that a discriminatory declaration of a local government body, which is also an employer, is contrary to Council Directive 2000/78/EC of 27 November 2000 establishing general framework conditions for equal treatment in employment and work,[66] in support of which it cited the theses of the judgment of the Court of Justice of 23 April 2020, in case C-507/18.[67]

6. Conclusions

The primary purpose of establishing administrative courts in Europe, including Poland, was to protect individuals' rights in relation to public administration. This objective has been reflected in the evolution of case law concerning challenges to local anti-LGBT resolutions, which are discussed in this paper. Although it was initially unclear how the courts could address these resolutions and who had the right to appeal against them, Polish administrative courts ultimately succeeded in annulling the contested resolutions.

Initially, the courts followed traditional patterns and refused to review resolutions that discriminated against the LGBT community. However, this approach was eventually challenged. The courts started to redefine certain concepts and reconsider their role in regulating local government bodies. This change may have been brought on by the realisation of the social and legal consequences of allowing discriminatory actions to take place. I firmly believe that recognising anti-LGBT resolutions as acts under Article 3(2) point 6 APAC is a significant step towards bringing more aspects of public administration activities under the jurisdiction of the court. The 'presumption

---

64 Cf. in particular the justification of the judgment of the PA Court in Gliwice judgment of 14 July 2020, III SA/Gl 15/20, LEX No. 3042555, as well as the judgments of the PA Court in Warsaw of 15 July 2020, VIII SA/Wa 42/20; PA Court in Lublin of 6 August 2020, III SA/Lu 7/20 and PA Court in Kielce of 11 September 2020, II SA/Ke 382/20, PA Court in Kraków of 10 January 2022, III SA/Kr 975/21, LEX No. 3291841.

65 Supreme Administrative Court judgment of 28 June 2022, III OSK 3746/21, LEX No. 3361734. Similarly, the Supreme Administrative Court judgments of 28 June 2022, III OSK 4041/21, LEX No. 3392456 and III OSK 4240/21, LEX No. 3395415.

66 Official Journal of the European Union, L series of 2000 No. 303, 16.

67 Judgment of the Court (Grand Chamber) of 23 April 2020 NH v Associazione Avvocatura per i diritti LGBTI - Rete Lenford., LEX No 2945628.

of jurisdiction' of the administrative court developed based on this case can certainly be used in other cases. Therefore, it has become possible to launch effective judicial review at the national level. It is worth adding that the ombudsman requested the court to consider whether the matter at stake should be submitted for a preliminary ruling to the CJEU, but the Polish courts didn't have to take this route.[68] The Polish administrative courts had no problem with creating substantive standards for controlling the legality of anti-LBGT resolutions using the principles contained in the Polish constitution and acts of European law.

The point was not to involve the court in ideological disputes, but to indicate to the public administration the legal limits of axiological freedom, which cannot be exceeded under the guise of 'subjective opinions of persons performing the functions of collegial bodies'. It should be noted that local government decision-making bodies act on behalf of the local government community, and not the private interests of its members. In my opinion, therefore, resolutions adopted by a public body cannot be considered as a private position. Councillors have the right to private views on controversial issues, but they should not impose them by issuing a resolution as a body of the local government community,[69] even if it has a different title (position, resolution, etc.). However, if this happens, there must be a way for the court to effectively verify whether or not such a resolution violates legally protected values.

The progressive approach of the courts in these issues is not kept in step with the views and legal provisions regarding the *locus standi* for a complaint. While the Ombudsman was able to file complaints successfully, this was the final resort. This serves as evidence that the criteria for filing a complaint before the administrative court need to be revised. The model based on the violation of individual legal interests turned out to

---

68 Marta Romańska, Agata Cebera, Jakub Firlus, "Between morality and discrimination by public administration: the case of so-called "LGBT free zones" in Poland", *Pécs Journal of International and European Law*, 2023 No. 1–2, 63–64, <https://doi.org/10.15170/PJIEL.2023.1.6>.

69 The doctrine has already correctly pointed out that the LGBT resolution was not signed by individual councillors who would like to make a statement about their views, but the resolution was marked with the symbol of the city council –Romańska, Cebera, Firlus (2023), 72.

be insufficient either to enable an LGBT person discriminated against by the authorities of their community to demand the right to go to court, or to enable NGOs fighting for the rights of LGBT persons to initiate a judicial review. Since administrative courts have noticed the need to conduct effective control of local government resolutions that do not have direct legal effects, the regulation of procedural *locus standi* should be adapted to this. In my opinion, the growing legal awareness of citizens who want to influence the legal acts in force in their local government community, as well as the second function of the administrative court (protection of legal order), require changes to the rules of procedural *locus standi* in the acts relating to local governments, and preferably, more broadly, in the act regulating proceedings before the administrative court. In my opinion, such actions are necessary to reduce the institutional vulnerability of LGBT people and communities.

Bibliography

Bodnar Adam (2021), "Polish Road toward an Illiberal State: Methods and Resistance", Indiana Law Journal No. 96.

Chmielnicki Paweł (Eds.) (2022), *Ustawa o samorządzie gminnym*, ed. Wolter Kluwer Polska (Warszawa).

Dąbek Dorota (2021) "Zakres sądowej kontroli administracji : aktualne tendencje na tle sporu o kognicję w sprawach stref wolnych od LGBT", in eds. Maksymilian Cherka, Piotr Gołaszewski, Jacek, Piecha, Marek Wierzbowski *Kryzys, stagnacja, renesans? Prawo administracyjne przyszłości. Księga jubileuszowa profesora dr hab. Jacka Jagielskiego*, Wolters Kluwer Polska (Warszawa).

Dolnicki Bogdan (Eds.) (2021), *Ustawa o samorządzie gminnym. Komentarz*, ed. Wolter Kluwer Polska (Warszawa).

Gurdek Magdalena (2007), "Glosa do wyroku TK z 13.03.2007 r., K 8/07", *Przegląd Prawa Publicznego*, No. 10.

Jaśkowska Małgorzata (2022), "Sądowoadministracyjna kontrola aktów z zakresu administracji publicznej, niebędących aktami prawa miejscowego, podejmowanych przez organy samorządu terytorialnego i ich związków", in: Marek Szewczyk, Maria Jędrzejczak, *Prawne formy działania stosowane przez organy samorządu terytorialnego. Księga jubileuszowa Profesora Krystiana Ziemskiego*, ed. C.H. Beck (Warszawa).

Kaniuka Andrea, Pugh Kelley C., Jordan Megan, Brooks Byron, Dodd Julia, K. Mann Abbey, L. Williams Stacey & Hirsch (2019), Jameson K., "Stigma and suicide risk among the LGBTQ population: Are anxiety and depression to blame and can connectedness to the LGBTQ community help?", *Journal of Gay & Lesbian Mental Health*, 23(2), DOI: 10.1080/19359705.2018.1560385.

Knysiak-Sudyka Hanna, Romańska Marta, Woś Tadeusz (2016), *Prawo o postępowaniu przed sądami administracyjnymi. Komentarz*, ed. Wolters Kluwer Polska (Warszawa).

Kowalski Michał (2019), *Prawo do sądu administracyjnego. Standard międzynarodowy i konstytucyjny oraz jego realizacja*, ed. Wolters Kluwer Polska (Warszawa).

Limantė Agnė & Tereškinas Artūras (2022), "Definition of Vulnerable Groups", in (Eds.) A. Limantė & D. Pūraitė-Andrikienė, *Legal Protection of Vulnerable Groups in Lithuania, Latvia, Estonia and Poland. European Union and its neighbours in a globalized world* (vol. 8), Springer, <https://doi.org/10.1007/978-3-031-06998-7_1>.

Meyerhoefer Chad, Bingjin Xue, Poznańska Anna (2023), "Implications of the Decline in LGBT Rights for Population Mental Health: Evidence from Polish LGBT-free zones", Cambridge, MA: National Bureau of Economic Research (No. 31702), <http://dx.doi.org/10.3386/w31702>.

Misztal Barbara A. (2011), "The Challenges of Vulnerability: In Search of Strategies for a Less Vulnerable Social Life", *Palgrave Macmillan London*, <https://doi.org/10.1057/9780230316690>.

Niżnik-Dobosz Iwona (2022), "Podstawy i znaczenie prawne rezolucji, deklaracji, apelów i oświadczeń organów stanowiących jednostek samorządu terytorialnego jako formy działania administracji publicznej", in: Marek Szewczyk, Maria Jędrzejczak, *Prawne formy działania stosowane przez organy samorządu terytorialnego. Księga jubileuszowa Profesora Krystiana Ziemskiego*, (Ed.) C.H. Beck (Warszawa).

Ploszka Adam (2023), "From human rights to human wrongs : how local government can negatively influence the situation of an individual : the case of Polish LGBT ideology-free zones", *The international journal of human rights*, Vol. 27, No 2, <https://doi.org/10.1080/13642987.2022.2121708>.

Romańska Marta, Cebera Agata, Firlus Jakub (2023), "Between morality and discrimination by public administration: the case of so-called "LGBT free zones" in Poland", *Pécs Journal of International and European Law*, No. 1–2, <https://doi.org/10.15170/PJIEL.2023.1.6>.

Russell Stephen T., Fish Jessica N. (2016), "Mental Health in Lesbian, Gay, Bisexual, and Transgender (LGBT) Youth", *Annual Review of Clinical Psychology,* 12:1, <https://doi.org/10.1146/annurev-clinpsy-021815-093153>.

Tarno Jan P. (2012) "Prawo o postępowaniu przed sądami administracyjnymi. Komentarz", ed. LexisNexis Polska (Warszawa).

Zhang Lei, Finan Laura J., Bersamin Melina, Fisher Deborah A. (2020), "Sexual Orientation-Based Depression and Suicidality Health Disparities: The Protective Role of School-Based Health Centers", *Journal of Research on Adolescence*, <https://doi.org/10.1111/jora.12454>.

Ziemski Krystian M. (2005), *Indywidualny akt administracyjny jako forma prawna działania administracji*, ed. Wydawnictwo Naukowe UAM (Poznań).

State Assistance to Dependents: The Precursor German System vs the Fragmentary Polish System

*Weronika Szafrańska**

Abstract: It is one of the norms of a democratic, rule-of-law state to support dependent people (mainly senior citizens) who are unable to work and need the care of others. Some of us will live to an age when we will need the constant help of another person, and the number of people with disabilities is also growing. In rapidly ageing societies, the lack of a comprehensive security system in the event of dependence may soon become the most significant challenge for individual governments due to the impending collapse of the system.

In this article, the author contrasts the German system for the protection of older adults with the Polish system, which is still developing. The former is considered one of the best in the world – the solutions adopted in Germany have been used, among others, in Japan. Particularly noteworthy in the German model is the incredible variety of measures created by the legislator to support dependent persons: these include not only cash benefits but also a range of benefits in kind, together with a developed network of care homes.

Keywords: dependent older adult, care insurance, social welfare centres, cash benefits

1. Introduction

The demographic crisis in Poland has been going on for a long time. Statistics Poland reported that, in 2023, the number of births was approximately 137,000 lower than the number of deaths. The 2023 data also shows that about 272,000 live births were registered, which is about 33,000 fewer than in the

* Ph.D., Assistant Professor at the Faculty of Law and Administration of the University of Silesia in Katowice, Poland. ORCiD: 0000-0002-6903-8758.

previous year.[1] However, such a rapidly ageing society is not only a Polish problem. The demographic processes taking place in this direction have led to the formation of a new conceptual category in legal systems. In addition to disabled people, dependent people have also begun to be distinguished, where this term is understood primarily as older people who have problems with functioning in everyday life or are even unable to live independently.[2]

Although the international human rights system does not have a separate treaty dedicated to older people, let alone dependent people, the problems of this section of society have been the subject of discussions at the UN,[3] the European Parliament,[4] and the Council of Europe.[5]

Such a significant acceleration in the ageing of the entire society is a massive test for subsequent governments to shape the social policy system with exceptional foresight to support dependent people. They constitute a group of vulnerable individuals, particularly susceptible to risks. The risk of threats significantly increases in countries like Poland, which lack fully structured legal and corresponding social support mechanisms. These people are exposed not only to social alienation but also to a faster progression of illnesses, including mental health disorders. Providing assistance on many levels requires, first and foremost, efficient organisation and financing from state budgets. Very often, the closest people are unable to take care of a family member, with these tasks being taken over by commercial entities operating professionally but for a fee. The state must, therefore, develop financial or organisational support mechanisms for people who cannot afford the help of private institutions.

In this article, the author briefly presents the system of social security regulations for dependent individuals in German social law, which is considered pioneering on a global scale, and compares it with the rules adopted

---

1 <https://stat.gov.pl/en/topics/statistical-yearbooks/statistical-yearbooks/demographic-yearbook-of-poland-2023,3,17.html> (accessed on 30 January 2025).

2 See Anna Gutowska, "(Nie)pełnosprawna starość – przyczyny, uwarunkowania, wsparcie", *Interdyscyplinarne Konteksty Pedagogiki Specjalnej*, No. 8, (2015): 9 ff.

3 <https://social.un.org/ageing-working-group/> (accessed on 30 January 2025).

4 <https://www.europarl.europa.eu/doceo/document/A-9-2021-0194_EN.html#_section1> (accessed on 30 January 2025).

5 See Recommendation CM/Rec(2014)2 of the Committee of Ministers to member States on the promotion of human rights of older persons, <https://rm.coe.int/1680695bce> (accessed on 30 January 2025).

in Poland. This comparison further highlights the need for states to develop comprehensive systems, which have become necessary in rapidly ageing societies, thereby minimising risks faced by vulnerable, dependent people. The Polish system's inefficiency in supporting dependent individuals indicates the necessity of systemic state involvement in alleviating the difficulties faced by this social group. Providing these individuals with comprehensive care is essential, and it requires a well-thought-out and stable financing system. Without well-considered state assistance and far-reaching systemic changes in many European countries, senior individuals, who are particularly vulnerable to risks, will remain without the support they are fully entitled to, as outlined in the EU Charter of Fundamental Rights.

2. Dependent person, concepts, degrees, and example models of protection

Although the definition of dependency, i.e. the development of a precise definition, criteria or degrees, is significant in planning various forms of social security in the world and the EU, no standard, unambiguous definition or methods of classifying dependency have yet been developed. Different countries adopt different rules and criteria for adjudicating dependency and its degrees.

It can be pointed out that a dependent person is a person who, due to the impairment of bodily functions, has limited activity causing the need for long-term or permanent support from another person in order to meet the basic needs of life.[6] Science has developed several scales for assessing the degree of dependence in performing simple and complex activities of daily living.[7] These include the Katz Activities of Daily Living, the Barthel Index, the Instrumental Activities of Daily Living, the Comprehensive Geriatric Assessment, and the Nurses' Observation Scale for Geriatric Patients. In

---

6 See Elżbieta Szwałkiewicz, "Co przemawia za potrzebą zdefiniowania 'osoby niesamodzielnej'? Definicja niesamodzielności i osoby niesamodzielnej", *Polityka Społeczna*, No. 2, (2018): 6–10.

7 Adam Zych, "Leksykon gerontologii", (Kraków: Oficyna Wydawnicza "Impuls", 2019), *passim*; Karol Pawlak, Agnieszka Ćwirlej-Sozańska, Agnieszka Wiśniowska-Szurlej, "Kryteria oceny stopni niesamodzielności – doświadczenia dotychczasowe i propozycje dla potrzeb polskiej praktyki", *Polityka Społeczna*, No. 2, (2018): 11–15.

addition, the WHO's International Classification of Functioning, Disability and Health,[8] along with the Disability Assessment Schedule developed from it,[9] are also used.

Individual countries tend to decide on adopting any of the developed theoretical models of care for dependents[10] and then adjust their legal solutions in this regard. However, the development of legislation in many European countries indicates a trend toward the institutionalisation and nationalisation of care for dependents – in such rapidly ageing national societies, the assistance of immediate family and relatives is no longer sufficient. Largely due to reasons of historical circumstance, the solutions that exist in individual EU countries vary widely.

Thus, for example, in individual EU Member States, there are widely varying solutions from a comprehensive benefits system (as in Germany) to those where such a system is lacking, and the regulation of benefits for dependents is fragmented and scattered (as in Poland).

The European country that first recognised the problem in question was the Netherlands, where as early as 1968, the institution of insurance against the 'extraordinary costs of illness/treatment' was introduced (since 2015, this has been regulated by the Long-Term Care Act[11]), forming an integral part of the Dutch health insurance system. The insured pays a premium, the amount of which depends on income, with a statutorily defined upper limit of the

---

8 <https://www.who.int/publications/m/item/icf-checklist> (accessed on 30 January 2025).

9 <https://www.who.int/standards/classifications/international-classification-of-functioning-disability-and-health/who-disability-assessment-schedule> (accessed on 30 January 2025).

10 Demi Patsios, Adam Davey, "Formal and Informal Community Care for Older Adults", in *The Cambridge Handbook on Age and Ageing*, (Malcolm Johnson, Cambridge: Cambridge University Press, 2005), 597-98: The book distinguishes five models of dependence and coupling between informal help provided within the kin and non-family support networks and formal help: the hierarchical compensatory model, the substitutional model, the specificity model, the supplementation model and the complementarity model.

11 Wet langdurige zorg (WIZ); (Official Journal of the Kingdom of the Netherlands 2014, Staatsblad 2014, 494); <https://wetten.overheid.nl/BWBR0035917/2024-01-01> (accessed on 30 January 2025).

premium assessment basis, they also bear their share of the costs of benefits. The long-term care fund is additionally fed by budget subsidies.[12]

Austria was the first European country to put a system to deal with the specific issue of dependency risk, which happened in 1993. Dependency was recognised and defined as a separate and independent social risk.[13] The entitlement to care allowance here is combined with the entitlement to other social security benefits.[14] The details are regulated by the care allowance laws of the individual states (*Landespflegegeldgesetz*) and also by the federal law on the introduction of care allowance (BPGG).[15] Generally, although predominantly paid by social security institutions, nursing care allowances are financed from budgetary funds.[16]

The provision of social services in the Czech Republic is based on the principle of contracting, which means that the beneficiary and the provider, after negotiations, enter into a contract specifying the purpose and scope of services, which should meet the needs of the dependent person. At the same time, the Social Services Law has been in effect since 2007,[17] introducing the possibility of collecting a care allowance (*príspevek na péci*). The legislator

---

12 Ralph Skuban, “Pflegesicherung in Europa. Sozialpolitik im Binnenmarkt”, (Wiesbaden: VS Verlag für Sozialwissenschaften, 2004), 161–162.

13 Walter Pfeil, “Die Pflegevorsorge in Österreich”, in: *Soziale Sicherung bei Pflegebedürftigkeit in der Europäischen Union*, (Klaus Sieveking, Baden-Baden: Nomos, 1998), 52.

14 Marta Luty-Michalak, Aleksandra Syryt, *Long-term care system for dependent people – Austrian experiences, Acta Universitatis Lodziensis. Folia Sociologica*, No. 71, (2019): 92–93; Daniel Eryk Lach, “Organizacja i finansowanie świadczeń opieki długoterminowej w wybranych krajach UE”, *Ruch prawniczy, ekonomiczny i socjologiczny*, No. 1, (2019): 161–162.

15 Bundesgesetz, mit dem ein Pflegegeld eingeführt wird (Bundespflegegeldgesetz — BPGG); BGBl. No. 110/1993.

16 Walter Pfeil, “Benefit Structures for Persons Dependent on Long-Term Care in Austria”, in *Long-Term Care in Europe: A Juridical Approach*, (Ulrich Becker, Hans-Joachim Reinhard, Berlin: Springer, 2018), 33–34.

17 Social Services Act No. 108/2006 of 14 March 2006: <https://www.zakonyprolidi.cz/translation/cs/2006-108?langid=1033> (accessed on 30 January 2025).

has distinguished four degrees of dependency – slight, medium, heavy and total dependence.[18]

France has a mandatory long-term care insurance system known as *Allocation Personalisée Autonomie* (APA) that was introduced in 2002. This system provides assistance to all residents over the age of 60 whose care needs exceed a threshold set by the government. It applies the AGGIR scale, which distinguishes as many as six degrees of loss of independence (with the lowest degree involving no restrictions on self-care activities, but only the need for support in maintaining the household).[19]

The various systems adopted in European countries allow practical comparative work to be carried out, which can translate into adopting the best possible solutions concerning the protection of dependents in each country.

3. The precursor German system

Germany was the first to establish a comprehensive institutional and legal system covering dependency through social insurance. The discussion on how to secure dependents lasted for 20 years and resulted in various proposals. One proposal was based on the provision method, which involved financing benefits from budgetary funds without prior contributions from beneficiaries. Another proposal was based on the insurance method, which had a wide range of proposals. Consideration was given to extending sickness insurance, pension insurance and voluntary or compulsory insurance.[20] The law on social insurance for dependency risk (literal translation from

---

[18] § 8 Zákon o sociálních službách. More about Czech solutions see: Iva Holmerová, Hana Vanková, Petr Wija, "Opportunities and Challenges for Integrated Provision of Long-term Care Services in the Czech Republic", in *Challenges of Ageing Societies in the Visegrad Countries: Hungary, Czech Republic, Poland, Slovakia*, (Zsuzsa Széman, Budapest: Hungarian Charity Service of the Order of Malta, 2013), 91 ff.

[19] Aleksander Surdej, Jan Brzozowski, "Rozwój systemu usług opiekuńczych dla osób niesamodzielnych we Francji: implikacje dla Polski", *Polityka Społeczna*, No.1, (2012): 10 ff.

[20] About history, see Gerhard Igl in *Sozialrechtshandbuch (SRH)*, (Franz Ruland, Ulrich Becker, Peter Axer, Baden-Baden: Nomos, 2022), 1177-80; Heinz Rothgang, "Ziele und Wirkungen der Pflegeversicherung", (Frankfurt: Campus-Verlag, 1997), 11 ff.

German: need for care) was passed on 26 May 1994.[21] As a result, on 1 January 1995, the Social Code was expanded with Book XI, entitled Long-Term Care Insurance.[22] The implemented solutions, which are unparalleled globally, have also served as a blueprint for other nations due to their highly progressive nature, especially considering that they were established in the 20th century.[23] The German legislature emphasised in the initial paragraphs of SGB XI the significance of considering gender-specific differences in care between men and women, as well as their needs in relation to benefits, when applying care insurance provisions. Furthermore, care needs arising from religious and cultural backgrounds must be taken into account.[24] This is especially important in a culturally diverse society like Germany.

The institutions of social care insurance are the care insurance funds (*Pflegekassen*), which are legal entities under public law (*Körperschaften des öffentlichen Rechts*) that carry out their tasks with the help of the staff and bodies of the health insurance funds (*Krankenkassen*; § 46).[25]

The basis for the care insurance was assuming it would cover everyone subject to statutory sickness insurance. Privately insured individuals must conclude a private care insurance contract (§ 23 SGB XI).

The provision of benefits for dependent persons is made possible through contributions collected from insured persons, or those who have entered into private contracts. These contributions have been collected since 1 January 1995, even though inpatient care, as a benefit provided from the care insurance funds, only started on 1 July 1996 (Section 68 (2–3) *Pflege-Versicherungsgesetz*).

---

21 Act of 26 May 1994: Gesetz zur sozialen Absicherung des Risikos der Pflegebedürftigkeit (Pflege-Versicherungsgesetz - PflegeVG), BGBl. I p. 1014; 2797.

22 Act of 26 May 1994: Sozialgesetzbuch (SGB XI): Soziale Pflegeversicherung, BGBl. I p. 1014); abb. SGB XI; In Poland, this issue has been worked on in detail by Ariel Przybyłowicz in "Ubezpieczenie pielęgnacyjne w Republice Federalnej Niemiec", (Warszawa: Zakład Ubezpieczeń Społecznych, 2017), *passim*.

23 E.g. Japan, Spain, Luxembourg; see Gerhard Igl in *Sozialrechtshandbuch (SRH)...*, 1180.

24 See Diana Auth, Simone Leiber, Sigrid Leitner, "Bedarfe und Bewältigungshandeln von sorgenden Angehörigen: Welche Rolle spielt Geschlecht in Wechselwirkung mit anderen Differenzkategorien?", *Sozialer Fortschritt*, No. 3, 2020: 163 ff.; Winfried Boecken, "Zur Frage eines Anspruchs von Pflegebedürftigen auf gleichgeschlechtliche Pflege", *Die Sozialgerichtsbarkeit*, No. 12, (2008): 698 ff.

25 Raimund Waltermann, Benjamin Schmidt, Katja Chandna-Hoppe, "Sozialrecht", (Heidelberg: C.F. Müller, 2022), 105.

With this arrangement, the required money was collected immediately without depleting the state or federal budgets.[26]

Contributions are calculated as a percentage of the base income, but not higher than the annual maximum contribution base of statutory sickness insurance. Once the base has been reached, there is an exemption from being subject to statutory sickness insurance and the obligation to conclude a private insurance contract is updated (Section 6(1)(1) in conjunction with Section 6(6) to (7) SGB V). The legislator has also opted for the traditional model of financing the contribution by placing equal shares of the burden on employees and employers (only Saxony has adopted a different solution, shifting more of the burden to the employee).

According to German law, the category of dependents includes those who require care due to a disability and those who, due to old age, have lost the ability to live independently. In this way, the state's care is also extended to older people whose disability is difficult to ascertain, whether as a result of a congenital or acquired illness or due to a sudden accident. To achieve this effect, the German legislator distinguished between the levels of care required and the degrees of disability. Although the German term *'Pflegegrad'* is often translated as 'degree of disability', it is, in fact, a broader concept: the degree defines the level of care required of a person in a general sense, which allows the scale to be extended to include older people who cannot live independently.

Degrees of care are regulated in § 14 and § 15 SGB XI. According to these regulations, people in need of care are those whose health leaves them with limited independence or abilities and who, therefore, require the assistance of others. They must be unable to compensate for or cope with physical, cognitive or mental impairments, or any stress or health-related demands on their own. The need for care concerning such people must be permanent, probably for at least six months and of a degree defined by law.

Until 2017, Germany distinguished between three levels of care needs. However, a new five-level system has since been introduced. The additional degrees were introduced to cater to the needs of people with dementia and

---

26 Frank Maschmann, "Grundzüge des Leistungsrechts der gesetzlichen Pflegeversicherung nach dem SGB XI", *Neue Zeitschrift für Sozialrecht*, No. 3, (1995): 109.

severe mental disorders. The aim of increasing the number of degrees of dependency was to improve the support process for dependent individuals.[27]

These regulations constitute the basis for the Sickness Insurance Medical Services (§ 18 SGB XI), unless experts are appointed by care funds in order to decide on the degree of independence. The test consists of checking the extent to which the subject can perform daily living activities and then specifying the type, scope, and expected duration of dependence. An essential element of the study is the presentation of proposals for preventive and rehabilitation measures, which take priority over care and nursing services in the German system (§ 5 SGB XI). The decision on the degree of dependence also includes the type and scope of recommended benefits, an individual care plan (*Pflegeplan*), and, if cash benefits are applied for, determining whether care in the home environment is being provided appropriately.[28] Classification to a given level of dependency and grants of specific benefits may be for a specified period.

In the event that the insured person disagrees with the decision made this way, which may also be a refusal decision, they may appeal against it to the relevant Social Court (*Sozialgericht*), which will then conduct the proceedings according to the rules of the Social Courts Act.[29]

The example of the provisions on granting care allowance shows how much the German legislator continuously makes efforts to improve the provisions. Over the past few years, the provisions concerning the assessment of the application and the granting of benefits (§ 18 - 18e SGB XI) have been considerably expanded, as have the provisions concerning the need to report to the National Association of Statutory Health Insurance Funds on the proceedings carried out or the possibility for the Federal Medical Service and the medical services to carry out pilot projects, research, and scientific expertise to further develop the tasks entrusted to the medical services about granting degrees of dependency and benefits. At this point, however, it is worth pointing out that the German statutory provisions have always been

---

27 Łukasz Jurek, "Reforma systemu orzecznictwa o niesamodzielności w Niemczech", *Ubezpieczenia Społeczne. Teoria i praktyka*, No. 3, (2020): 7–8.

28 Gerhard Igl, "Das neue Pflegeversicherungsrecht: Soziale Pflegeversicherung (Sozialgesetzbuch – Elftes Buch)", (Munich: C.H. Beck Verlag, 1995), 57.

29 Act of 3 September 1953: Sozialgerichtsgesetz (SGG), BGBl. 1975 I p. 2535.

characterised by a very high degree of casuistry when compared to, for example, the Polish equivalents.

First, abuses of the right to care benefits is prevented by a waiting period, i.e. the time during which the insured person must be subject to social insurance in order to obtain the right to benefits at all. As a rule, benefits are granted if the insured person was covered by social care insurance for at least two years in the last ten years before applying for the benefit – either as a member of a care fund or covered under the insurance of a member of their family (§ 33(2) SGB XI). The second 'safety feature' is the insurance abuse clause introduced in 2007 (§ 33a SGB XI). This is intended to prevent benefits from being granted to anyone residing in Germany and acquiring insurance coverage as family members of the insured person, i.e. essentially to immigrants where the sole purpose is to obtain benefits for dependents.[30]

4. Care insurance benefits in Germany

As indicated above, in Germany, one of the insurance principles is the priority of preventive measures and rehabilitation (§ 5 SGB XI). In accordance with this principle, care funds check in individual cases which medical rehabilitation and complementary services are appropriate and justified to overcome or reduce the need for care. This is assessed during the initial examination and again later, during periodic examinations while accepting care insurance benefits. The essential provision of care insurance is the provision of community care, i.e. home care (§ 36). These services are generally provided by caregivers employed by outpatient care facilities authorised to provide services, or by caregivers employed directly by care funds.[31]

Instead of in-kind community care services, dependents may receive a care allowance (§ 37 SGB XI) that allows them to freely choose and decide how to use the funds obtained to provide care for themselves. In practice, the benefit is usually given to carers in exchange for providing care. This benefit is intended to strengthen the potential and readiness of loved ones to provide care. However, the benefit can be used in any way, as long as it

30 Constanze Janda, *Migranten im Sozialstaat*, (Tübingen: Mohr Siebeck, 2012), 176.

31 Andreas Wahl, "§ 36", in *SGB XI. Soziale Pflegeversicherung. Kommentar*, (Peter Udsching, Bernd Schütze, Munich: C.H. Beck Verlag, 2018), 275 (Rn. 2).

is used to provide necessary and appropriate primary care and household assistance, whether by relatives, volunteers, or professional providers.[32] The amount of the care allowance in 2024 ranged from €332 to €946 per month. The above two benefits may be granted as a combined benefit (§ 38 SGB XI).

In the regulations, the legislator further provided for unique benefits to support creating communities of dependent people (at least three). The incentive for this is a cash allowance to cover additional costs related to building and operating such communities (§ 38a; § 45e).[33]

The provision of community care also comes in the form of respite care, which allows for a replacement to be found when a caregiver who permanently takes care of a dependent person cannot provide care due to holidays, illness or other reasons (§ 39 SGB XI). In such a situation, the care fund covers the costs of care provided by a foster carer in an amount not exceeding €1,612 per year, and for a period not longer than six weeks in a calendar year. The condition is that the replaced caregiver must have previously taken care of the dependent person for at least six months.

Finally, community care services include auxiliary measures (e.g. bandages, plasters, incontinence pants, disposable gloves, disinfectants, wheelchairs, and specialised anti-decubitus beds) and measures to improve living conditions. Care funds assess, in cooperation with the Medical Services of the Sickness Insurance or a qualified caregiver, whether the requested measure is necessary.[34]

When community care and the care allowance are insufficient resources, a dependent person may use institutional care, i.e. semi-stationary care that includes daycare and night care (§ 41 SGB XI) and a short-term stay in a stationary care facility (§ 42). In the case of daycare, a dependent person stays in a care facility and returns home at night, where a caregiver takes care of them. The same with night care. As part of this benefit, the care fund covers the costs of benefits conditioned by independence, the costs of social care (understood, for example, as conversations, keeping company during walks

---

[32] Otto Krasney, "Pflegegeld des § 37 SGB XI", *Die Sozialgerichtsbarkeit,* No. 6, (1996): 254.

[33] Stephan Muckel, Markus Ogorek, Stephan Rixen, "Sozialrecht", (Munich: C.H. Beck Verlag, 2019), 204.

[34] Anne Barbara Lungstras, "§ 40", in *SGB XI. Soziale Pflegeversicherung…*, 325 (Rn. 13).

or organising joint social events), and the costs of necessary medical care services provided in each centre.[35]

Residential care services (§ 43 SGB XI) are only financed by care funds if home or semi-residential care is impossible or out of the question due to exceptional circumstances. For example, placement in a stationary care facility will be justified when there are no people able and willing to provide care in the place of residence, or in the case of dependent people who are bedridden.[36] A permanent stay in a stationary care facility is a benefit provided in kind, without the possibility of obtaining a care allowance in return.

In addition to the examples mentioned above, care insurance finances several other benefits for dependent people and guarantees certain rights for caregivers, such as:

- advice and information obligations of care funds (§§ 7–7b SGB XI),
- care for people requiring care if the caregiver uses preventive or rehabilitation services (§ 42a),
- lump sum benefit for caring for a disabled person (§ 43a),
- additional care and activation in inpatient care facilities (§ 43b),
- pension insurance for carers (§ 44 SGB XI). Here, it is required that the carer takes care of at least one dependent person for a minimum of 14 hours a week, and the ward is entitled to benefits from care insurance,
- accident insurance for caregivers (§ 44 section 1)
- co-financing of sickness and care insurance contributions during the carer's leave (§44a),
- free courses and training for caregivers organised by care funds (§ 45 SGB XI)
- benefits for people with a significant need for general care (including offers providing targeted assistance and advisory support for caring relatives and similarly close carers as carers – offers aimed at relieving carers of work, help from volunteers) – benefits further specified by government regulations individual states (§ 45a)
- 'targeted' allowance (*Entlastungsbetrag*) used for the specific purpose of quality-guaranteed services to relieve the burden of caring relatives and

35 See Andreas Wahl, "§ 41–42", in *SGB XI. Soziale Pflegeversicherung…*, 336–46.
36 See Britta Wiegand, "§ 43", in *SGB XI. Soziale Pflegeversicherung…*, 348–50.

similarly close persons acting as caregivers and to support the independence and self-determination of people in need of care in organising their daily life (§ 45a–§ 45b SGB),

- benefits supporting the development of infrastructure and new forms of care, such as creating, developing, and supporting groups of volunteers and other people willing to engage in civic activities and appropriate volunteer structures (one of many forms of action provided for in § 45c SGB XI); promoting and developing self-help groups, organisations and contact points whose aim is to support people in need of care, as well as their relatives and people of a similar nature (§ 45d),
- special care leaves of up to 10 calendar days or of six months.

The monetary benefit is also known as the personal budget. This benefit is based on an individual assessment of the need for social benefits regulated in SGB XI. However, following § 35a SGB XI, at the request of a dependent person, the benefits, such as in-kind community care services, care allowance, combined benefits, night and daycare services, and coverage of the costs of auxiliary measures, may be included in the personal budget, as a comprehensive benefit covering the benefits of various social law institutions. A personal budget is a cash benefit granted to meet the individually determined needs of dependent persons. Benefits in kind are taken into account here in the form of special care checks that a dependent person can use in a care facility of their choice. A personal budget is intended to be a benefit that emphasises the independence of the person using it and implements their right of free choice. By better considering the individual needs of people with mental, physical, or psychological disabilities, it contributes to social reintegration.[37]

An overview of various benefits offered to dependent persons in the German system indicates the advantages of the contributory system (the introduction of additional insurance). Less economically developed countries, such as Poland, should consider whether they can afford to maintain and develop benefits for dependent people without this type of additional financial support.

---

[37] Eva-Maria Rothenburg, "Das Persönliche Budget: Eine Einführung in Grundlagen, Verfahren und Leistungserbringung", (Munich: Juventa, 2009), 47.

5. Selected benefits for dependent persons in Poland

When comparing both systems, the first striking difference is the lack of a comprehensive regulation of the described issues in Polish law. Systemic solutions are still missing. Problems with benefits for dependent people (and also disabled people) tend to be 'patched' by introducing new benefits – mainly cash ones.

Although Poland has an institution of long-term care provided in the form of home care, community care – stationary care offered in facilities, or day care that provides assistance during the day, as well as activation and rehabilitation activities for dependent persons, the regulations governing these services are fragmented across various legal acts, such as the Act on Social Assistance, the Act on Family Benefits, the Act on General Health Insurance, and the Act on Health Care Services Financed from Public Funds. This fragmentation leads to a lack of coordination between different institutions, inconsistency and difficulties in accessing the available forms of support.

It is worth noting that, in Polish law, the term 'long-term care' is explicitly used in reference to nursing and care services within the healthcare system (for bedridden patients), while care services provided within the social assistance system are formally referred to as various types of care services. In the latter case, these services are primarily directed toward individuals living alone who, due to age, illness, or other reasons, require assistance from others. However, it is important to emphasise that decisions regarding the allocation of these services are often discretionary, meaning that the extent of the dependent person's needs frequently clashes with the financial capabilities of the state or the respective local government unit.

The current, insufficient implementation of the institution of care services, as regulated in the Act on Social Assistance,[38] includes specialised care services for lonely people who, due to age, illness or other reasons, are deprived of the help they require, which demonstrates the inefficiency of the Polish system. Social welfare homes are overcrowded and more specialised staff members are required. The provisions in this area need to be clarified because they

[38] Act of 12 March 2004 o pomocy społecznej (Social Welfare Act; Dz.U.2023.901), abbreviated as "u.p.s.".

are too general.[39] Importantly, in the Polish system, many benefits are conditional on a low income threshold, exceeding which limits or excludes the possibility of receiving additional funds. Additionally, the eligibility for some benefits depends on holding a recognised degree of disability. For example, in the case of the highest caregiver allowance, the disability must have arisen before the age of 25.

As highlighted in numerous reports on the subject, the Polish system of care for dependent individuals is inefficient, primarily due to chronic underfunding in both the healthcare and social assistance sectors. Local governments, which are responsible for financing many care services, often lack sufficient resources, limiting both the availability and quality of these services. Additionally, low wages for professional caregivers lead to severe staff shortages, with many choosing to emigrate to countries offering better working conditions. The process of granting assistance is complex and discretionary, resulting in many people not receiving the support they need, or not knowing where to seek help. The system of social care homes is inefficient, with a shortage of places in public facilities and private care remaining too expensive for many. The state tends to shift the responsibility for caregiving onto families without providing adequate financial support or respite services. For these reasons, the Polish model of senior citizen care is recognised as a form of familism without support.[40]

The ongoing need to develop the system of assistance for dependent persons in Poland is demonstrated through various legislative initiatives undertaken by lawmakers. It was only in 2019 that the Sejm passed the Act on Supplementary Benefits for People Unable to Live Independently,[41] specifying the conditions for acquiring the right to a 'supplementary

---

39 Łukasz Jurek, "Opieka nad osobami niesamodzielnymi: model realizowany a model pożądany", *Polityka Społeczna*, No. 2, (2018): 25.

40 See the Batory Foundation Report "Towards Fair Care: Elderly Care in Poland", 2022: <https://www.batory.org.pl/publikacja/w_strone_sprawiedliwej_troski/> (accessed on 30 January 2025); The Coalition "Helping the Dependent" Report: "Long-Term Care in Poland Today and Tomorrow. Updated and Expanded Edition" (2020): <https://niesamodzielnym.pl/index.php?page=raporty&utm_source=chatgpt.com> (accessed on 30 January 2025).

41 Act of 31 July 2019 o świadczeniu uzupełniającym dla osób niezdolnych do samodzielnej egzystencji (on supplementary benefit for persons incapable of self-sufficiency), Dz.U.2023.156.

benefit', the procedure for granting it and the rules for paying and financing benefits for people unable to live independently.[42] This benefit is given to anyone over the age of 18 whose inability to live independently has been confirmed, for example, by a decision on a total incapacity for work and the inability to live independently. A care allowance is another benefit for dependent people in Poland (currently approximately PLN 295 per month). It is available in two situations: to people who are utterly incapable of work and independent living (they must have a certificate to this effect from the medical examiner or medical committee at the Social Insurance Institution (ZUS) and also to people who are over 75 years of age, who receive the allowance automatically.

On 1 November 2023, an attempt to patch the system was introduced in the form of what are known as 'neighbourhood services'.[43] This solution is familiar in the Polish system – they have been provided as part of various projects, including those co-financed by the EU. Still, the introduction of their framework as a form of providing care services has been postulated for years. These services include assistance in meeting basic life needs, basic hygiene and nursing care, which should be understood as support that does not require specialised knowledge and skills and, where necessary and possible, ensuring contact with the environment. The organiser of neighbourhood services is the relevant municipality for the place where the person using the neighbourhood services resides, or an independent entity authorised by the municipality (Article 50(3a) et seq. of the u.p.s). The legislator provided that the organisation of these services will be entrusted to municipalities. Since this was a government project, it seems clear that, once again, the national legislator decided to use the 'hands' of local government units to patch up the imperfections in the nationwide system.[44] The forms of assistance within the framework of neighbourhood services are specified in resolutions of individual units of local government. Municipalities that decide to provide care

---

42 Commonly referred to as '500 plus for seniors'.

43 Act of 28 July 2023 o zmianie ustawy o pomocy społecznej oraz niektórych innych ustaw (Dz.U.2023.1693).

44 Shifting problems to local authorities is a common action of government authorities in Poland, see Anita Richert-Kaźmierska, "Organizacja systemu opieki nad seniorami wyzwaniem dla samorządów lokalnych", *Acta Universitatis Lodziensis. Folia Oeconomica*, No. 3, (2020): 25 ff.

services in the form of neighbourhood services will have the opportunity to obtain additional financial resources for their implementation in 2024 under the 'Senior Support Corps' programme.

At the same time as the introduction of the institution of neighbourhood services, the legislator significantly amended the provisions regarding protected housing (Article 53 u.p.s.),[45] replacing this negatively associated name with the term 'training and supported housing,' which is intended to emphasise their distinctiveness, making a clear division into two forms of support. Training and assisted living apartments are a form of assistance that, with the support of specialists, prepares the people staying there to lead an independent life, or which supports them in their day to day functioning. These apartments are intended to serve not only disabled people but also those who are dependent.[46]

Together with the above services, the legislator also introduced the possibility for social welfare homes to provide short-term support services in the form of a twenty-four-hour or daily stay to adults who require support due to their age, illness, or disability, and who are not residents of the home (Article 55a–55c u.p.s.). This is the quasi-equivalent of a German carer's leave/respite care.[47] Short-term support services provided in the form of a 24-hour stay may be granted for a fixed period of up to thirty days in a calendar year, with the possibility of extending the stay to a maximum of sixty days in particularly justified cases. Short-term support services provided daily may be granted for between four and twelve hours a day (also no more than sixty days per year). The applicant may declare their readiness to pay the whole fee. In that case, the authority conducting the proceedings is not obliged to determine the applicant's income situation. If the interested party claims that they cannot fully cover the costs of a short-term stay in a social welfare home, the head of

---

45 This is in line with the directions of the Strategy for the Development of Social Services, Public Policy until 2030 (with an outlook until 2035), adopted by Resolution No. 135 of the Council of Ministers of 15 June 2022 (M.P.767).

46 Ministry of Family data for 2022 shows that there were 1,623 sheltered (training and supported) housing units, with 4,278 people living in them; <https://www.prawo.pl/samorzad/mieszkania-treningowe-i-wspomagane-rozporzadzenie,523150.html> (accessed on 30 January 2025).

47 On the need for such solutions, see Daniel Eryk Lach, "Zabezpieczenie społeczne nieformalnych opiekunów osób niesamodzielnych", *Forum Prawnicze*, No. 5, (2018): 3 ff.

the social welfare centre or social services centre will determine the applicant's contribution to the costs. The municipality will bear the remaining costs of the service. If a person using short-term support services has an income not exceeding the income criterion for a single person, they will not be expected to contribute. The municipal council will issue a resolution (i.e. an act of local law) determining the detailed conditions for granting short-term support services provided daily and in the form of a twenty-four-hour stay, as well as the terms of payment for these services and the detailed conditions of a partial or total exemption from fees, as well as the procedure for collecting them. The issue of the municipality's participation in the costs of a short-term stay in a social welfare home may turn out to be a factor that determines the availability of the service for anyone who exceeds the income criterion but does not have sufficient resources to pay the total amount.

6. Comparison and conclusions

Poland and Germany, like many other European countries, face various challenges related to their ageing populations. While both countries aim to provide care for dependent individuals, their approaches to organising and financing this system differ significantly. Germany has established a comprehensive long-term care insurance system that provides both financial support and a wide range of care services. On the other hand, Poland relies on a fragmented and often discretionary social assistance system, leading to significant limitations in access to benefits.

The primary difference between the two care systems lies in their structure and funding methods. In Germany, the long-term care insurance system ensures access to various benefits funded by contributions. As a result, support is systematic and predictable. By contrast, in Poland, assistance for dependent individuals is often financed by local governments, which frequently lack sufficient funds. This results in a limited availability of care services, leaving many individuals without adequate support. In rapidly ageing societies, the lack of a comprehensive system to address dependency risks could soon become a significant challenge for governments, threatening systemic collapse. One criticised yet 'tempting' solution for policymakers, due to its simplicity, is raising health insurance premiums. However, as noted by D. E. Lach, citing H. Neseker, in an underfunded healthcare system, such funds would likely be directed primarily toward healthcare services, rather than the intended purpose of supporting dependent individuals.[48]

Significant differences also exist in the organisation of care services. Germany offers a flexible system that includes both institutional care (nursing homes) and an extensive range of home-based services, allowing dependent individuals to remain in their familiar environment. There is also the possibility of combining various types of support, such as cash benefits and care services. In Poland, care services are fragmented and decisions regarding their allocation are often discretionary. In addition, the system of social care homes is inefficient – there is a shortage of places in public facilities, while private care remains too expensive for many individuals.

Another crucial difference concerns working conditions for caregivers and support for family caregivers. In Germany, the long-term care insurance system ensures professional caregivers and support for family members who provide care, including training, caregiving leave and financial benefits. In Poland, wages in the care sector are low, leading to severe staff shortages and the emigration of qualified workers. Family caregivers also do not receive adequate support, care allowances are limited and the lack of well-developed respite care services leaves families struggling to cope on their own.

Equally important is the availability and quality of benefits. In Germany, the system clearly defines the support for dependent individuals and levels of dependency are classified according to uniform criteria, ensuring predictability and a consistent standard of assistance. In Poland, there is no unified definition of a dependent person and various legal regulations lead to administrative chaos and difficulties in accessing benefits. Many forms of assistance are means-tested, meaning that some individuals, despite being in genuine need, do not qualify for support.

In recent years, Poland has taken steps to improve the situation of dependent individuals, introducing a supplementary benefit for dependent persons and neighbourly services. However, compared to Germany, these measures are temporary solutions and do not create a cohesive support system. The German system has a broad range of solutions, including long-term care insurance, flexible support options and high-standard institutional and home-based care. The German model is based on stable funding and a well-organised structure,

---

[48] Daniel Eryk Lach, "Organizacja i finansowanie…", 167.

ensuring predictability and broad access to care services. Poland still relies on inconsistent and fragmented solutions, placing the primary responsibility for care on families. To move closer to the German model, Poland would need comprehensive reforms in funding, service organisation and caregiver support. Without these changes, the gap in care for dependent individuals in Poland will continue to widen, posing one of the greatest challenges to the country's social care system in the context of an ageing population.

Optimal solutions should also include obligations to make additional contributions to help build a robust support system for dependent individuals, with an extensive range of benefits and a guarantee of their availability. It is equally necessary to pressure the authorities to focus on foundational work, such as creating conditions (including financial incentives) that encourage young people to pursue careers in caregiving, expanding the network of care homes and establishing appropriate regulations to provide respite for family caregivers.[49] Until the system is repaired, Poland should also consider developing a private care insurance market, which, despite the lack of state solutions, remains underdeveloped in the country.[50]

For years, Polish literature has been calling for adopting a model resembling the German solutions, recognising their effectiveness.[51] Introducing mandatory care insurance, developing support for family caregivers and investing in in-kind and technological benefits would be key steps toward creating a more efficient and equitable system for older adult care. With proper legislative and financial support, these changes could ensure dignified living conditions for dependent individuals and relieve families of the caregiving burden, making the system more sustainable and effective in the long term.[52]

The analysis has led to the conclusion that the optimal solution is introducing an additional contribution obligation and, on this basis, constructing

---

[49] Agnieszka Furmańska-Maruszak, "Równowaga między pracą i opieką. Wsparcie nieformalnego opiekuna osoby starszej na rynku pracy w porównaniach międzynarodowych", *Acta Universitatis Lodziensis, Folia Oeconomica,* No. 2, (2015): 111–26.

[50] Łukasz Jurek, "Zapotrzebowanie na prywatne ubezpieczenie opiekuńcze w Polsce", *Rozprawy Ubezpieczeniowe. Konsument na rynku usług finansowych* 33, No. 3, (2019): 68–80.

[51] Daniel Eryk Lach, "Organizacja i finansowanie…", 165.

[52] See Daniel Eryk Lach, "Few remarks on constructing a system to cover the risk of long-term care in Poland", *Praca i zabezpieczenie społeczne*, No. 9, (2020): 44 ff.

a solid system of support for dependent persons with an extensive system of benefits and the certainty of obtaining them. It is necessary to develop the entire care system with state support, from encouraging young people to receive training to provide the best care for dependants to creating a comprehensive network of care facilities and homes.

Bibliography

Auth Diana, Leiber Simone, Leitner Sigrid, "Bedarfe und Bewältigungshandeln von sorgenden Angehörigen: Welche Rolle spielt Geschlecht in Wechselwirkung mit anderen Differenzkategorien?", *Sozialer Fortschritt*, No. 3, 2020.

Boecken Winfried, "Zur Frage eines Anspruchs von Pflegebedürftigen auf gleichgeschlechtliche Pflege", *Die Sozialgerichtsbarkeit*, No. 12 (2008).

Furmańska-Maruszak Agnieszka, "Równowaga między pracą i opieką. Wsparcie nieformalnego opiekuna osoby starszej na rynku pracy w porównaniach międzynarodowych", *Acta Universitatis Lodziensis, Folia Oeconomica*, No. 2 (2015).

Gutowska Anna, "(Nie)pełnosprawna starość – przyczyny, uwarunkowania, wsparcie", *Interdyscyplinarne Konteksty Pedagogiki Specjalnej*, No. 8 (2015).

Holmerová Iva, Vanková Hana, Wija Petr, "Opportunities and Challenges for Integrated Provision of Long-term Care Services in the Czech Republic", in *Challenges of Ageing Societies in the Visegrad Countries: Hungary, Czech Republic, Poland, Slovakia* (Zsuzsa Széman, Budapest: Hungarian Charity Service of the Order of Malta, 2013).

Igl Gerhard in Sozialrechtshandbuch (SRH) (Franz Ruland, Ulrich Becker, Peter Axer, Baden-Baden: Nomos, 2022).

Igl Gerhard, "Das neue Pflegeversicherungsrecht: Soziale Pflegeversicherung (Sozialgesetzbuch – Elftes Buch)" (Munich: C.H. Beck Verlag, 1995).

Janda Constanze, Migranten im Sozialstaat (Tübingen: Mohr Siebeck, 2012).

Jurek Łukasz, "Opieka nad osobami niesamodzielnymi: model realizowany a model pożądany", *Polityka Społeczna*, No. 2 (2018).

Jurek Łukasz, "Zapotrzebowanie na prywatne ubezpieczenie opiekuńcze w Polsce", *Rozprawy Ubezpieczeniowe. Konsument na rynku usług finansowych* 33, No. 3 (2019).

Jurek Łukasz, "Reforma systemu orzecznictwa o niesamodzielności w Niemczech", *Ubezpieczenia Społeczne. Teoria i praktyka*, No. 3 (2020).

Krasney Otto, "Pflegegeld des § 37 SGB XI", *Die Sozialgerichtsbarkeit*, No. 6 (1996).

Lach Daniel Eryk, "Few remarks on constructing a system to cover the risk of long-term care in Poland", *Praca i zabezpieczenie społeczne*, No. 9 (2020).

Lach Daniel Eryk, "Organizacja i finansowanie świadczeń opieki długoterminowej w wybranych krajach UE", Ruch prawniczy, ekonomiczny i socjologiczny, No. 1 (2019).

Lach Daniel Eryk, "Zabezpieczenie społeczne nieformalnych opiekunów osób niesamodzielnych", *Forum Prawnicze*, No. 5 (2018).

Lungstras Anne Barbara, "§ 40", in *SGB XI. Soziale Pflegeversicherung. Kommentar* (Peter Udsching, Bernd Schütze, Munich: C.H. Beck Verlag, 2018).

Luty-Michalak Marta, Syryt Aleksandra, Long-term care system for dependent people – Austrian experiences, *Acta Universitatis Lodziensis. Folia Sociologica*, No. 71 (2019).

Maschmann Frank, "Grundzüge des Leistungsrechts der gesetzlichen Pflegeversicherung nach dem SGB XI", Neue Zeitschrift für Sozialrecht, No. 3 (1995).

Muckel Stephan, Ogorek Markus, Rixen Stephan, "Sozialrecht" (Munich: C.H. Beck Verlag, 2019).

Patsios Demi, Davey Adam, "Formal and Informal Community Care for Older Adults", in The Cambridge Handbook on Age and Ageing (Malcolm Johnson, Cambridge: Cambridge University Press, 2005).

Pawlak Karol, Ćwirlej-Sozańska Agnieszka, Wiśniowska-Szurlej Agnieszka, "Kryteria oceny stopni niesamodzielności – doświadczenia dotychczasowe i propozycje dla potrzeb polskiej praktyki", *Polityka Społeczna*, No. 2 (2018).

Pfeil Walter, "Benefit Structures for Persons Dependent on Long-Term Care in Austria", in Long-Term Care in Europe: A Juridical Approach (Ulrich Becker, Hans-Joachim Reinhard, Berlin: Springer, 2018).

Pfeil Walter, "Die Pflegevorsorge in Österreich", in: Soziale Sicherung bei Pflegebedürftigkeit in der Europäischen Union (Klaus Sieveking, Baden-Baden: Nomos, 1998).

Przybyłowicz Ariel in "Ubezpieczenie pielęgnacyjne w Republice Federalnej Niemiec" (Warszawa: Zakład Ubezpieczeń Społecznych, 2017).

Richert-Kaźmierska Anita, "Organizacja systemu opieki nad seniorami wyzwaniem dla samorządów lokalnych", *Acta Universitatis Lodziensis. Folia Oeconomica*, No. 3 (2020).

Rothenburg Eva-Maria, "Das Persönliche Budget: Eine Einführung in Grundlagen, Verfahren und Leistungserbringung" (Munich: Juventa, 2009).

Rothgang Heinz, "Ziele und Wirkungen der Pflegeversicherung" (Frankfurt: Campus-Verlag, 1997).

Skuban Ralph, "Pflegesicherung in Europa. Sozialpolitik im Binnenmarkt" (Wiesbaden: VS Verlag für Sozialwissenschaften, 2004).

Surdej Aleksander, Brzozowski Jan, "Rozwój systemu usług opiekuńczych dla osób niesamodzielnych we Francji: implikacje dla Polski", *Polityka Społeczna*, No. 1 (2012).

Szwałkiewicz Elżbieta, "Co przemawia za potrzebą zdefiniowania 'osoby niesamodzielnej'? Definicja niesamodzielności i osoby niesamodzielnej", *Polityka Społeczna*, No. 2 (2018).

Wahl Andreas, "§ 36", "§ 41-42" in *SGB XI. Soziale Pflegeversicherung. Kommentar* (Peter Udsching, Bernd Schütze, Munich: C.H. Beck Verlag, 2018).

Waltermann Raimund, Schmidt Benjamin, Chandna-Hoppe Katja, "Sozialrecht" (Heidelberg: C.F. Müller, 2022).

Wiegand Britta, "§ 43", in *SGB XI. Soziale Pflegeversicherung. Kommentar* (Peter Udsching, Bernd Schütze, Munich: C.H. Beck Verlag, 2018).

Zych Adam, "Leksykon gerontologii" (Kraków: Oficyna Wydawnicza "Impuls", 2019).

The Vulnerability of a Municipality Regarding VAT

Sławomir Owczarczuk[*,1]

Abstract: In carrying out public tasks to meet the needs of their residents under conditions of increasing tax risk and competition with private entities, municipalities, as value added tax (VAT) payers, are particularly vulnerable participants in tax law relationships. The legal structure of the municipality and the specificity of its action in the sphere of imperium and dominium, with the help of many different organisational units, means that the tax status of municipalities in the EU VAT system, despite extensive CJEU case law, still raises important legal questions. It is not defined clearly enough in the VAT Directive and is not uniformly regulated in the laws of EU Member States. The lack of harmonisation of the law in this area leads to the non-uniform application of VAT rules to municipalities in the Member States, resulting in municipalities not having sufficient protection under the current VAT system. This chapter aims to show the specificity of the legal construction of municipalities as VAT payers based on selected examples and to indicate in which areas of municipalities' activities in the EU their rights in the VAT system are infringed. In particular, the nature of these infringements and the measures that need to be taken to ensure that municipalities exercise their rights, particularly the principles of VAT neutrality and deductibility.

Keywords: tax law, VAT, municipality, taxpayer, vulnerability

1. Introduction

Due to its fiscal efficiency, VAT is a major source of budgetary revenue for EU Member States and the phenomenon of the way it has spread round the world

---

* PhD, Assistant Professor at the Faculty of Law and Administration of the University of Silesia in Katowice, Poland ORCID: 0000-0003-3486-0028.

1 The publication uses materials obtained within the research project, entitled "The theoretical legal model of taxation of the metropolis with turnover taxes, in particular VAT"; no. 2023/07/X/HS5/00495, funded by the National Centre of Science (NCN), Poland.

over several decades has been noted and appreciated by many researchers.[2] As revenue for the State budget, this indirect tax is collected not only from private companies but also from municipalities, even though they do not act as VAT payers in every area of their activity and incur high VAT costs in the price of purchased goods and services when making infrastructure investments.

Tax authorities are interested in maximising indirect tax revenues, especially during periods of global crises, which increases the risk of applying a pro-fiscal interpretation to municipalities and violating the principles of VAT. The legal structure of the municipality is complex. The municipality consists of several organisational units of different legal status, performing various paid and unpaid activities in civil law and public law. This causes serious problems with the correct classification of transactions carried out by the municipality and its organisational units for VAT purposes as taxable, exempt or non-taxable activities. Furthermore, municipalities, acting in the sphere of *imperium* and *dominium*, are not able to reduce their tax liabilities by deducting the input tax to the same extent as private companies. The existing model of VAT taxation of local government, formally harmonised, leads to significant differences in the tax status of municipalities in the Member States due to differences in the implementation of Article 13(1) of the VAT Directive[3] and non-uniform organisational and legal forms of municipal activities.[4]

---

2 See: Alan Tait, *Value Added Tax: International Practice and Problems* (IMF, Washington DC, 1988), p. 3; Alan Schenk and Oliver Oldman, *Value Added Tax: A Comparative Approach* (rev. edn. Cambridge University Press, Cambridge, New York, 2007), p. 33; Richard Bird and Pierre-Pascal Genderon, *The VAT in Developing and Transitional Countries* (Cambridge University Press, New York, 2007), p. 20 (citations omitted); Liam Ebrill, et. al., *The Modern VAT* (IMF, Washington DC, 2001), p. xi; Michael Keen & Ben Lockwood, "The Value Added Tax: Its Causes and Consequences", Journal of Development Economics 92(2) (2010), p. 138; Kathryn James, *The Rise of Value-Added Tax* (Cambridge University Press, New York, 2015), pp. 148–149 (citations omitted).

3 Council Directive 2006/112/EC of 28 November 2006 on the common system of value added tax (OJ EU.L.2006.347.1), hereinafter referred to as the VAT Directive.

4 Sławomir Owczarczuk, "Model opodatkowania usług komunalnych podatkiem od towarów i usług – wnioski na przykładzie dostaw wody i odbioru ścieków". *Ruch Prawniczy, Ekonomiczny I Socjologiczny*, Year LXXXIV – volume 1 – (2022), p. 153. <https://doi.org/10.14746/rpeis.2022.84.1.12>.

The majority of these provisions have remained unchanged since their introduction in 1977.[5] The existing law in this area does not follow the dynamic changes and has been too complex since its inception, leaving the VAT status of municipalities unclear.[6] This means that the CJEU case law, while providing valuable interpretative guidance, is not able to solve all the growing problems that arise while the municipalities perform the tasks of a public utility nature, the aim of which is to satisfy the collective needs of the population on an ongoing and uninterrupted basis through the provision of services accessible to the public. The experience of the 'old' and 'new' EU Member States reinforces the conviction that the current VAT system with respect to municipalities is inefficient and constitutes a permanent state of uncertainty as a result of which municipalities are particularly vulnerable participants in tax law relationships under the VAT Directive and require special legal protection.

2. Inaccuracies in the current legislation

In accordance with Article 13(1) of Council Directive 2006/112/EC of 28 November 2006 on the common system of VAT: states, regional and local government authorities, and other bodies governed by public law shall not be regarded as taxable persons in respect of the activities or transactions in which they engage as public authorities, even where they collect dues, fees, contributions, or payments in connection with those activities or transactions. However, when they engage in such activities or transactions, they shall be regarded as taxable persons in respect of those activities or transactions where their treatment as non-taxable persons would lead to significant distortions of competition. In any event, bodies governed by public law shall be regarded

[5] See: Rita de la Feria, "The EU VAT Treatment of Public Sector Bodies: Slowly Moving in the Wrong Direction". *Intertax*, Vol. 37, Issue 3, (Kluwer Law International BV, The Netherlands 2009), pp. 148–149. Sijbren Cnossen, "Is the VAT's Sixth Directive Becoming an Anachronism?", European Taxation (International Bureau of Fiscal Documentation, December 2003), p. 434.

[6] For example, the expression "significant distortions of competition" in Article 13(1) of the VAT Directive continues to raise questions of interpretation and application. Ibid., p. 151. See also Alan Schenk, Victor Thuronyi, Wei Cui, *Value Added Tax. A Comparative Approach* (Cambridge University Press 2015), p. 298.

as taxable persons in respect of the activities listed in Annex I, provided that those activities are not carried out on such a small scale as to be negligible.

According to the VAT Directive, municipalities:

1) are not regarded as VAT payers where they carry out activities in their capacity as public authorities. The public-law nature of the activities is a condition for excluding municipalities and other bodies governed by public law from being taxable persons, subject to the wording of the second and third paragraphs of Article 13(1) of the VAT Directive;
2) are regarded as taxpayers in respect of the activities and transactions they carry out in their capacity as public authorities, even if they collect dues, fees, contributions or payments in connection with those activities or transactions, if their exclusion from the category of taxpayers would lead to significant distortions of competition;
3) are regarded as taxpayers in respect of the activities set out in Annex I to the VAT Directive, unless the small scale of these activities means they can be omitted.[7]

In other words, municipalities are recognised as VAT payers in three possible situations, namely when:

1) they do not act as public authorities but as private entities,
2) they are acting as public entities, but treating them as non-taxable entities would lead to a significant distortion of competition, in particular between private and public sector entities,[8]
3) they perform the activities set out in Annex I, unless the small scale of these activities is such that they may be omitted.[9]

Under the last condition, municipalities are considered taxpayers (whether or not they act as a public authority) as long as they carry out the activities enumerated in Annex I, unless the small scale of these activities means that they can be disregarded. This applies to activities such as: telecommunication services, the supply of water, gas, electricity and heat; the transport of goods;

---

7 See Sławomir Owczarczuk, *Status podatnika VAT w samorządzie terytorialnym* (Taxpress, Warszawa 2012), pp. 65–67.

8 See Article 13(1), paragraph 2 of the VAT Directive.

9 See Article 13(1), paragraph 3 of the VAT Directive.

the provision of services by seaports and airports; the transport of persons; the supply of new goods manufactured for sale; transactions concerning agricultural products carried out by agricultural intervention agencies in accordance with the regulations on the common organisation of the market as regards products; the organisation of trade fairs and exhibitions of a commercial nature; warehousing; the activities of commercial advertising agencies; the activities of travel agencies; the operation of staff canteens, buffets, cafeterias and other similar establishments; and the activities of radio and television stations insofar as they are not exempted under Article 132(1)(q) of the VAT Directive.

The literature emphasises that the principle of equality of competition in tax law is aimed at preventing distortions of competition, as tax should not be a determinant of economic decisions.[10] Therefore, it is fully understandable that treating municipalities as VAT-exempt entities would lead to a significant distortion of competition between them and private companies in, for example, the real estate trade, the supply of water, gas, electricity and heat, the collection of sewage, rental, lease, etc.

As Juliane Kokott notes: 'Article 13(1)(1) (providing for such exclusion from VAT) therefore has to be interpreted strictly'.[11] Ben Terra/Julie Kajus emphasises that: 'According to Article 13 (formerly Article 4(5) of the Sixth Directive), bodies governed by public law are not regarded as taxable persons in respect of activities or transactions in which they engage as public authorities'.[12] However, in the activity of municipalities as public sector entities, we can distinguish, in addition to the 'redistribution of income and wealth (transferring money, through taxation, social transfers, grants subsidies)' and 'provisions of public goods and services' also 'competitive services (provision of other goods and services similar to those supplied by the private sector)'.[13]

---

[10] Juliane Kokott, Pasquale Pistone, *Taxpayers in international law: international minimum standards for the protection of taxpayers' rights* (C.H. Beck, Hart Publishing, Nomos 2022), p. 380.

[11] Juliane Kokott, *EU Tax Law* (C.H. Beck, Hart Publishing, Nomos 2022), p. 440.

[12] Ben Terra, Julie Kajus, *A Guide to the European VAT Directives*. Vol. 1 (IBDF, 2023), p. 379.

[13] Ibid.

Individual types of services are subject to VAT to the extent set out in Article 13(1), paragraphs of 2 and 3 of the VAT Directive.

This requires municipalities to define the boundaries between activities subject to VAT (taxable and exempt) and activities excluded from the VAT system, as well as to apply a proportionate deduction of VAT, which is a significant problem for municipalities, tax authorities and courts.

3. Various ways of implementing the provisions of the VAT Directive

It is up to each Member State to choose the appropriate legislative technique to transpose into national law the principle of treating municipalities and other bodies governed by public law as non-taxable persons for VAT purposes, as an exception to the principle of the universality of VAT taxation.[14]

There are some variations in the way Article 13 of the VAT Directive has been transposed into the laws of the Member States, leading to different ways of implementing it.[15] The existing discrepancies between national and EU law distorted the performance of public tasks and the equal conditions of competition between municipalities. Most EU countries have, over time, adopted a solution that does not deviate in its normative construction from the provision of Article 13(1) of the VAT Directive. For example, the list of activities that refer to Annex I of the VAT Directive is contained in the acts of Ireland, Latvia, Slovakia, Malta, Cyprus, Croatia, Bulgaria, Belgium, France, the Czech Republic, and other Member States. Some countries have even included a definition of a local authority in their VAT law.[16]

Regardless of how Article 13(1) of the VAT Directive has been transposed in individual Member States, the status of municipalities under the EU VAT system continues to pose practical problems, as evidenced by the ongoing tax disputes involving municipalities. Initially, most of the CJEU rulings on

---

[14] Judgment of the CJEU of 17 October 1989, Case 231/87 and 129/88, *Ufficio distrettuale delle imposte dirette di Fiorenzuola d'Arda and others v. Comune di Carpaneto Piacentino and others*, ECR 1989/9/03233.

[15] Ismael Jiménez, "VAT and Public Bodies in EC Member States", Intertax, Vol. 36, Issue 6/7 (Kluwer Law International 2008), p. 281.

[16] For example in Cyprus: («local authority» municipality council, improvement council, village authority and community council) – Art. 2(1) VAT Law 2000–2013.

the interpretation of Article 13(1) of the VAT Directive focused on the scope of the freedom of transposition granted to Member States under this provision.[17] Later rulings have examined the scope of the concept of 'significant distortions of competition'.[18]

As Rita de la Feria emphasised: 'In the last thirty years, the ECJ has struggled with the meaning of expressions such as "engaged in as public authorities" (Article 13(1), first paragraph), "significant distortions to competition" (Article 13(1), second paragraph)'.[19] Despite new CJEU rulings in recent years, this struggle is not over and reflects significant problems with the application of controversial legislation in the 'new' Member States.[20]

The current EU VAT system is still not neutral for municipalities. The legal systems of many Member States lack provisions for refunding part of the undeducted VAT, or for its compensation outside the VAT system in order to protect the interests of municipalities. When carrying out public investments in a situation where the municipality, in a given transaction, does not have the status of a VAT payer, the local government incurs significant costs due to undeducted VAT and needs financial support from the State, which should ensure the implementation of the principle of adequacy. In addition to providing budgetary revenue to Member States, the purpose of the VAT system is to reduce the distortions of competition that occur and to increase the neutrality of VAT.[21]

---

17 De la Feria (2009), p. 151.

18 Ibid., p. 152. For example: Case C-102/08, *Salix*, [2008] OJ C142/12.

19 De la Feria (2009), p. 157.

20 As municipalities are not able to ensure full tax neutrality due to the non-deductibility of the unput VAT, which becomes a hidden cost in the performance of municipal investments ("tax cascading"), some Member States have compensation funds from which a refund is made outside the VAT system, where municipalities are entitled to recover non-deductible VAT related to their activities as public authorities.

21 Oskar Henkow, *The VAT/GST Treatment of Public Bodies* (Alphen aan den Rijn, 2013), p. 185.

Poland's VAT Act[22] does not have a regulation relating directly to the activities set out in Annex I to the VAT Directive, which generates tax interpretation difficulties. In the post-accession period, the phenomenon of municipalities and tax authorities incorrectly identifying VAT payer status was widespread. VAT-registered taxable entities were often the municipalities' offices rather than the municipalities themselves. This changed under the influence of the case law of the administrative courts, which, unlike the tax authorities, applied a pro-EU (systemic external) interpretation. The implementing provisions of the VAT Act in force at the time did not correspond to the requirements of correct legislation and were not in line with EU legislation. The lack of systemic lawmaking became particularly apparent when the fiscal distinctiveness of the municipality and its budgetary units, and the interpretation applied by the tax authorities, were the main obstacles to implementing the principle of VAT neutrality and deductibility in municipalities.[23] Polish administrative courts apply a pro-EU interpretation when resolving tax disputes between municipalities and tax authorities, quite often referring preliminary questions to the CJEU, which interprets the provisions of the VAT Directive.

4. The municipality as a vulnerable VAT payer

As confirmed by CJEU case law, difficulties in the application of the provisions of the VAT Directive by municipalities and tax authorities caused and continue to cause:

---

22 Act on the Tax on Goods and Services of 11 March 2004 (consolidated text: Journal of Laws 2023, item 1570 with subsequent amendments) hereinafter referred to as the ATGS. In spite of the legislative changes made between 2004 and 2023, the Polish legislator did not exclude municipalities from the VAT system when they carry out public law tasks simultaneously on the basis of public law provisions and civil law contracts. See Article 15(6) of the ATGS.

23 Sławomir Owczarczuk, "Ewolucja statusu gminy jako podatnika z perspektywy 25 lat funkcjonowania podatku od towarów i usług w Polsce – wnioski de lege lata i postulaty de lege ferenda". *Samorząd Terytorialny*, No. 6, June 2020, p. 12.

1) either the unauthorised exclusion of municipalities from the category of VAT payers,[24]
2) or the unauthorised attribution of VAT status to them in a given transaction.[25]

In the first case, the CJEU case law *de facto* concerned the tax authorities' infringement of the principle of neutrality and the deductibility of VAT in municipal activities of a public utility nature whose objective is to meet the collective needs of the population on an ongoing and uninterrupted basis through the supply of services open to the public, as listed in Annex I to the VAT Directive (water supply), which was carried out by the municipality through its own budgetary organisational unit or a municipal company. The tax authorities denied municipalities the right to deduct the input tax in situations where the investor in the construction of a water supply or sewerage system was a municipality and the VAT-taxable sales of the water supply or sewerage were made by its budgetary organisational unit that, having at its disposal assets received from the municipality free of charge, was regarded as a taxable entity separate from the municipality under national VAT legislation. The municipalities were deprived of the right to deduct VAT due to an incorrect implementation of the provisions of the VAT Directive,[26] leading to distortions in competition between the municipalities themselves and between the municipalities and private entities.

Tax authorities have also taken the position that municipalities do not act in a 'VAT-taxable capacity' when constructing public buildings, and do not have the right to deduct the input tax when this municipal infrastructure was not initially used for VAT-taxable activities, but was subsequently used for VAT-taxable activities.[27]

---

[24] See judgments of the Court of Justice EU of 29 September 2015, C-276/14, *Gmina Wrocław v. Minister Finansów*, (ECLI:EU:C:2015:635) and of 25 June 2018, C-140/17, *Szef Krajowej Administracji Skarbowej v Gmina Ryjewo*, (ECLI:EU:C:2018:595).

[25] See judgments of the Court of Justice EU of 30 March 2023, C-612/21, *Gmina O. v Dyrektor Krajowej Informacji Skarbowej*, (ECLI:EU:C:2023:279) and of 30 March 2023, C-616/21, *Dyrektor Krajowej Informacji Skarbowej v Gmina L.*, (ECLI:EU:C:2023:280).

[26] There was a similar situation in Belgium. See Patrick Wille, "VAT Grouping in Belgium, VAT and Bodies Governed by Public Law", Bulletin For International Taxation (IBDF, August/September 2008), p. 428.

[27] E.g. rent or lease of real estate.

However, the municipalities' position was confirmed in the CJEU judgment of 25 July 2018, *Szef Krajowej Administracji Skarbowej vs Gmina Ryjewo*, in which the court found a violation of the principle of VAT neutrality.[28] The court ruled that Articles 167, 168, and 184 of the VAT Directive do not preclude a public law body from correcting the deduction of VAT paid on real property when it was initially used for non-taxable activities and the public body did not expressly indicate any intention to use the real property for taxable activities, but where it could have been used for both VAT taxable and non-taxable activities at the time of its acquisition and the public body did not rule out the possibility that it would be used for such purposes.[29]

In the second situation, the tax authorities treated the municipality as an entity acting as a VAT payer and enjoying the right to deduct the input VAT, but as a result of the CJEU ruling of 30 March 2023, *Gmina O. vs Dyrektor Krajowej Informacji Skarbowej*, its status as a VAT payer was challenged.[30] The request was made in proceedings between the municipality of O. and the Director of the National Treasury Information (Poland) for a tax interpretation addressed to that municipality with regard to its liability to pay VAT on activities consisting of that municipality concluding a contract with certain of its residents for the installation of renewable energy systems on their real properties, in return for monetary compensation from those residents.

Similarly, in a judgment of 30 March 2023, *Dyrektor Krajowej Informacji Skarbowej vs Gmina L.*, the CJEU ruled differently from the tax authorities.[31] In his advance tax ruling of 13 March 2020, the Director of the National Treasury Information Bureau took the view that the municipality of L. acted as a taxable entity for VAT purposes and that it should consequently be allowed to deduct the input VAT paid.[32] By contrast, the court ruled that: Articles 2(1), 9(1), and 13(1) of the VAT Directive must be interpreted as meaning that the fact that a municipality has contracted out the removal of asbestos and the collection of products and waste containing asbestos for the benefit of its residents who are owners of their real properties and who so wish, does not constitute a supply of services subject to VAT where those

---

28 See Case C-140/17.

29 Ibid., point 59.

30 See Case C-612/21.

31 See Case C-616/21.

32 Ibid., point 17.

activities are not intended to generate a regular income and do not give rise to any payment by those residents and where those activities are financed out of public funds.[33]

Taking into account the indicated CJEU rulings of 2023, the municipalities' settlements of VAT on investments for the benefit of residents in renewable energy sources, largely financed with EU funds, are currently being analysed in detail.

Adopting the CJEU's theses would mean that municipalities do not have to charge the VAT due on subsidies and on residents' participation in the costs of installing renewable energy installations. The municipalities are also not entitled to deduct VAT, as there is no connection between the expenses incurred and economic activity. The effect of these rulings is to diametrically change the line of interpretation of the tax authorities in Poland. The problem affects more than 2,000 municipalities that do not know how they are supposed to act in this area of public utility activity. This is because the position of the national tax authorities was completely different in previous years, and the collective needs of the local government community must be met.

The question as to whether or not previous tax settlements should be reviewed. The normative construction of the notion of a VAT payer adopted by the Polish legislator with regard to local government units differs from the EU regulations. The Polish legislator has strictly connected the notion of a VAT payer in relation to municipalities with the performance of activities by these units on the basis of civil-law contracts concluded,[34] whereas Article 13(1) of the VAT Directive does not contain any such limitation.

Municipalities are left uncertain about their VAT rights and obligations. Deciding whether a municipality is subject to VAT in a given transaction, and thus whether its non-taxation of VAT distorts or is likely to distort competition significantly, leaves room for interpretation and requires case-by-case

33 Ibid., point 52.

34 See Article 15(6) of the TGS: "Taxable persons shall not include public authorities and the offices of such bodies as regards tasks established by specific provisions for the performance of which they have been appointed, with the exception of transactions carried out under private law contracts." See also the judgment of the CJEU, C-616/21, point 12.

decisions.[35] As the presented CJEU rulings on municipalities (C-276/14; C-140/17; C 612/21; C 616/21) indicate, this uncertainty does not serve either the tax authorities, the courts or the local communities. From the point of view of the principles of law, it is unacceptable to have a position in which one municipality, acting on the basis of an individual interpretation received, is treated as a VAT payer and has the right to deduct input tax, while another municipality that has not applied for such an interpretation does not have this status.[36]

The differences between the legislation of the Member States and that of the EU result in the case law of the CJEU on municipalities based on EU tax law diverging from national regulations. Concepts of EU law confronted with concepts of national tax law are not always directly supported by the court's rulings, which then affects the implementation of the principle of effectiveness of EU law.

The system of exclusions or exemptions for public entities can create an advantage or disadvantage for municipalities on the market. The reference in Article 13(1) of the VAT Directive to the clause: 'acting of a given entity as a public authority' leads to the Member States defining this category of entity, and thus of VAT taxable entities, differently. In this way, national regulations become a barrier to VAT harmonisation. Moreover, discrepancies in the application of EU VAT rules arise both when municipalities are obliged to bear the cost of input VAT on investments made, and when they have the possibility to recover it.

Problems with determining the tax status of municipalities under the EU VAT system concern issues such as the taxation or non-taxation of: subsidies and compensation paid to commercial companies, the activities of

---

35 In some countries, such as Belgium, specific procedures have been established for the determination of a potential significant distortion of competition (a turnover threshold of more than €25,000 per year for a given activity, at which the tax authority had to decide whether the municipality's activity had VAT taxable status or not, after hearing arguments presented by the municipality). See Aurélie Soldai, Camille De Neyer, Alexander Vandendries, "Le cinquantenaire de la TVA: rétrospectives et perspectives", Revue Générale de Fiscalité et de Comptabilité Pratique, RGFCP (Wolters Kluwer 2021/1), p. 20.

36 Owczarczuk (2020), p. 15.

wholly-owned municipal companies,[37] transactions between municipalities, various forms of cooperation in local government; the extent of the proportional deduction of the input tax in the provision of public services; the causal link between purchases made and individual types of activities; adjustments to multi-annual fixed assets; gratuitous benefits in local government, etc.

Since the distinction between activity in a 'public authority capacity' and economic activity can only be defined in accordance with the applicable law of an EU Member State,[38] the maze of legal pitfalls associated with the activities of municipalities under the EU VAT system is steadily increasing along with the volume of legislation.[39] Therefore, as Christian Amand rightly points out: 'Since constitutional law is not harmonised, the VAT treatment of public bodies is not harmonised either'.[40]

The distortions are even more pronounced in metropolitan areas. In Poland, for example, the tax authorities demanded the taxation of the contribution paid by the municipalities to the only metropolitan association so far (the Upper Silesian and Zagłębie Metropolis), which was a levy under the public law regime. It was only a decision of the Supreme Administrative Court that brought an end to the violation of the law by the tax authorities, in particular the principles of universality and neutrality of VAT.[41] The Supreme Administrative Court held that the conclusion of such public-law agreements between a metropolitan association and the municipalities, as well as their subject matter, are strictly regulated by administrative law, so it is impossible to consider them even close to civil-law contracts. In the case of the municipalities' membership fees, the legal relationship between

---

37 See, for example, the judgment of the Court of Justice EU of 22 February 2018, C-182/17, *Nagyszénás Településszolgáltatási Nonprofit Kft. v Nemzeti Adó- és Vámhivatal Fellebbviteli Igazgatósága*, (ECLI:EU:C:2018:91).

38 Christian Amand, "VAT for Public Entities and Charities – Should the Sixth Directive Be Renegotiated?", International VAT Monitor (November/December 2006), p. 436 and ECJ judgments: of 17 October 1989, Joined Cases 231/87 and 129/88, *Ufficio distrettuale delle imposte dirette di Fiorenzuola d'Arda and others v. Comune di Carpaneto Piacentino and others*, [1989] ECR 3233; of 15 May 1990, C-4/89, *Comune di Carpaneto Piacentino and others v. Ufficio provinciale imposta sul valore aggiunto di Piacenza*, [1989] ECR I-1869.

39 De la Feria (2009), p. 165.

40 Amand (2006), p. 436.

41 Judgment of the Supreme Administrative Court of 3 March 2021, I FSK 830/20 (CBOSA).

the Upper Silesian and Zagłębie Metropolis and the municipalities that are part of the metropolitan association was not based on civil law contracts, but on acts of generally applicable law (acts, regulations, and acts of local law). Such legal relationships between the metropolitan association and the municipalities belonged to the sphere of *imperium*, which are not related to economic activities subject to VAT.

The noticeable lack of legal certainty in the activities of municipalities where the VAT system is concerned, despite the considerable body of CJEU case law, is not diminishing at all. This is despite the fact that the CJEU constantly makes use of 'soft law' – opinions, guidelines, and explanations when resolving tax disputes.[42] The rights of municipalities are not sufficiently protected at the national and EU level, which is due to the structure of Article 13(1) of the VAT Directive, which weakens the VAT system.[43] There is a constant struggle concerning the VAT Directive, as it is based on budgetary considerations rather than on fundamental principles of constitutional law common to all Member States, meaning that it is not able to guarantee the equal treatment of all entities as regards tax matters.[44]

5. Conclusions

As the discussion above demonstrates, given the current EU legal framework, legal scholarship and the CJEU 2023 case law, a municipality in the VAT system is a weaker party to tax law relationships and particularly vulnerable. Therefore, it needs special legal protection, if only because of the social aspect of its activities: meeting the collective needs of the local government community. Under the law, the status of a VAT payer in the municipal activities of municipalities **should be clearly defined** and not raise major doubts. This is the main *de lege ferenda* postulate addressed to the legislator.[45]

Despite the rich body of CJEU case law, the current VAT system is still unsatisfactory as regards the activities of municipalities, requiring reform

42 Kokott, Pistone (2022), p. 480.

43 Giangiacomo D'Angelo, "New Frontiers in the EU VAT Regime for Public Bodies", Intertax, Vol. 46, Issue 12, (2018 Kluwer Law International BV, The Netherlands), p. 1021.

44 Amand (2006), p. 443.

45 Owczarczuk (2020), p. 16.

and simplification.[46] This is because the wording of Article 13 of the VAT Directive remains unchanged (despite the fact that the European Commission has examined proposals to change the VAT system for municipalities).[47]

Taking into account the rapid changes in society and the economy, regardless of the unpredictable political situation, the CJEU will continue to try to adapt the VAT system to the municipal activities of municipalities with new reinterpretations of Article 13 of the VAT Directive,[48] but is there a 'Solomonic' way out of the impasse?

Maciej Szpunar's diagnosis is apt here: The levying of VAT on activities carried on by bodies governed by public law in their capacity as public authorities may appear to be pointless because it leads to significant administrative complications without any evident effect on public finances, apart from the movement of funds from one account to another. However, there are two major reasons for levying tax in this way where the activities carried on by the public bodies are similar in nature to ordinary economic activities.[49]

Among other things, the advocate general gives the following reasons: first, the principle of the universality of VAT requires, wherever possible, that VAT must be levied on all economic activities; second, if activities are carried on by public bodies on the same basis as they are or may be carried on by private bodies, but without tax being levied, this will lead to a different type of distortion of competition.[50]

He goes on to conclude, however, leaving no illusions that it is for that reason that the EU legislature provided for the taxation of activities carried on by public bodies where the absence of such taxation would lead to distortions of competition. The Court has already addressed that principle in a series of judgments, but it still causes problems in practice.[51]

---

46 Zob. Katarzyna Feldo, *VAT w partnerstwie publiczno-prywatnym* (Wolters Kluwer, Warszawa 2011), pp. 280–281.

47 Giangiacomo D'Angelo (2018), pp. 1011–1012.

48 See also Giangiacomo D'Angelo (2018), p. 1021.

49 Opinion of Advocate General Maciej Szpunar delivered on 8 September 2016, C 344/15, *National Roads Authority v The Revenue Commissioners*, point 1, (ECLI:EU:C:2016:661).

50 Ibid. point 2. See the Opinion of Advocate General Juliane Kokott delivered on 23.12.2015, C 520/14, *Gemeente Borsele and Staatssecretaris van Financiën*, points 22 to 27 (ECLI:EU:C:2015:855).

51 See Szpunar (2016), point 3.

This is why there have been many *de lege ferenda* proposals made to the EU legislator over the years in favour of the full inclusion of municipalities in the VAT system, with the option to exempt certain activities or to tax them at a 0% rate.[52] When comparing the advantages and disadvantages of various models of VAT/GST taxation,[53] the literature points out that the most favourable model is that of full taxation of public entities.[54]

First, this would be in line with the structure and nature of VAT. Second, it would not raise so many interpretation problems under the VAT Directive. Third, it would reduce administrative costs.[55] Consequently, Article 13(1) of the Directive should be repealed.[56] To this end, experience from Australia and New Zealand, where a system of full taxation of public entities has been adopted and publicly funded services are taxed at a zero indirect tax rate (Australia), could be used. For many researchers, the system used in these countries would be the best alternative.[57] However, for social reasons (e.g. price increases for certain goods and services) and, above all, political reasons, it remains difficult to adopt.

It is therefore necessary to eliminate those factors that distort the conditions of competition between municipalities and private entities in the legislation of the Member States and at the EU level. Municipalities are not tax evaders and, as the CJEU case law shows, their rights are still being violated by tax authorities and courts, which are not always able to correctly recognise the tax status of municipalities in the VAT system.[58]

---

52 See Sijbren Cnossen, *Modernizing General Consumption Taxes in the Caribbean* (Posted On Dec. 14, 2020), pp. 25–26. The author notes that Australia and Canada avoid distortions by returning input tax.

53 Good and Service Tax.

54 See Michel Aujean, Peter Jenkins, Satya Poddar, "A New Approach to Public Sector Bodies", 10 International VAT Monitor 144 (July/Aug. 1999), pp. 144–149 and Michel Aujean, Peter Jenkins, Satya Poddar, "A New Approach to Application of VAT to Public Sector Bodies", The Tax Journal (Monday, 28 June 1999), p. 17.

55 Henkow (2013), p. 187.

56 Ibid.,186. See also Jiménez (2008), p. 281.

57 Pierre-Pascal Gendron, "VAT Treatment of Nonprofits and Public-Sector Entities", in *The VAT Reader, What a Federal Consumption Tax Would Mean in America*, Special Supplement Managing Editor: Cathy Phillips (Tax Analysts 2011), p. 247.

58 See from the perspective of 25 years of Polish experience: Owczarczuk (2020), pp. 7–17.

Hence, to reduce tax disputes in the EU VAT system, a specific solution was to compensate municipalities for non-deductible VAT outside the VAT system. However, the municipality's vulnerability under tax law is evident in the systems of EU Member States with a compensation fund and those without such regulation[59]. It can be concluded that it is primarily the very legal structure of the municipality and the specificity of its operation, consisting in meeting the needs of its inhabitants in the sphere of imperium and dominium, with the help of many different organisational units, which makes the municipality a very vulnerable participant in legal and tax relations. For this reason, in the area of many other public levies, municipalities benefit from subjective and objective exemptions[60]. Therefore, to reduce the high costs of VAT tax disputes involving municipalities, especially in EU Member States that do not have VAT compensation systems, a new regulation that considers the specificities of municipalities and the public tasks performed by these entities is necessary. It is high time to make an effort to build new legal solutions at the EU and national level that would allow municipalities to overcome the current legal and institutional barriers and constraints in conducting municipal activities.

As entities of the public finance sector, local government units generally perform fiscal obligations and carry out public tasks in order to satisfy the collective needs of the local community. They can expect from the state and the EU a stable, transparent and fair tax system, respect for the principles of legal certainty and VAT neutrality, as well as the principle of adequacy.[61] In recent years, a special role of the CJEU has been prominent in interpreting the provisions of the VAT Directive in relation to the current socio-economic situation, in which the distinction between the public and the private sector is increasingly difficult.[62] The role of the case law of the Member States is also important, which comes down to countering distortions of competition in the VAT system, respecting principles of law and upholding constitutional values.[63]

59 For example, in Poland.
60 Examples include Polish laws on CIT, excise duty, stamp duty.
61 Owczarczuk (2020), p. 15.
62 Giangiacomo D'Angelo (2018), p. 1011.
63 Owczarczuk (2020), p. 16.

Bibliography

Amand Christian, "VAT for Public Entities and Charities – Should the Sixth Directive Be Renegotiated?", International VAT Monitor (November/December 2006).

Aujean Michel, Jenkins Peter, Poddar Satya, "A New Approach to Application of VAT to Public Sector Bodies", The Tax Journal (Monday, 28 June 1999).

Aujean Michel, Jenkins Peter, Poddar Satya, "A New Approach to Public Sector Bodies", 10 International VAT Monitor 144 (July/August 1999).

Bird Richard, Genderon Pierre-Pascal, *The VAT in Developing and Transitional Countries* (Cambridge University Press, New York, 2007).

Cnossen Sijbren, "Is the VAT's Sixth Directive Becoming an Anachronism?", European Taxation (International Bureau of Fiscal Documentation, December 2003).

Cnossen Sijbren, "Modernizing General Consumption Taxes in the Caribbean" (Posted On Dec. 14, 2020).

De la Feria Rita, "The EU VAT Treatment of Public Sector Bodies: Slowly Moving in the Wrong Direction". Intertax, Vol. 37, Issue 3 (Kluwer Law International BV, The Netherlands 2009).

Ebrill Liam, et al., *The Modern VAT* (IMF, Washington DC, 2001).

Feldo Katarzyna, *VAT w partnerstwie publiczno-prywatnym* (Wolters Kluver, Warszawa, 2011).

Gendron Pierre-Pascal, "VAT Treatment of Nonprofits and Public-Sector Entities", *in The VAT Reader, What a Federal Consumption Tax Would Mean in America*, Special Supplement Managing Editor: Cathy Phillips (Tax Analysts 2011).

Giangiacomo D'Angelo, "New Frontiers in the EU VAT Regime for Public Bodies", Intertax, Vol. 46, Issue 12 (2018 Kluwer Law International BV, The Netherlands).

Henkow Oskar, *The VAT/GST Treatment of Public Bodies* (Alphen aan den Rijn, 2013).

James Kathryn, *The Rise of Value-Added Tax* (Cambridge University Press, New York, 2015).

Jiménez Ismael, "VAT and Public Bodies in EC Member States", Intertax, Vol. 36, Issue 6/7 (Kluwer Law International 2008).

Keen Michael & Lockwood Ben, "The Value Added Tax: Its Causes and Consequences", Journal of Development Economics 92(2) (2010).

Kokott Juliane, *EU Tax Law* (C.H. Beck, Hart Publishing, Nomos 2022).

Kokott Juliane, Pistone Pasquale, *Taxpayers in international law: international minimum standards for the protection of taxpayers' rights* (C.H. Beck, Hart Publishing, Nomos 2022).

Owczarczuk Sławomir, "Ewolucja statusu gminy jako podatnika z perspektywy 25 lat funkcjonowania podatku od towarów i usług w Polsce – wnioski de lege lata i postulaty de lege ferenda". Samorząd Terytorialny, No. 6 (June 2020).

Owczarczuk Sławomir, "Model opodatkowania usług komunalnych podatkiem od towarów i usług – wnioski na przykładzie dostaw wody i odbioru ścieków". Ruch Prawniczy, Ekonomiczny I Socjologiczny, Year LXXXIV – volume 1 – (2022). <https://doi.org/10.14746/rpeis.2022.84.1.12>.

Owczarczuk Sławomir, *Status podatnika VAT w samorządzie terytorialnym* (Taxpress, Warszawa 2012).

Schenk Alan, Oldman Oliver, *Value Added Tax: A Comparative Approach* (rev. edn. Cambridge University Press, Cambridge, New York, 2007).

Schenk Alan, Thuronyi Victor, Cui Wei, *Value Added Tax. A Comparative Approach* (Cambridge University Press 2015).

Soldai Aurélie, De Neyer Camille, Vandendries Alexander, "Le cinquantenaire de la TVA: rétrospectives et perspectives", Revue Générale de Fiscalité et de Comptabilité Pratique – RGFCP (Wolters Kluwer 2021/1).

Tait Alan, *Value Added Tax: International Practice and Problems* (IMF, Washington DC, 1988).

Terra Ben, Kajus Julie, *A Guide to the European VAT Directives*. Vol. 1 (IBDF, 2023).

Wille Patrick, "VAT Grouping in Belgium, VAT and Bodies Governed by Public Law", Bulletin For International Taxation (IBDF, August/September 2008).

Conclusions

Institutional vulnerability may be understood in a number of ways, primarily as there are diverse ways of applying protection mechanisms within different areas of law. Recognising that there is insufficient protection, or none at all, for individuals or groups allows us to presume that those affected may be identified as vulnerable. However, the lack of legal protection does not create the vulnerability. The simultaneous existence of specific features of a group and particular environmental issues or circumstances may result in vulnerability. With this in mind, the authors of this volume try to broadly identify entities, groups or circumstances that allow for the recognition of vulnerability.

When attempting to present the essence of vulnerability, the authors conduct theoretical and legal considerations on the various faces of sensitivity in the first part of the volume.

'The history of law is a history of discrimination – law has introduced and preserved social inequalities. At the same time, the evolution of law shows its efforts to rise above prejudices to respect equality and diversity and to recognise human rights'. This sentence, taken from the article by Olga Sitarz, illustrates well the problems that legislators and law enforcement bodies face regarding anti-discrimination. When trying to define the essence of discrimination and answer fundamental questions about the factors that should be taken into account when qualifying a given phenomenon as discrimination, the criteria that should be used to assess someone as 'vulnerable', and the role played by social, cultural and civilisational changes in shaping discrimination, the author introduces readers to the problematic world of eliminating discrimination by law, bearing in mind that both discrimination and its prohibition constitute a restriction of human rights.

One of the hallmarks of discrimination is specific characteristics common to a particular group of people, usually vulnerable. In his chapter, Marcel Piterman presents the concept of antifragility as the ability of a system or individual to benefit from stress and grow stronger. Based on historical, sociological and legal analysis, Marcel explains the intersection between vulnerability, resilience and antifragility in legal decision-making, pointing out the challenges and opportunities of integrating these concepts into legal practice, as well as the potential benefits for disadvantaged groups.

Counteracting vulnerability through law should begin from a constitutional point of view. In his contribution, Mauro Arturo Rivera León touches on the specific issue of supermajorities while voting in the constitutional courts and tribunals. He questions whether supermajorities make it harder for courts to fulfil their task of protecting human rights and prevent them from striking down legislation that disproportionally affects vulnerable groups. The author presents arguments in favour of this thesis and then challenges them individually. In his eyes, the vulnerability argument does not appear to be an objection conclusively refuting the feasibility of supermajority rules in constitutional adjudication.

The reflections contained in this volume reveal yet another form of vulnerability, manifested in the powerlessness of various marginalised groups or individuals in the face of multiple types of legal solutions or decision-making in matters that affect them.

As has been shown, the reasons for vulnerability can be rooted in poverty and the inability to get out of it, as well as in ignoring people experiencing poverty by the social policies of both the state and society. Being poor limits social participation and excludes people experiencing poverty from society. Poverty results from human rights violations and leads to the inability to exercise several human rights, both social and civil. The game is thus about human dignity. For this reason, in this volume Maria d'Oliveira Martins proposes a rethinking of the protection of the poorest and the concept of minimum income. She proposes an existential minimum as a right that can be directly invoked when challenging the absoluteness of budgetary entitlements and deserves special attention. The obligation of a state should be seen as part of the re-establishment of the right to poverty; since universal preventive instruments do not fulfil their mission to eradicate poverty, it is necessary to develop support that meets people's needs, minimises their suffering, and restores their dignity. The proposal to unconditionally grant a minimum income to those in the group of people identified as being in extreme poverty and to dispense with other eligibility criteria, by a simple and comprehensive system, makes it possible to reintegrate the poorest back into society and make them full members of society.

The research in this volume also revealed a vulnerability in the context of machine-learning processes, as the increasing digitisation of private and civil services leads to new forms of vulnerability. Big-tech companies are investing heavily to increase their significance in the global markets, including the social sector. Machine-learning processes do not usually consider the specific needs of vulnerable people and tend to treat everyone equally, which does not mean righteously. These individuals are unable to protest decisions made in the MLDM process, because the process is non-transparent. Dominika Iwan-Sojka proposes to improve the transparency of MLDM processes in the public domain by focusing on the right to receive reasons for decisions and access to legal remedies if the decision is flawed and inexplicable. The key here is a human rights-based approach from the design stage of MLDM processes. These processes should consider such premises as disability, age, socioeconomic status, gender, gender identity, etc., which can take the form of consultation, feedback from potential users, or active participation in this phase. Addressing vulnerability in MLDM processes by ensuring transparency is only one step in the many complex processes involved in human-centred ML models.

Another challenge concerns the standard of protection that an AI system provides each victim. Here again, one can identify the powerlessness of the aggrieved party in the clash with the algorithms, with the entire system of AI deciding, for example, on the allocation of social assistance to the poorest. Iwona Gredka-Ligarska identifies a severe imbalance between the legal situation of professional operators of AI systems and the legal situation of individuals affected by such systems. Thus, the possibility of taking AI to court and claiming compensation, and on what basis, is problematic. This is because it is unclear whether we are dealing with responsibility or liability here. Yet, the social consequences of algorithmic activities are already so extensive that such activities might be considered hazardous.

All of the issues raised in the section on 'powerlessness' pose a formidable challenge to states, international organisations and researchers. Many specific solutions may exist, but they should have a common denominator: a human rights-based approach.

The last part discusses various entities that may become vulnerable in a clash with legal systems. The authors consider various circumstances in which legal protection needs to be introduced or strengthened in order to protect the diverse interests of individuals or groups in the context of institutional vulnerability.

The criminal policy is strictly based on the protection of some victims considered particularly vulnerable, such as victims of gender-based violence, children, victims with disabilities, elderly victims, victims of hate crime and terrorism, as well as victims of human trafficking. Although protecting vulnerable individuals and groups has recently expanded notably in criminal law, specific issues still elicit further reflection. Criminal Codes occasionally use the wording 'abusing a situation of vulnerability', although the prevailing criterion seems to be that aggravations based on abuse are different from those based on the 'particular vulnerability' of the victim. Dyango Bonsignore explains this is a relevant regulatory debate for European legislators, as there are examples of technical approaches within the EU. Concerning vulnerable groups, national legislators should provide exceptional care to avoid jurisdictional uncertainty and, above all, the risk of deviation and co-opting that is present in anti-discrimination offences such as hate speech. However, trying to resolve vulnerability solely through criminal law will not be efficient, as it is usually ill-equipped to provide integrative and long-lasting solutions. Furthermore, vulnerability protection should not become a playground for struggles for labels, nor foster spurious competition over which stakeholders can appear as the more significant victims.

The next issue under analysis is the need to create new European mechanism standards to guarantee the ecological safety of vulnerable entities. Ewa Radecka and Gabriel Radecki focus on determining whether vulnerable people have the tools to protect their fundamental human right to a clean, healthy environment in a proper state of equilibrium. As a result of the research, the chapter concludes that legal solutions regarding social participation do not adequately protect the needs of individuals, where only social and environmental entities are admitted to be involved in administrative proceedings. Consequently, the interest of the vulnerable may be protected only indirectly, provided that this interest is consistent with the general interest raised by any ecological organisation involved in the proceedings. These provisions do not provide mechanisms to protect individual interests, which are particularly vulnerable in cases where an ecological organisation acts contrary to these interests.

Identifying vulnerable groups in company law may seem non-viable at first glance, but the analysis of the practical application of specific instruments proves the opposite. Shareholders are not, in principle, a vulnerable group, as they are investors who decide to take up shares and participate in the company in light of contractual freedom. In the practice of a company's operations, circumstances may arise in which shareholders can be considered vulnerable due to potential conflicts of interest. Piotr Pinior emphasises the need to introduce additional protective mechanisms for shareholders when their interests are violated, and where there are no instruments to protect their rights. The violation of the interests of a minority shareholder appears when a shareholder is deprived of the right to a dividend for a long time, at the same time as the company's assets are being transferred to the majority shareholders or board members, and there is no possibility of selling or redeeming the shareholder's shares (known as a 'corporate prisoner'). Such circumstances allow the identification of the shareholder as a vulnerable person due to the lack of legal protection. The mechanisms enabling a shareholder to exit the company on the basis of a court decision help guarantee the proper protection of minority shareholders in conflict situations and constitute a remedy for 'trapped' shareholders. These instruments should also ensure appropriate remuneration (fair value) for the purchased shares. The mechanism of a shareholder's right to exit the company is undoubtedly a desirable institution, and one that should also be considered in all types of companies, particularly in limited liability companies, where the problem of shareholders' vulnerability frequently occurs in trade practice.

The tenth chapter refers to a situation in Poland where the local government entities declared themselves 'LGBT-free zones' and unfriendly towards the LGBT community. Dawid Grzegorczyk focuses on the need to protect this vulnerable group in relation to local government bodies and the interaction with the judiciary, where courts are expected to defend human rights against discriminatory actions by public administration. The author specifically examines whether LGBT individuals and LGBT organisations had effective means of challenging such discrimination under current laws and judicial practices. In contrast to the initial judgments of the first instance administrative courts, declaring that the resolutions could not be challenged because they had not been adopted 'in matters relating to public administration', the Supreme Administrative Court stated that all activities of local government are subject to the judicial system and the administrative court has the presumption of jurisdiction in this respect. Another question was the legitimacy of starting the proceedings since, in the Polish model, only citizens with 'a legal interest in filing a complaint' are granted the right to challenge such resolutions. The research proves that, despite the initial uncertainty of how the courts could address these resolutions and who had the right to appeal against them, the Polish administrative courts ultimately succeeded in annulling the contested resolutions, mainly due to the involvement of the ombudsman. Nevertheless, these cases serve as evidence that the criteria for filing a complaint before the administrative court need to be revised. The model based on the violation of individual legal interests turned out to be insufficient, either to enable an LGBT person discriminated against by the authorities of their local community to demand the right to go to court, or to enable NGOs fighting for the rights of LGBT persons to initiate a judicial review. The function of the administrative court (protection of legal order) requires changes to the rules of procedural *locus standi* in acts relating to local government entities and, preferably more broadly, in the act regulating proceedings before the administrative courts, which will be necessary to reduce the institutional vulnerability of LGBT community in the future.

The significant acceleration in the aging of the entire society is a massive test for subsequent governments to shape the social policy system with exceptional foresight to support dependent people. These people are exposed not only to social alienation but also to a faster progression of illnesses, including mental health disorders. As a group particularly vulnerable to risks, dependent individuals should be provided with special care by the state through efficient organisation and financing from state budgets. The comparison of the fragmented Polish solutions to the German system clearly shows that the best results are achieved in legal systems that comprehensively approach the protection of such people, creating a well-thought-out, structured support system predominantly funded by citizens. Weronika Szfrańska proposes introducing mandatory care insurance, which could ensure funding of a stable system and enable the development of infrastructure for dependent care. It is recommended to precisely define levels of dependency, allowing for a better alignment of assistance with individual needs. Developing support for family caregivers would also be a crucial step. Educational and training programmes for caregivers, along with pension and health benefits, could encourage more individuals to take on caregiving roles. Providing medical equipment, improving living conditions and implementing technological innovations, such as care management applications, could significantly enhance the quality of life for dependent individuals and ease the workload of caregivers. Additionally, introducing community support programmes that promote neighbourhood cooperation and the integration of older adults into local communities would be beneficial.

The last form of institutional vulnerability is the situation of local government entities (municipalities) as VAT payers. Despite extensive CJEU case law, the tax status of municipalities in the EU VAT system still remains doubtful, mainly due to the lack of harmonisation of the law in the Member States and non-uniform legal forms of municipal activities. As confirmed by CJEU case law, difficulties in applying the provisions of the VAT Directive have caused, and continue to cause, either the unauthorised exclusion of municipalities from the category of VAT payers, or the unauthorised attribution of VAT payer status in a given transaction. Deciding whether a municipality is subject to VAT in a given transaction, and thus whether its non-taxation of VAT distorts or is likely to distort competition significantly, leaves room for interpretation and requires case-by-case decisions. The system of exclusions or exemptions for public entities can create an advantage or disadvantage for municipalities on the market. As Sławomir Owczarczuk points out, a municipality in the VAT system is a weaker party, requiring special legal protection because of the social aspect of its activities: meeting the collective needs of the local government community. Thus, it is high time to build a new system at EU and national levels to allow municipalities to overcome the current legal and institutional barriers and constraints in conducting municipal activities.

These considerations confirm that vulnerability is not reserved for individuals, but can be understood differently and can occur in non-obvious situations, affecting a wide range of entities, groups or institutions. For this reason, various protection measures tailored to the specific situation are necessary to counteract vulnerability.

Ius, Lex et Res Publica
Studies in Law, Philosophy and Political Cultures

Edited by
Barbara Janusz-Pohl

Vol. 1 Anna Jaron: Socio-Economic Constitutional Rights in Democratisation Processes. An Account of the Constitutional Dialogue Theory. 2012.

Vol. 2 Stanisław Filipowicz: Democracy – The Power of Illusion. 2013.

Vol. 3 Teresa Dukiet-Nagórska (ed.): The Postulates of Restorative Justice and the Continental Model of Criminal Law. As Illustrated by Polish Criminal Law 2014.

Vol. 4 Agnieszka Kupzok: Enforcement of Patents on Geographically Divisible Inventions. An Inquiry into the Standard of Substantive Patent Law Infringement in Cross-Border Constellations. 2015.

Vol. 5 Alicja Jagielska-Burduk / Wojciech Szafrański: Legal Issues in Cultural Heritage Management. A Polish Perspective. 2016.

Vol. 6 Maciej Mataczyński (ed.): The Takeover of Public Companies as a Mode of Exercising EU Treaty Freedoms. 2017.

Vol. 7 Maciej Barczewski (ed.): Value of Information. Intellectual Property, Privacy and Big Data. 2018.

Vol. 8 Pawel Smoleń, Marcin Burzec: Introduction to Polish Tax Law. 2018.

Vol. 9 Łukasz Pohl, Konrad Burdziak: Judicial Interpretation of the 1997 Criminal Code Provisions on Self-Defence. 2019.

Vol. 10 Adam Szot: Judicial Review of Administrative Discretion. The Influence of Court Decisions on Administrative Actions. 2019.

Vol. 11 Michał Peno / Konrad Burdziak (eds.): The Concept of Modern Law. Polish and Central European Tradition. 2019.

Vol. 12 Leszek Leszczyński / Bartosz Lińewski / Adam Szot (eds.): Potential of Precedent in the Statutory Legal Order. 2019.

Vol. 13 Łukasz Bolesta: In Search of a Model for the Legal Protection of a Whistleblower in the Workplace in Poland. A legal and comparative study. 2020.

Vol. 14 Paweł Chmielnicki / Adam Sulikowski (eds.): New Perspectives on Legislation. A Comparative Approach. 2020.

Vol. 15 Marcin Burzec / Beata Kucia-Guściora / Paweł Smoleś: Agricultural Activity in Poland: A Fiscal and Legal Study. 2020.

Vol. 16 Magdalena Półtorak / Ilona Topa (eds.): Women, Children and (Other) Vulnerable Groups. Standards of Protection and Challenges for International Law. 2021.

Vol. 17 Josef Albert Fox: Die polnische Verfassung vom 3. Mai 1791. Hintergründe der Entstehung und der Außerkraftsetzung. Stellung Polens im Zeitalter der Aufklärung. 2021.

Vol. 18 Barbara Janusz-Pohl (ed.): Juvenile Justice Systems: Poland-Brazil-Portugal. 2021.

Vol. 42 Jakub Kępiński: The impact of Directive 2005/29/EC on Polish law on combating unfair competition. 2025.

Vol. 43 Paul von Chamier Cieminski: Hostile Cyer Operations between States and International Law. 2025.

Vol. 44 Monika Jagielska / Barbara Mikołajczyk / Piotr Pinior (eds.): Institutional Vulnerability in Law. 2025.

www.peterlang.com

www.ingramcontent.com/pod-product-compliance
Ingram Content Group UK Ltd.
Pitfield, Milton Keynes, MK11 3LW, UK
UKHW021831100926
8556IPUK00004B/275

9 783631 931752